Around the World in 175 Days

# The First Round-the-World Flight

# AROUND THE WORLD IN 175 DAYS

CARROLL V. GLINES

SMITHSONIAN INSTITUTION PRESS
Washington and London

Editor: Ruth W. Spiegel
Designer: Janice Wheeler
Library of Congress Cataloging-in-Publication Data
Glines, Carroll V., 1920
Around the world in 175 days: the first round-the-world flight/
Carroll V. Glines
p. cm.
Includes bibliographical references and index.
ISBN 1-56098-967-X (alk. paper)
1. Flights around the world. 2. United States. Army. Air Corps. 3. World records.
I. Title: Around the world in one hundred seventy five days. II. Title.
TL721.U6 G55 2001
629.13′09–dc21 2001020583

British Library Cataloguing-in-Publication Data available
Manufactured in the United States of America
08 07 06 05 04 03 02 01 5 4 3 2 1

∞ The paper used in this publication meets the minimum requirements of the American National Standard for Information Sciences—Permanence of Paper for Printed Library Materials ANSI Z39.48-1984.

# Contents

Foreword, by Walter J. Boyne vii
Acknowledgments ix

Introduction 1
1. The Challenge 7
2. The Preparation 22
3. The Adventure Begins 34
4. Daring the Aleutians 46
5. *Seattle* Is Lost 59
6. First across the Pacific 74
7. To China and the "Paris of the Orient" 84
8. On to Calcutta 95
9. Paris by Bastille Day 105
10. Preparing for the North Atlantic 116
11. North America at Last! 126
12. Mission Accomplished 142
Epilogue 160

**Appendix: The Route of the Flight** 173

**Notes** 176

**Further Reading** 189

**Index** 191

# Foreword

The 1924 flight around the world by the Air Service Douglas World Cruisers was one of the most important events of the Golden Age of Flight. While Charles Lindbergh's famous solo transatlantic flight in May 1927 captured the imagination of the world, the flight of the World Cruisers had further importance in many ways.

The 1924 flight of 26,000 miles was far more ambitious, calling upon the resources of the Air Service, the U.S. Navy, the State Department, and many other agencies to make it possible. It was this concerted effort that made the flight so important, for it demonstrated on the one hand how difficult such a journey was, and on the other, how it was possible to solve the problems with sufficient foresight and effort. As impressive as the flying and navigation feats were on the World Flight, the logistics effort was even greater. It created a pattern, a modus operandi, for Air Service operations that were passed on, first to the Air Corps, then to the Army Air Forces.

The Douglas World Cruiser was basically a much modified version of the very successful DT-2 that set a number of records for its class and was used in a variety of roles by the U.S. Navy. Of the original four aircraft that began the historic flight in April 1924, two survive. It has been my privilege to have had a close relationship with both the *Chicago* and the *New Orleans.*

The *Chicago* was restored at the National Air and Space Museum's Silver Hill facility, which now bears the name of Paul Garber, the distinguished curator who accepted the *Chicago* for the Smithsonian Institution in 1925. In the ensuing years, it deteriorated and had to be restored for exhibition in the new National Air and Space Museum that opened in July 1976. Walter Roderick, a brilliant craftsman, was assigned the restoration task, working with his equally skilled friend, Ed Chalkley.

Walter was a quiet, intense person with unbelievable skills that he dedicated wholeheartedly to the restoration of the *Chicago.* Through Ed, he drew upon the expertise of the other craftsmen at Silver Hill as required, but the *Chicago* was strictly his baby and he restored it with a meticulous attention to detail that is still startling today. An example: Biplanes of the period often used cloth tape to run from rib to rib in the wings for strength and conformity. The tape in the *Chicago*'s wings was pinked but it was pinked in a unique, nonstandard manner. Walter first made pinking sheers which duplicated the original tape pinking, then spent countless hours, personally pinking every inch of the hundreds of feet of cloth tape in the wings. He then carefully proceeded to cover his workmanship with fabric, knowing that it would probably not be seen for maybe fifty years—but also knowing that when anyone saw it again, he would know that it had been authentically copied from the original.

It was my task to supervise the installation of aircraft and I was pleased to give the *Chicago* the honor of being the first aircraft to be installed in the new National Air and Space Museum in the summer of 1975. Chalkley and Roderick were there to superintend its movement from the old Castle. We placed it on the second floor of the Milestones of Flight Gallery in the new building, an inspiration to us all.

It later fell to Ed and Walter to supervise the movement of the *New Orleans* from the Air Force Museum in Dayton to its new home in the Museum of Flying at Santa Monica. Although there was not enough time to give the *New Orleans* the same degree of restoration that had been lavished on the *Chicago,* the two men saw to it that it was moved safely, given a cosmetic touch-up, and then hung securely in the new museum.

Working with Ed and Walter, it was obvious that they were of the same stripe as the men who had planned and made the original flight. They planned meticulously, executed their work with care and distinction, and did the job with a minimum of fanfare. And when the *Chicago* was given its place of honor in the National Air and Space Museum, no one appreciated the work of Ed Chalkley and Walter Roderick more than Leigh Wade, a surviving pilot of the flight and a great American gentleman. With tears in his eyes, Leigh congratulated both for the genuine triumph of restoration. It was a moving moment, one that no one present has ever forgotten.

Walter J. Boyne, Former Director<br>National Air and Space Museum

# Acknowledgments

This book is about the courageous effort put forth six years after World War I by the U.S. Army Air Service to have its planes encircle the globe and preserve for all time the honor of being first. The Air Service kept accurate records at every step of the mission from idea conception to eventual success. The official records and correspondence are in the National Archives in Washington, D.C., and the U.S. Air Force Historical Research Agency at Maxwell Air Force Base, Alabama. Diaries of two participants are available at the U.S. Air Force Museum, Dayton, Ohio, and the U.S. Air Force Academy, Colorado Springs. Memorabilia, photographs, and personal artifacts from the flight are on display in several museums in the United States. The archives of the Mobil Corporation, known previously as the Vacuum Oil Company and now Exxon Mobil, contain information on its role in furnishing petroleum products and cooperation throughout the flight.

The National Air and Space Museum in Washington, D.C., and the Museum of Flying at Santa Monica, California, are, respectively, the final resting places of the *Chicago* and the *New Orleans,* two of the nation's most distinguished aircraft. The manufacturer aptly designated them World Cruisers even before the flight. They rank with the Wright *Flyer* and the *Spirit of St. Louis* as representatives of the progress of fixed-wing aviation during its first quarter-century.

One of the foremost sources of personal reminiscences about the flight was the book written by the late Lowell Thomas, world famous adventurer, author, and radio/television commentator who was the flight's official historian. He based his book on the personal narratives of six participants. His files containing the notes made during interviews with them are located at the Marist College, Poughkeepsie,

New York. In order to preserve the immediacy and accuracy of the events they describe, I chose to use the stories as they appeared in the book, *The First World Flight,* subtitled *Being the Personal Narratives of Lowell Smith, Erik Nelson, Leigh Wade, Leslie Arnold, Henry Ogden, and John Harding,* and published to much acclaim in 1925. I am greatly indebted to Lowell Thomas Jr. for his permission to quote liberally from the narratives obtained by his father. It is these personal anecdotes told during and shortly after the flight that provide a special insight into the personalities of the men and the way they met and handled the unusual hazards they faced. Other valuable sources were the diaries of John Harding Jr. and Leslie P. Arnold and the memoirs of Alva L. Harvey.

It was my privilege during my military career to meet and talk at length with Leigh Wade in Washington, D.C., and Erik Nelson in Alaska about their experiences during the World Flight. Their candor and willingness to discuss the details of their life experiences was what encouraged me to begin collecting documentation about the first World Flight and the many flights by others that followed. That research resulted in a book entitled *Round-the-World Flights* (Van Nostrand Reinhold, 1982; TAB Books, 1990; and updated again by Brassey's, 2001). It was that first World Flight that continued to hold my interest and eventually led to the present work.

The official reports written during and after the flight were the major sources for the facts about the planning and preparation that took place. Of special interest was how the unique problems encountered in traversing foreign countries were solved by the crews with the assistance of the Army Air Service staff in Washington, the State Department, the engineering officers at McCook Field, Ohio, and especially the advance officers who encountered unprecedented challenges under primitive conditions in strange places to prepare facilities for the planes' arrival. I am indebted to the curators who made these records available for study, especially Duane Reed of the Air Force Academy's Special Collections Department, guardian of the Leigh Wade/Cole Morrow files. Dave Menard and Jerry Rep of the Air Force Museum are due my thanks for their help in locating information in those archives. Peter M. Bowers, prolific aviation writer, has my appreciation for providing some World Flight photographs from his large collection. Other sources of information and photographs, for which I am also appreciative, include the historical offices of the U.S. Navy, U.S. Coast Guard, and the National Marine Fisheries Service of the National Oceanic and Atmospheric Administration, formerly the Bureau of Fisheries of the Department of Commerce.

I am grateful to the Smithsonian Institution Press for the opportunity to bring the facts about this epochal flight into print and thus provide an in-depth view into what made it such a successful and memorable venture for the struggling predecessor of today's United States Air Force.

Carroll V. Glines
Colonel, USAF (Ret.)

# Around the World in 175 Days

# Introduction

Ever since Christopher Columbus theorized that the world was round, there were other intrepid seafaring souls who also wanted to prove this by sailing westward until they reached their starting point. Ferdinand Magellan, a Portuguese navigator, was determined to try. With the backing of Charles I of Spain, he set out with five ships from Seville on 10 August 1519 to search for a western route to the Spice Islands of the East Indies. He headed southwest across the Atlantic Ocean, explored the Rio de la Plata, and wintered in Patagonia. He then sailed through the strait, named for him, at the tip of South America and headed northwest across the Pacific, reaching the Marianas and Philippine Islands in 1520.

Magellan never returned to his adopted land; he was killed by natives at Macatan. But on 8 September 1522, his flagship *Victoria* with eighteen men aboard returned to Spain, thus completing the first circumnavigation of the globe. It had taken the crew 1,088 days to complete the voyage.

The first expedition leader to succeed was Sir Francis Drake, an English navigator, who set out in 1577 sailing westward and returned to England in 1580 after pillaging the coasts of South and North America. In the more than four millennia since, others have circled the earth by ship, dirigible, and aircraft, many vying to make the trip faster than their predecessors.

One of the first persons to circle the earth in a deliberate attempt to establish a record was Nellie Bly, a newspaper reporter who had become well-known for her exposés of social conditions in the United States in the nineteenth century. Born Elizabeth Cochrane on 5 May 1867, she took "Nellie Bly" as a pen name when she began writing for the *Pittsburgh Dispatch*. In 1887, she pretended to be insane so she would be committed to an asylum. Her series of articles on conditions there, published in the *New York World,* made her famous.

Joseph Pulitzer, the paper's publisher, in a continued effort to outdo his competitors with sensational and unusual news accounts, had been impressed by Jules Verne's novel, *Around the World in Eighty Days,* which had been published in 1873. Would Nellie be interested in trying to beat Phineas Fogg's record by using available commercial transportation?

It was the opportunity of a lifetime for Nellie. She studied shipping schedules and in mid-November 1889, with a minimum of baggage, left New York and sailed across the Atlantic and Mediterranean. She proceeded to Aden, Colombo, Singapore, Hong Kong, Tokyo, San Francisco, and reached New York on 25 January 1890, 72 days, 6 hours, and 11 minutes after her departure.

Pulitzer gave much front-page space to Nellie's adventures by train, ship, ricksha, and sampan. Clothes, games, songs, and dances were named for her. She later wrote three books, one of them titled *Nellie Bly's Book: Around the World in Seventy-Two Days.*

The public attention paid to Nellie encouraged others to try to beat her record. George Francis Train duplicated her trip in 1890, setting a new mark of sixty-seven days. Charles Fitzmorris, Chicago's chief of police, left the city in 1901 and returned 60 days, 13 hours, and 29 minutes later to brief acclaim. Round-the-world fever was contagious. J. W. Sayre of Seattle became the first to make the trip in less than two months when he set a new mark of 54 days, 9 hours, and 42 minutes in 1903. Later that year Henry Frederick bested Sayre's mark by a scant 2 hours and 40 minutes. In 1907, a new record of 40 days, 9 hours, and 30 minutes was set by Colonel Burnley-Campbell of Great Britain. This was broken four years later by André Jaeger-Schmidt, a one-legged Parisian newspaperman, who encircled the globe in 39 days, 19 hours, 42 minutes, and 38 seconds.

The celebrity given these trips, however brief, continued to fascinate the few Americans who could afford the trip and who wanted the glory and publicity anticipated in setting a new record. John Henry Mears, a New York theatrical producer and writer, carefully analyzed world shipping schedules in 1913 and went around the world in 35 days, 21 hours, and 36 minutes, much of the trip by ship. Mears has the distinction of being first to use an airplane as one of the means of transportation. It was a stunt arranged by the Seattle *Post-Intelligencer* to gain this honor for Mears since he flew only about forty miles while approaching the West Coast by sitting on the wing of a chartered plane and clinging to the wing struts.

The Mears short flight may have inspired others to think about the potential of aircraft to establish new records. In February 1914 the Bureau of Aeronautics of the Panama-Pacific Exposition Company announced sponsorship of a race around the world by "aeroplane." The race was to start and end in San Francisco and be completed within ninety days, with a starting date of 15 May 1915. Prizes totaling $150,000 were offered to the first three successful world circlers. Confidence that the trip could be made entirely by air was shown in an article in *Aero and Hydro* magazine:

Considerable discussion has been launched as to the possibility of accomplishing the voyage within the prescribed limit of 90 days, traveling only by some sort of motored aero vehicle for the entire distance. . . . To win the race, and the Exposition's cash prize of $100,000 . . . it will be necessary to average 250 miles a day. The world's record for one day's flying is 1,350 miles.[1]

The only restrictions were that the course outlined by the race's organizers had to be followed and the entire distance had to be by aircraft. The race was to be flown eastward from San Francisco with prescribed stops at six cities in the United States and then designated points between Newfoundland and Labrador, Greenland, Iceland, and the Hebrides. The route next included stops in England, France, Germany, Poland, and Russia, then along the Trans-Siberian Railway, down into Manchuria and Korea, and across Japan. The prescribed route was then from northern Japan to Kamchatka, with varying routes across the gap which separates Asia from North America, then on to Vancouver, Seattle, Tacoma, and Portland to San Francisco.

The route of the flight would take the fliers over numerous uninhabited areas where no airplane had ever been seen before. Airfields were most likely to be a polo field, parade ground, or city park. Automobiles were rare and gasoline was in short supply or nonexistent in many areas of the world. Orville Wright, writing in a popular aviation magazine of the day, felt that "it would be foolish for an aviator to risk his life in attempting a nonstop flight across the ocean with such a machine until the motor has been perfected to the point where it could be depended upon." He noted that the longest single flight to date (1914) was less than 900 miles.[2]

In the same issue, the editor wrote: "Is the trip worth making? Yes, emphatically, yes. And even if the hazardous voyage is tried several times, with loss of life and consequent failure, it will still be worth trying, and there is no doubt that one of these days—in 1915 or 1925—it will be accomplished."[3]

The growing conflict in Europe that became World War I temporarily canceled the idea. But the war did have a beneficial effect on aviation progress, especially long-distance flying. Aircraft, engines, and airfield facilities improved rapidly in the warring countries. Hundreds of pilots were trained and a desire to continue flying in either the military services or pursuing commercial ventures using surplus military aircraft was not going to be denied.

In 1919 two private organizations dedicated to the growth of aviation in the United States—the Aero Club of America and the Aerial League of America—joined forces. They appointed a commission to ascertain the extent of interest in civilian aeronautics throughout the United States. A number of aeronautical authorities were selected to make a survey and the group traveled by Pullman car to forty-nine cities in the United States. They reported that the nation was indeed interested in aviation and noted that several national and international aviation contests were scheduled for 1920, with a total of more than two million dollars in prizes offered. Typical was the prize of $100,000 announced by the Aero Club of America, "to be awarded to the person who evolves and demonstrates the first heavier-than-air aircraft which will rise from and land on the ground vertically and will, in other words, make it possible to rise from and land on the roof of a medium-size house," according to *Flying,* the journal of the Aero Club and Aerial League. The prize was offered by the French millionaire André Michelin.[4]

This expression of interest encouraged the commission members to expand their survey. They appointed a special three-man committee to tour the world and organize the "First Aerial Derby around the World." The group traveled (mostly by ship and train but never by air) more than 40,000 miles and visited thirty-two countries. Twenty-seven new aero clubs were organized in the nations they passed through. When the commission reached Paris on 20 May 1920, it was dissolved by mutual consent. In its place, the World's Board of Aeronautical Commissions was established to perpetuate the work of the original aerial derby commission and act in an advisory capacity to those interested in aviation, to advance it as rapidly as possible, and to encourage aerial navigation in all parts of the world.

The rules for the derby reflected an optimism about the future of aviation based on the fact that a few aircraft had already flown great distances without refueling and now seemed reliable enough to make such an arduous trip. The race was never held but the idea remained fast in the minds of pilots of many nations.

Strange as it may seem today, most people in the United States had never seen an airplane when World War I ended. Although the airplane had proven effective as a war machine, the American public, although interested in seeing airplanes, did not accept them as a safe, reliable means of transportation. There were a few American government leaders who fortunately believed that a dedicated core of military airmen must be retained for national defense but there were less than 1,000 Army Air Service pilots, about 10,000 enlisted men, and 800 obsolescent planes left over from World War I available to help prove that the airplane had an unrealized potential for peace as well as for war. That potential had to be proven. The few airmen who remained in uniform were deeply troubled that the nation that had given birth to the first heavier-than-air flying machine was unable to capitalize on this technological advance. To attract the public's attention they would have to keep the public focused on aviation through the media by continually seeking national and international speed, altitude, distance, and endurance records.

Among the first Army Air Service achievements after the war were three successive world altitude records set in 1919 in an experimental LePere biplane designed by Capt. Gene LePere, a French engineer on loan by the French government, and built at the Air Service's Engineering Division at McCook Field, Dayton, Ohio. Although altitude records were important, there were other achievements that captured more public interest. That year a Martin bomber was flown completely around the perimeter of the United States for the first time. A U.S. Navy Curtiss seaplane, the NC-1, made a flight with fifty passengers and another, the NC-4, had completed the first flight across the Atlantic. The next year, four de Havilland DH-4s, led by Capt. St. Clair Streett, completed the first aerial round trip between New York City and Nome, Alaska.

One of the first American solo record-setters was Lt. James H. "Jimmy" Doolittle who flew coast-to-coast with one stop in 21 hours, 19 minutes, the first to do so in less than a day. In May 1923, Lts. Oakley T. Kelly and John A. Macready made the first nonstop coast-to-coast flight, setting a new record for the greatest distance ever made in a single cross-country flight up to that time. That summer, Lt. Lowell H. Smith and Lt. John P. Richter captured headlines with their 37¼-hour endurance flight in a de Havilland DH-4B using midair refueling for the first time. The world speed record, set by Navy Lt. A. J. Williams in November 1923, was over 260 mph.

Other nations were also testing the potential of aircraft at the beginning of the nineteen-twenties. Argentina appropriated two million dollars for aviation development; Luis Barrufaldi, one of its military pilots, set a South American altitude record of more than 24,000 feet. Belgium was operating passenger planes on four European routes. China had trained 125 pilots and had 140 planes. France was leading the world in the development of civil aviation. At the same time, Germany claimed to have the most up-to-date, complete, and regularly scheduled air traffic routes in the world, despite the restrictions imposed by the Allied Aerial Control Commission as the result of the Treaty of Versailles. Great Britain was pushing ahead in aircraft development, experimentation, and development of mail routes. Italy was developing aerodromes and encouraging aircraft production. Japan was strengthening its naval and army air arms and increasing production of war machines.

Shortly after the Smith-Richter endurance flight, Maj. Gen. Mason M. Patrick, chief of the Army Air Service, and assistant chief Brig. Gen. William "Billy" Mitchell, became concerned that the United States was beginning to fall dangerously behind in research and development of military aircraft. Both encouraged the pilots to attract public attention to aviation by participating in air races and seeking more speed, altitude, and distance records. Other nations reported preparations to fly around the world in an effort to capture the honor of being first to do so. The time had come for Americans to consider the challenge of a World Flight.

# 1. The Challenge

Four years after World War I was over, the focus of the participating nations as they turned from wartime to peacetime pursuits was on increasing the speed and range of aircraft. France, Great Britain, Italy, and Russia were creating military aeronautical organizations and forging ahead with the development of new aircraft for commercial air transportation. Germany, although it had limits placed on its military forces by the 1919 Treaty of Versailles, began concentrating on scheduled airline operations with planes and dirigibles.

U.S. Army Air Service planners were rightly worried that American supremacy in the air was being sadly outpaced. The aircraft manufactured in the United States during the war, mostly trainers, were obsolete by the beginning of the twenties decade and were rapidly used up through crashes or through sale as surplus to barnstorming pilots. And they were not being replaced with more modern machines. Assistant Secretary of War John M. Wainwright summarized the situation this way:

> The Army Air Service is faced with this condition of affairs: Its wartime manufactured equipment has been practically used up. The amounts of money appropriated for new aircraft are so small that within two years it will have on hand less than one-half the number of aircraft necessary for its normal peacetime emergency, no reserve on hand, and it will be impossible in less than a year to expand the remnant of the aircraft industry which may be left or to create it anew so that this material can be manufactured in sufficient quantity for use in such an emergency. This situation is not only serious, but it is actually alarming.[1]

It was this message of concern from Wainwright and a few other government leaders that although the United States had the distinction of being the birthplace of the airplane, it was being left behind in developing its potential for military and commercial uses. Something had to be done to stimulate public interest and support.

The Army Air Service had only about 975 officers and less than 10,000 enlisted men assigned at the beginning of 1923. This relatively small force had its advantages in that most of the officers knew each other and their qualifications. The pilots wanted to continue flying and were encouraged to think of ways to keep public attention focused on the potential of airplanes as other nations were doing. One way to do this was to set new marks for speed, distance, and altitude. By the end of 1922, thirty-three out of the forty-two world aviation records established during the year were credited to American pilots, most of them military. Yet when the French undersecretary of state for air was informed that the United States had established a new speed record of nearly five miles a minute, he was unimpressed. "Records, yes," he said, "but they are a façade; back of them there is nothing!"[2] Assistant Secretary of War Dwight F. Davis, when asked at a congressional hearing about the Frenchman's criticism, explained: "I think what he had in mind was that one cannot fight with records, that you need planes."[3]

The American pilots who remained in uniform were kept aware of the progress being made by other nations, especially by Maj. Gen. Mason M. Patrick, chief of the Army Air Service. An 1886 graduate of West Point, he had a varied military career in the Corps of Engineers and had sailed to France in 1917 as head of the famous First Engineers, charged with all engineer construction for the American Expeditionary Forces (AEF). He was a no-nonsense, efficient officer who had extensive experience with military and civilian engineering projects. At the time, the Air Service was trying desperately to get units trained and into the air war. Brig. Gens. Benjamin D. Foulois and William "Billy" Mitchell, the two ranking Air Service officers in France, were at odds over organizational matters. To settle the rift, Gen. John J. Pershing, chief of the AEF, designated Patrick as chief of the Air Service, AEF, with the mandate to get American units into combat.

"In this army," Pershing told Patrick, "there is but one thing that is causing me anxiety, and that is the Air Service. In it are a lot of good men, but they are running around in circles. Someone's got to make them go straight. I want you to do it."[4]

The decision to assign Patrick, although not a pilot, to command all of the American flying units in France influenced development of the Air Service favorably for the next decade. An effective leader with a genius for organization, he was able to place the Air Service on a more efficient working basis quickly and enabled the United States to do its part in the air war. When he returned to the United States, he was appointed head of the entire Army Air Service. Realizing that he could command better respect of his young pilots if he qualified as a pilot, he did so and soloed in 1922 at age sixty under the instruction of Maj. Herbert A. Dargue, chief of the Air Service's Training and War Plans Division. General Patrick was cautious, however, and never flew without an experienced pilot to accompany him.

The experience in France had made Patrick a proponent for a strong air force. It was this conviction, spoken frequently in staff meetings, that encouraged his subordinates to think and plan for the future. It was reinforced by his assistant, the irrepressible Brig. Gen. William "Billy" Mitchell, who would express the virtues of a strong, separate air force so boldly and publicly that he would be court-martialed later for accusing the U.S. War and Navy departments of "incompetency, criminal negligence, and almost treasonable administration."

Patrick agreed with Mitchell on most of his theories and concepts about the potential of air power and the need for appropriations to develop the Air Service but chose not to express them so offensively. Patrick quietly spread the word among the pilots to do what they could to bring aviation to the people by participating in air shows and seeking aviation records with the attendant publicity.

The first written record that anyone in the Air Service was thinking about a world flight was a personal letter written in 1919 by Mitchell to Lt. Col. Henry H. "Hap" Arnold, then commanding Rockwell Field, an Air Service base at San Diego. "I am very anxious to push through a flight to Alaska with land planes," he wrote. "Better get oriented along that line as to the possibilities from your department north. This might develop into a round-the-world flight."[5]

The first *official* documentary evidence about such a flight appears in a short April 1922 memorandum from Major Dargue to Lt. Robert J. Brown Jr., a young flying officer assigned to the Training and War Plans Division of the Office of Chief of Air Service. "You are familiar with the fact that several lighter-than-air projects are under consideration at the present time and but few heavier-than-air projects," said Dargue. He continued:

"It is desired that you look into the possibilities of a flight to Asia by way of Alaska, and furthermore, the possibility of carrying this flight on around the world to England with a probable return to the United States by way of Iceland, Greenland, and Newfoundland. . . . The two Australians [brothers Ross and Keith Smith] who made the flight from London to Australia [in 1919] have been interested in a flight around the world, but it is improbable that this flight will be completed. It is also improbable that such a flight could be made during this coming summer on account of the attitude of the General Staff; however, the details of such a flight should be looked into with the possibility of accomplishing it before the end of the next fiscal year. It is believed that the only section of such a flight that has not been flown is from Alaska to Japan."[6]

The seemingly innocuous memorandum from his superior turned into a full-time study for Brown. As he proceeded with his assignment, he soon realized that some basic questions had to be answered and vital decisions made which would affect any detailed planning for such a task. Should a World Flight head east to take advantage of the prevailing winds in the northern hemisphere? Or west at a time when the weather would be most favorable in the Aleutians, the Middle East, and across the Atlantic? Whatever the general direction, where should fueling stops be made along the route chosen? What type and how many aircraft should make the flight? Should they be land planes or sea planes? How would they be serviced in remote areas? Who should be chosen for such an important flight? How much would the flight cost? Where could accurate maps be obtained? Would other government agencies, especially the navy, cooperate?

Brown worked for weeks studying all the possibilities. He queried the navy, marine corps, coast guard, and other government agencies, oil companies, aircraft manufacturers, the notes of military attachés of other governments, and civilian sources of information on foreign countries such as the National Geographic Society and the Smithsonian Institution. He followed the news about the world flights announced by members of foreign air services, especially those planned by British, Portuguese, and Argentine pilots. What preparations had they made? What type of planes were they planning to fly?*

Lieutenant Brown was completing his preliminary study in the summer of 1922 and had briefed Generals Patrick and Mitchell giving alternatives and options that should be considered before the basic decisions were made. The matter was considered confidential and no word was passed to the press about what Brown was doing. In an interview with reporters at Selfridge Field, Michigan, in October 1922, Mitchell was asked by a newspaper reporter if a flight around the world was possible. Mitchell, never one to duck a question from the media, responded that the Air Service was indeed planning a World Flight but did not give any details. In a follow-up article, an Associated Press reporter learned that plans were in a preliminary stage for "a considerable aerial squadron" to make the flight but it would not be carried out until the secretary of war approved it.

The reporter was insistent and wrote that the concept for the Army Air Service to make such a flight "was in line with the reasons that prompted President [Theodore] Roosevelt to send the fleet around the world in 1908. It would have value both as a step in providing aerial defense through training and in giving the world a better understanding of American postwar developments. Fliers of other nations have undertaken, up to this time without success, world-girdling flights, while the American Air Service project would call for a fleet of aircraft and careful preparations involving considerable expenditures. Possibly a special act of Congress to authorize a flight and make necessary appropriations would be required should administration officials approve the scheme. For this reason it is not expected any definite step will be taken for a year or more."[7]

Such a news leak from Mitchell generated immediate response from Secretary of War Weeks who directed Maj. Gen. J. G. Harbord, Army deputy chief of staff and one of Mitchell's chief antagonists, to investigate. In a memorandum to Patrick,

---

*The first nonstop air crossing of the Atlantic was made by Capt. John Alcock and Lt. Arthur Whitten Brown in June 1918 in a Vickers Vimy. The first airship crossing and the first double-crossing of the Atlantic took place the following month in a British R-34 flown by Squadron Leader G. H. Brown and thirty crew members. In May 1919 the Curtiss NC-4, an American Navy seaplane, completed the first transatlantic flight in stages. The Smith brothers and two mechanics completed a flight of 11,294 miles from London to Melbourne, Australia, in December 1919 in a Vickers Vimy bomber. The first air crossing of the South Atlantic was made in several stages from Portugal to Brazil by Portuguese fliers Gago Cotinho and Sacadura Cabrál using three British-built Fairey floatplanes.

Harbord said Secretary Weeks wanted to know the truth about such a statement and quoted Weeks as saying that "such a plan should have his approval before arrangements are even begun, much less given publicity. If the Air Service can independently plan and publish such events, we could hardly deny the same privilege to the chiefs of other arms."[8]

Patrick replied that Mitchell told him the remark was "made conversationally and with no intention on his part that it would be given newspaper publicity." Yet Patrick acknowledged that one of the divisions in his office had been studying the possibility of making long flights—"transcontinental, to Panama by several routes, and also several routes which might be followed by aircraft which would circle the globe. As a matter of fact, the Secretary of War himself indicated to me his desire to have investigated the possibilities of such flights to the Panama Canal Zone." Patrick added: "It is difficult for me to believe that the above memorandum means that such studies should not be undertaken without the prior sanction of the War Department. It is, of course, understood that no project of the kind would be actually executed until all of the details had been laid before the Department and the necessary sanction obtained. . . . Until any such plan or project is found to be feasible and all the details are worked out, I have seen no reason for submitting the matter to the Department."[9]

There had been rumors that the navy and marine corps were considering a World Flight using aerial refueling and these rumors were given credibility by Rear Adm. William A. Moffett in a *New York Times* interview. He told a reporter that a World Flight "was within the realm of possibilities" and implied that it would be accomplished by navy pilots because of their experience with seaplanes. After the reporter checked with the U.S. Navy and War departments, the story was immediately squelched by spokesmen who acknowledged a World Flight might be a possibility at some future date but did not regard it as a safe venture at that time.[10]

There were no further public inquiries about the World Flight but preliminary plans were shaping up for submission to the War Department staff by the Air Service. Major W. H. Frank, Air Service executive officer, presented the staff's collective opinion about the choice of aircraft for such a flight to the chief of the Air Service Engineering Division at McCook Field, Dayton, Ohio.

"The best airplanes to be used for such a flight are at present undoubtedly DH-4Bs with extra gas capacity and other lesser refinements [Frank wrote]. Although this airplane, as it stands today, is practically an American product with an American engine, nevertheless, its basic design is that of the British de Havilland, together with Handley-Page wheels [which] makes this airplane essentially a British product. A long flight such as contemplated will be given considerable publicity and will display American postwar development. While all due credit must be given to the country which designed the de Havilland airplanes, in view of their seven years of satisfactory performance, still it would be highly desirable to make a flight of this nature in a thoroughly American airplane. . . . In view of the structural changes we have made in the de Havilland airplane, it might be feasible to give it an American name. Consideration should be given to the possibility of modifying the LePere airplane and changing its name in the same manner. The recommendation of the Engineering Division is requested as to the possibilities of making this flight within two years with an all-American airplane."[11]

The response from McCook Field was that the names of both types of aircraft could be changed but only the uninformed would think they were new. There would be no new airplanes scheduled for the Air Service inventory within two years if an all-American type were desired. Still, if the Air Service were willing to expend the necessary funds, it was feasible to have a newly designed one available during that time. The Engineering Division at McCook stood ready to "collect the necessary data from the various manufacturers and others."[12]

At McCook Field, Lt. Erik H. Nelson, an engineering officer, was assigned to study the several types of aircraft that might be used on a World Flight and recommended a Fokker T-2, the same type of aircraft that Lts. John A. Macready and Oakley G. Kelly were planning to fly nonstop across the country in the spring of 1923. Nelson reported that there was also a newer Fokker, the F.5, and a civilian transport, the Davis-Douglas Cloudster, that could be considered. Lt. Clarence E. Crumrine in the Airways Section of the Air Service at McCook collaborated with Nelson and submitted a detailed report to Major Dargue in the Training and War Plans Division. Crumrine, a member of the successful round-trip flight of four aircraft from Mitchel Field, New York, to Nome, Alaska, in 1920, noted that he understood his superiors were thinking that the flight would be made by only one aircraft and recommended the route be divided into three divisions for planning purposes. The flight could start from Seattle and proceed eastward across Canada and the Atlantic to Ireland and England. The plane would make many stops proceeding across Europe and Russia to Japan, then to Alaska, and return to Seattle. Crumrine cited one reason against crossing Russia was "Bolshevik troubles" but the reasons in favor were the shorter distance and the fewer countries to have to negotiate with for assistance and landing permissions. He covered many details including sending "thoroughly seasoned" flyers as advance men along the route, asking for assistance of the navy and a 20- to 25-week flying training program for the crews "practicing great circle courses, night flights, flights over clouds in daytime, and a few flights over Lake Erie, testing the sextant on the horizon."[13]

Several weeks later, Nelson and Crumrine submitted a follow-up report after Nelson had checked further on the Fokker F.5, which offered two alternative wing arrangements—one a monoplane and the other a biplane. It also had wide cockpits, increased visibility fore and aft, and a unique engine arrangement that permitted "certain minor adjustments in flight." They also stated that the flight should be started on 1 April 1924 and that special training should be given "in an entirely practical form" to include training with the most modern flight instruments available.[14]

After Crumrine's report was received in Washington, General Patrick asked for input from other experienced pilots, including Lt. St. Claire Streett who had led the 1920 flight to Nome. Streett suggested three routes be considered, one starting and ending at Washington, D.C., and proceeding westward through Alaska to Japan, China, India, Europe, Greenland, and Canada, completely avoiding Russia. A second shorter route was suggested heading eastward through Russia, beginning and ending at Mitchel Field, New York. A third possibility was a route beginning in Detroit and proceeding eastward to Greenland, through Europe, the Middle East, and Japan with one stop in Russia, before going to Alaska and ending in Detroit.[15]

The suggestions that were received from other pilots were carefully weighed and by May 1923 it was time for some basic decisions. Lt. Col. J. E. Fechet, chief of the Training and War Plans Division, after studying Crumrine's report, prepared a long memorandum for General Patrick suggesting that a committee be formed of the five officers who had already been working nearly a year on the project; the suggestion was quickly approved. He assigned Capt. William F. Volandt to research financial and transportation arrangements, as well as carry on correspondence with agencies in parts of the world along the flight route and ascertain the cost of distributing supplies and fuel to the advance bases. Capt. Lorenzo L. Snow was instructed to coordinate diplomatic relations. Lt. Robert J. Brown Jr. was appointed chairman of the committee and placed in charge of organization, coordination, and liaison. Brown and Lt. St. Claire Streett were to determine and plan the route, obtain maps, coordinate with other services and the State Department, oversee distribution of supplies, and obtain data on climate, terrain, and facilities. Later, Lt. Elmer E. Adler was charged with negotiating for and procuring the gas and oil from companies like Tidewater, Vacuum, and Shell from their subsidiaries around the world. Lt. Erik H. Nelson was designated equipment and engineering officer while Crumrine was requested to investigate all ground support and flying equipment that might be used and then be designated as one of the advance officers.

The choice of planes to be used was the most urgent decision to be made because of the lead time involved in procuring and testing a new aircraft. Lieutenant Colonel Fechet noted that the Fokker T-2, "due to its sluggishness and weight, is not considered feasible." Instead, the Fokker F.5 and Davis-Douglas Cloudster should both be considered because they were adaptable to landing gears and pontoons and had a large fuel- and weight-carrying capability. Fechet "strongly" recommended that Nelson proceed to California to obtain firsthand information about the Cloudster, obtain one, and make extensive gas consumption tests with wheels and pontoons. The first model had made its initial flight on 21 February 1921 and was the first plane capable of carrying a useful load exceeding its own weight.[16]

With every decision, the cost to the government would always be a factor and Volandt studied the possible expenses as each element was being considered. His preliminary bottom-line estimate was that $100,000, in addition to the cost of aircraft, would finance a flight of six aircraft around the world without having to obtain special appropriations. Until the type and number of aircraft, the route, support equipment, and the facilities needed were decided, no accurate total estimates could be made.

Fechet recommended that six advance officers should be appointed to supervise the distribution of supplies along the route and make arrangements with foreign governments and local vendors. He felt that Lt. Col. Streett should be authorized to proceed immediately to Labrador, Greenland, Iceland, England, France, and Italy.

Streett was not available to travel at that time, however, and Crumrine was substituted. At the same time, Lt. Clifford C. Nutt, stationed in Manila in the Philippines, should be authorized to travel to China, Japan, and the Aleutians to obtain all available information relative to weather, tides, landing, harbor and anchorage facilities, airways, and distribution of supplies.

Fechet believed only four aircraft should make the flight but if six were to be used, they might go in two groups, possibly one going eastward and the other westward. He was not enthusiastic about this option because it "might develop into a race." He felt initially that the flight should go eastward to take advantage of the prevailing winds and depart from the West Coast "thus allowing an opportunity while on home soil to eliminate possible difficulties with the engines and airplanes prior to the final departure from this country." In laying out a route, long hops should be considered so that landings in Greenland and Iceland could be avoided. He "assumed that the United States did not desire to enter into negotiations with Russia for the purpose of making an airplane flight over that country." He favored the southern route through Asia Minor and India, although such a route was much longer than through Russia. He stated the best possible time period for the flight was between May 1 and October 1, but "a more detailed study of the itinerary must necessarily be a part of the completed project."[17]

Fechet recommended that the project be approved "at least in principle," and asked that a letter be forwarded to the Adjutant General of the Army in order that instructions might be issued to the advance officers at the earliest possible date.[18] The project was approved verbally by General Patrick at the end of May 1923.

Lt. Jimmy Doolittle was at the time assigned to the engineering division at McCook Field and had become widely known for his record-setting 1922 coast-to-coast flight in less than twenty-four hours. Now he submitted his own request for permission to make a world flight. He recommended another pilot accompany him on a route that would begin in Sacramento, California, and proceed westward to Hawaii, Midway, Wake, Guam, Manila, India, Egypt, Greece, Rome, Europe, Newfoundland, New York, Kansas City, and return to Sacramento. He suggested that another possible route was across the South Atlantic from Africa to South America rather than across the North Atlantic. He estimated such a flight could be accomplished in one and a half to three months and that it could be made in a Fokker T-2 or a Davis-Douglas Cloudster "provided slight modifications were made to allow solar and astronomical observations to be readily taken."[19] Doolittle's request was not approved as he was chosen to attend Massachusetts Institute of Technology to pursue a master's degree in mid-1924, and a doctor of science degree the following year.

Lt. Erik Nelson was meanwhile authorized to travel to Santa Monica to check on the Cloudster and obtain information on the Fokker T-3 transport that was then being manufactured by the L.W.F. Company for the Air Service. The preceding model, a Fokker T-2, had been flown coast-to-coast nonstop by Air Service Lts. John A. Macready and Oakley G. Kelly in May 1923.

A new Fokker transport model then being developed in Europe, the F.5, was thought to have long-distance possibilities because it offered two wing arrangements on the same fuselage. The first arrangement was a monoplane wing that could be used as an ordinary land plane; it would then be fitted with biplane wings and special pontoons for the ocean flying. It was dropped from consideration when the decision was made to use an all-American airplane. Only one model was ever built.

Lieutenant Nelson inspected the Douglas-Davis Cloudster at Santa Monica that had attempted a nonstop flight across the United States in June 1921 but had not succeeded. Although it was the first plane to carry a useful load exceeding its own weight, he was more impressed during his visit with the Douglas DT-2, a biplane, single-engine, two-place, open cockpit torpedo bomber being produced for the U.S. Navy.[20]

It was on 1 June 1923 that General Patrick officially notified the Adjutant General of the Army that the Air Service was considering the possibilities of making a flight around the world. He noted that British aviators had made one attempt which had failed and were contemplating another soon. French fliers were already en route but were using only one plane so Patrick considered their chances of success small. He believed that with proper preparation, the Army Air Service could make the flight first before the other nations. He requested authority to send two officers on a pathfinding expedition, one officer to cover each ocean and obtain information on climatic conditions, transportation, harbor and landing facilities, and tides. He estimated the expenses of the officers would be $4,400.[21]

Without waiting for top-level approval, plans went ahead to choose the aircraft for the flight. Lieutenant Nelson forwarded a detailed analysis of the DT-2 from McCook Field to Air Service headquarters that contained a number of changes he had suggested to company president Donald W. Douglas. Douglas agreed to make these changes and Nelson urgently requested $23,721 be authorized to purchase one DT-2 for extensive tests at McCook. He recommended the Fokker T-3 at the same time be eliminated from consideration.[22]

The request was approved. Nelson's experience on both the Alaskan and Puerto Rican flights enabled him to recommend essential modifications to make the plane stronger and much lighter than the original design. His choice was based on the ruggedness and weight-carrying features of the DT-2s. These would give them a radius of action of about eight hundred miles, sufficient to make a round trip between practically any two adjacent stops on the chosen route if a destination were closed. Nelson was authorized to test the DT-2 after changes were made that included increased gas capacity to 644 gallons by adding fuel tanks in the upper wing, over the wing roots, behind the fire wall, and under the pilot's seat. This capacity would increase the range to nearly 2,200 miles.

Nelson also recommended an oil tank with a capacity of thirty gallons, a larger radiator and engine cowling redesign, strengthened wing bracing, increased rudder surface for better control with heavy loads, a cut-out in the upper wing for increased visibility for the pilot, and moving the observer's seat forward for easier communication between the two crew members. He also asked for pontoon strengthening, and most important, that the rear fuselage be made of steel tubing instead of wood as required by the U.S. Navy.

Douglas agreed to all these changes and began modification of a DT-2 on the production line which would be flown to McCook Field by Nelson and thoroughly tested. Prices to produce four aircraft with these modifications was requested of the company, as well as the cost to the government of overhauling thirty-five Liberty twelve-cylinder engines and ten of other engine makes. The Liberty engines, all manufactured during World War I, were rated at 400 to 425 horsepower. When updated to the 1923 model, the engineers promised a top aircraft speed of 105.1 mph at 1,650 rpm. Cruising speed with pontoons was estimated at 70 mph, and 85 mph as land planes. An electric starter was to be provided and a ten-gallon reserve water tank would be required in the pilot's cockpit. The latest type of navigation instruments were to be provided, including an earth inductor compass.[23]

After negotiations with Nelson, the Douglas Company proposed to produce four more planes with all of Nelson's modifications and equipment requirements at $22,221 each. It was the first time the modified model was referred to in official documents as "D-WC" for "Douglas World Cruiser."[24] Later, the hyphen was dropped.

By 1 September 1923, procurement of the four additional aircraft was approved in addition to the one to be tested at McCook Field. Nelson flew the prototype there in October and after a rigorous series of performance tests and a few more minor changes, he was satisfied that it was the right plane for the job. He made suggestions for improvements in the engine cooling, fuel and oil systems, flight controls, and steel tubular construction in the tail sections in the four production models. Attaching points for handling and lifting the aircraft on board ship were added. The thirty-five Liberty engines in storage were fitted at the same time with the latest improvements, such as stub-tooth gear trains, reinforced bolted-on cylinders, a new type of fuel pump, and a standard ignition system. Both electric and hand starters and a hand-operated fuel "wobble" pump for emergencies was placed in the rear cockpit. This addition later proved its value on the flight across the North Atlantic.

While these activities were going on, the westward route against the prevailing winds recommended by Lieutenant Streett was approved because it was more logical in view of the weather conditions that could be expected during the various seasons in all the countries over which the planes would pass if they left in early April. It was planned at first that the flight would begin in Washington, D.C., but the official starting point was changed to Seattle on the West Coast. Instead of back-tracking from the factory across the country, the flight would then proceed down the Aleutian Islands to take advantage of the best weather conditions usually experienced there that time of year. As the typhoon season off the Chinese coast usually began about the middle of June, an early start would permit passage through this area before it started. The flight through Japan, China, French Indochina, and India would not be difficult if it were made before or during the early part of the monsoon season. The weather from India through Europe usually presented the best yearly weather patterns in midsummer and could enable the flight to arrive at the Faeroe Islands and prepare for the Atlantic crossing to Labrador with stops in Iceland and Greenland before the winter weather began.

With the route now set, Streett made a detailed study of the Pacific and Atlantic Pilot Books published by the U.S. Navy and Great Britain, together with the U.S. Navy, U.S. Coast Guard, British, Danish, and German admiralty hydrographic charts, as well as the U.S. Geodetic Survey charts. These charts contained information that was used to determine the best possible harbors and bays where water landings could be made. All landings across the Pacific and along the coast of Asia, as far as Calcutta, India, and the Atlantic Ocean crossing were to be made on floats or pontoons. Wheels were to be used for the overland European and United States flights.

Secretary of War Weeks meanwhile approved the plan to send two officers on a pathfinding expedition "for the purpose of gathering data required in connection with a proposed flight around the world." Expenses for their travel were to be met from Air Service funds.[25]

Lieutenants Crumrine and Nutt were given their instructions by General Patrick. They were directed to proceed immediately by the best means available to the countries specified in their orders and request the assistance of the authorities there in making arrangements for the flight through their respective countries. They were required to make frequent reports which would contain "all possible data and information that you would consider essential if you were detailed to make a flight through the countries which you are visiting." They were provided extensive multipage questionnaires to serve as guides to obtain this information.[26]

Other advance officers were meantime being selected and military attachés in each country over which the flight would pass were asked to obtain information on land transportation, meteorological conditions, airways, airplane and seaplane facilities, and means of communication, together with maps of the route and sketches of the landing areas. They were asked to provide their opinions of the best routes to be followed between landing points.

The information obtained was used by Streett to compile an airways guide book similar to a green or blue book then used by early automobile operators giving comprehensive information about a route. These were to be given to the fliers, along with maps, so they could be studied before departure for each segment.

The instructions to the two officers were specific. Crumrine would visit Labrador, Greenland, Iceland, and Denmark, while Nutt was to go from the Philippines to Japan, China, and Southeast Asia. "You have been selected for this important duty because of your experience in cross-country flights and the excellent manner in which you have performed duties to which you have been assigned," Patrick wrote to each. "The success of the proposed flight around the world will depend to a large extent upon the information you gather. You will be required to work practically entirely upon your own initiative in traveling as expeditiously as possible through unknown and uncharted territories. Bear in mind the fact that as an officer in the

U.S. Army, you are backed by the authority of one of the largest nations in the world and use every tactful means possible to obtain the required information. I know that you will encounter great difficulties during this mission, but I am confident that you will be successful."[27]

The flight as originally planned would be made over twenty-eight different foreign countries, including protectorates and colonial mandates which were controlled by twenty-five separate governments. There were international agreements among many nations at this time for landing rights or permission for flights across borders so the secretary of war sent an official notification to the secretary of state of the flight's intended itinerary and requested that American embassies along the route be informed. The countries to be visited were asked to cooperate with the pathfinding officers and assist in preparations for the flight's arrival. Every country except Japan cordially expressed its desire to furnish any information needed about facilities and any data required to fulfill the mission. Danish vessels agreed to assist the effort in the Atlantic, the British Royal Air Force would assist the travel of the advance officers over the airways in Asia Minor, and the French Air Ministry turned over much valuable information on France, Syria, and French Indochina. In securing visas on the passports for the members of the flight, it was necessary to increase the number of pages in each passport from four to six to accommodate the unusual number of countries in which the flight would land.

In the case of Japan, Jefferson Caffrey, the American chargé d'affairs there, was asked "whether proposed flight over Japanese territory could be arranged for under present law, and whether request could, in your judgment, be made without antagonizing Japanese opinion, both official and unofficial."[28] It was known that the Washington naval treaties of 1921 and 1922 had offended the Japanese.

When no reply was received by mid-November, Caffrey was informed that a response was necessary by 30 November 1923. "For your discreet use you are confidentially informed that of all the governments from which permission for flight across territory was requested, the Japanese government is the only one which has not yet replied."[29]

The Japanese had good cause for not replying promptly. The country had experienced a devastating three-day earthquake and fire on 1 September 1923, leaving half a million people dead and several million destitute and homeless; one-fifth of the city of Tokyo alone was destroyed. American help had been offered immediately by President Calvin Coolidge and relief ships and U.S. Navy vessels were immediately dispatched with aid supplies. Recognizing the Japanese government's desire to take care of its own problems and avoid friction between the Americans and the sensitive Japanese about distribution, relief supplies were to be delivered to Japanese authorities at several main ports and no attempt was to be made by Americans to issue them directly to the public.

The relief materials were gratefully received in Japan. Ambassador Cyrus E. Woods notified the secretary of state that the promptness and efficiency with which the emergency was met by the United States "not only made a great impression on the Japanese but was an inspiration to them to meet the emergency with like promptness and like efficiency." He also noted that the U.S. Navy ships had not only delivered the supplies but departed promptly, leaving the Japanese regretting their departure.[30]

There was a growing urgency to get a response from Japan for the World Flight so the State Department again inquired of Caffrey what Japan's answer was. The Vice Minister for Foreign Affairs told him that the Japanese War Department "did not look with favor on the particular flights proposed, but if the American government would not urge the government of Japan to grant permission for American officers to visit Japan on such an expedition it was his personal belief that the Japanese War Department would not raise objections to the projected flight across Japanese territory."[31]

A letter reply from Caffrey was finally received in Washington on 7 January 1924 stating that the Japanese would offer no objection to American army aircraft flying over or landing in Japanese territory but imposed three conditions: "(1) The only landing place permitted on the flight from the Aleutian Islands to the Island of Honshu is one on the Island of Shumushu. (2) Certain details relating to fortified zones and naval stations shall be settled by agreement between the Japanese military authorities and an American officer detailed for the purpose. (3) In case of a similar request being made by the Japanese authorities, the United States shall permit Japanese military or naval aircraft to fly over or land in American territory."[32]

In a follow-up reply, the state department told Caffrey to assure the Japanese that if Japan were to make a request to make a similar flight over the United States, "the Department would be glad to recommend to the Governors of the States . . . that permission to fly over and to land [should] be granted to the Japanese."[33]

China then had second thoughts about permitting a flight over its territory. Word had been received in Peking that the planes were military types and Chinese regulations prohibited military aircraft of foreign nations from flying over China.[34] In a return message, Secretary of State Charles Evans Hughes reiterated a letter from the war department which explained the purpose of the flight was to obtain information concerning the operation of aircraft in various climates of the world, and increase scientific knowledge of aeronautics. He added, "Naturally, this government is also desirous of being the first to circumnavigate the globe by air."

Hughes mistakenly noted that the type of plane was "a modification of a commercial airplane which has been used for some time as a commercial air transport along our East Coast. The plane is in no way a military type. It was built only for the purpose of the accomplishment of this flight."[35] The Chinese then granted permission for the flight to land at Shanghai.

Germany came back with a proviso that while it would permit the flight to cross German territory, no photographs were to be made of fortifications at Ingolstadt and Ulm, and that a copy of any photographs taken during the flight over Germany be furnished to the German government.[36] This restriction was agreed to in a follow-up telegram.

Turkey was also tardy in granting permission to enter and cross the country. The Turkish representative in England told American officials that it was probably because neither the Turkish Grand National Assembly nor the United States had yet ratified the treaty between the two nations. The U.S. High Commissioner in Turkey was informally told that the Turkish government was "desirous of having Turkey omitted from the itinerary, giving as reasons that safety to machines and crews could not be assured, or that the flight over Turkey should be postponed until appropriate arrangements can be made." The message also stated that an identical refusal had been given to a British request of a similar nature. It was pointed out to the Turks, however, that they could derive distinct benefits from such a visit by American planes but did not explain what those benefits were.[37]

There were other matters being examined on a worldwide basis. Lieutenant Crumrine, advance officer for the Sixth Division of the flight, sent a memorandum to Brown suggesting plans for the assistance of the U.S. Navy in his area of responsibility across the North Atlantic. He thought four vessels would be needed to patrol and provide communications.[38] Later, after discussions with the U.S. Navy, six vessels were made available.

By this time Lt. Clifford Nutt was in Japan and had reached agreement that two Japanese destroyers would be authorized to carry 1,000 gallons of gasoline and oil for the planes wherever it would be requested. This was only half of what would be needed, however; the rest would have to be carried by chartered ship which would take thirty days at a cost of three hundred dollars per day, payable in gold. This exorbitant price was applied because the weather in April and May in Japanese waters was so hazardous that it was almost impossible to find a ship captain willing to make the trip. One shipping firm replied that "this journey must be undertaken by those who are prepared to die."[39] Nutt then proposed that two American destroyers be dispatched with additional fuel and oil. This was acceptable to the Japanese provided one Japanese army and one naval officer would be allowed on board each American ship during the trip to the Kurile Islands.

On 2 April 1924, the commander-in-chief of the U.S. Asiatic Fleet notified United States Navy headquarters in Washington that the destroyers USS *Pope* and USS *Ford* would arrive at Yokohama, Japan, on 6 April. In addition, four other destroyers, USS *Truxton,* USS *Perry,* USS *Paul Jones,* and USS *Pillsbury,* would arrive there on 15 April to assist in patrolling the Japanese area of the World Flight.[40]

In addition to being suspicious of American intentions that the World Flight crews would be spying on their military installations, the Japanese had another reason to be contentious. For many years, American legislation establishing federal immigration and naturalization policy had been particularly harsh on Asian immigrants. The Immigration Act of 1917 barred immigration from a large geographical zone consisting mostly of Asian regions. In 1923 Congress was considering the National Origins Act, also called the Johnson-Reed Act, which would bar entry to any alien ineligible for citizenship. Since Asian immigrants were not eligible for citizenship, this law would end Asian immigration to the United States.

In the next session of Congress, the 1924 Immigration Act was being considered that confirmed the earlier law barring immigration from a large geographical zone consisting mostly of Asian regions. The Japanese, although grateful for the assistance rendered to the earthquake victims, were especially incensed about this act of rejection and blatant discrimination. Emotional reaction was very widespread and intense in Japan. If the act were passed before the World Flight, it was possible that they would refuse any incursions into Japanese air space and the entire flight would have been jeopardized. Japanese Ambassador Hanihara Masanao warned Secretary of State Charles Evans Hughes that excluding his people was "unworthy and undesirable" and would have "grave consequences upon the otherwise happy and mutually advantageous relations between" Japan and the United States.[41]

The 1924 Immigration Act was enacted with the exclusionary provisions still in effect. It was signed into law by President Coolidge on 26 May and became effective on 1 July 1924. Japanese protesters promptly designated July 1 as a so-called *Kokujokubi* or "National Humiliation Day" because, in their opinion, the Japanese people had been insulted by being singled out for exclusion. As a gesture of protest against the law, a Japanese octogenarian donated 100,000 yen ($50,000) to the Japanese Army Aviation Service, requesting that it be used to promote a round-the-world flight by Japanese airmen.[42] To prepare for such a long-distance flight, on 1 May 1925 two Japanese airmen, Yukichi Goto and Minezo Yonezawa, completed a 2,727-mile flight around Japan in a Kawanishi K-6 seaplane in 33 hours, 48 minutes flying time with eight stops.

There was one more reason that the Japanese were reluctant to allow American planes to fly over their home islands. There was the possibility of the crew members reporting visually or photographically any military buildup, especially naval shipbuilding. In 1921–1922, the question of naval disarmament had resulted in the Washington Naval Treaty after a conference between the British, American, and Japanese whereby the navies of the three nations would restrict their strengths of warships to a ratio of five, five, and three, respectively. The Japanese Navy was by no means united in its willingness to accept these relative strengths. There is evidence from deciphered Japanese cables that the Japanese planned to construct a fleet with America as the hypothetical enemy. At the time of the World Flight they would not want any military buildup detected.[43]

There were, in short, strong reasons why the Japanese Army and Navy departments objected to the Americans flying through Japan but they did relent on one point: there would be no objection if a nonstop flight were made from the Aleutian Islands directly to Aomori, a seaport in the northern part of the main island. The Vice Minister of Foreign Affairs finally prevailed over the military and the flight was approved with the stipulation that Japanese officers would accompany the American ships that would be used to refuel the planes. When there was no objection to this from the United States, the last diplomatic hurdle was cleared and detailed planning could continue in earnest.

# 2. The Preparation

One of the major dates in the history of the first World Flight was 6 November 1923. On that date, General Patrick formally and confidently requested authority from the War Department to send a flight of four Army Air Service airplanes around the world in the spring and summer of 1924. "This matter has been under consideration for several months," he wrote, "and sufficient data is now available to indicate the entire feasibility of such a project and to allow an estimate of the cost to be made."

The purposes of the flight were to "gain for the Air Service added experience in long-distance flying, and particularly in the supply problems connected therewith, to complete an airplane flight around the world in the shortest practicable time, to demonstrate the feasibility of establishing an airway around the globe, and incidentally to secure for the United States, the birthplace of aeronautics, the honor of being the first country to encircle the world entirely by air travel."

In further rationalization for the flight, the letter added, "the Air Service has endeavored during the last few years to foster the development of aviation in spite of the limited funds available, and though we still lag behind the world powers in the size of our air force and in the commercial use of aircraft, the Army Air Service has brought to this country many aeronautical records of importance and has done much to place America in the lead in airplane performance and development. The successful completion of the proposed flight will further stimulate interest in commercial aviation and will likewise demonstrate the importance of aircraft in national defense. Several unsuccessful attempts have been made by foreign countries to make such a flight. This feat can now be accomplished by the Army Air Service, though heretofore it has scarcely been practicable, because in spite of their other achievements, the aircraft industry had, until recently, failed to develop an all-American airplane believed to be suitable for such a flight."[1]

The flight was approved by the Army Chief of Staff and the Secretary of War. When it was announced to the public, there were critics who held strong reservations about the success of such an undertaking. The airplanes selected for this endurance flight were open-cockpit biplanes untested in the weather extremes expected. They were constructed of wood, fabric, and wire and the engines were surplus World War I Liberties that rarely could be run for more than fifty to seventy-five hours before failure or needing replacement. There were only three cockpit instruments for navigation in addition to the compass: altimeter, bank-and-turn indicator, and airspeed indicator. The gist of the argument against the flight was that the United States would be risking its national reputation on a hazardous undertaking.

To counter these criticisms, an announcement was handed out to the press that rationalized the attempt and explained the route of flight, the selection of personnel, and the training they had undergone. To alleviate concerns that there might not be sufficient information for the crews to make such a flight, it was stated that "the officers and men making this flight will be provided with accurate charts and maps which will eliminate largely the element of uncertainty, but, undoubtedly, these men will encounter many of the trials of the early explorers. . . . While the round-the-world flight appears to be a stupendous undertaking, from the data that have been compiled the Army Air Service is confident that it will bring to a successful conclusion the greatest aviation achievement yet attempted."[2]

A major conference of the World Flight planners was held at the Air Service Engineering Division at McCook Field, Ohio, on 10 November 1923. Enough information had been received from the state department and the pathfinding officers to allow more definitive decisions regarding the westbound route. The flight would pass through at least twenty-two countries and the cost, excluding the aircraft, was estimated at $127,832.71. This amount would include per diem and transportation for the advance officers, gasoline, oil, landing-field preparation, and an allowance for contingent expenses. The four planes and the necessary spares such as wings, pontoons, wheels, propellers, struts, and crating for overseas shipment, plus a fund for unexpected maintenance, were estimated at $230,000.

It had been planned at first there would have be a radio installed in at least one plane, although it was recognized that this would increase the weight, require generators and batteries with increased capacity, and a skillful operator. The radios of that day had a range of only about 150 miles under favorable conditions. This was deemed inadequate for the distances from the receiving stations anticipated on the flight. The difficult decision was made that none of the planes would have radio receivers or transmitters.

There was a question about photography for historic and publicity purposes. A fifth aircraft was suggested for this purpose but was quickly rejected. A follow-up question was whether cameras should be taken by each crew to record the flight's progress. Again, weight was the deciding factor. In those days the official World

War I Army Graflex aerial cameras, film packs, and accessories were too heavy so only small hand-held cameras would be used.

The Pacific and Atlantic crossings presented the greatest logistic difficulties. Long over-water flights were not considered practical with the equipment then available and preparation of landing sites over the entire route could not be undertaken because of the expense and the time available for the work. It was therefore decided that the portion of the flight from Seattle to Calcutta would be flown in aircraft equipped with pontoons, as would that portion of the flight from Brough near Hull, England, to the United States. The rest of the flight would be flown as land planes with wheels.

The route would be divided into six divisions and officers assigned to each were to oversee the establishment of depots and subdepots at major stops for stocking gas and supplies and routine maintenance. A seventh division was added later and each advance officer assigned was to make the necessary arrangements for refueling, quarters, meals, security, public relations, and maintenance when stops at cities across the country were decided after the flight's return to the United States.

The advance officers assigned and their divisions were:

| | |
|---|---|
| First Division | Lt. Clayton L. Bissell (Seattle to Attu) |
| Second Division | Lt. Clifford C. Nutt (Kashiwabara, Japan, to Kagoshima) |
| Third Division | Lt. Malcolm S. Lawton (Shanghai, China, to Calcutta, India) |
| Fourth Division | Lt. Harry A. Halverson (Calcutta, India, to Constantinople, Turkey) |
| Fifth Division | Maj. Carlyle H. Wash (Constantinople, Turkey, to London, England) |
| Sixth Division | Lt. Clarence E. Crumrine and Lt. LeClair D. Schulze (Brough, England, to Icy Tickle, Labrador) |

A seventh division would be organized for the flight across the United States if it appeared that at least one of the planes would be successful in reaching Labrador.

Each of these officers, all pilots, was charged with making all local arrangements necessary to ensure quick passage of the flight through his division. They were to remain in their respective areas after the flight passed to settle all bills and arrange for the return of government equipment and supplies to the United States.

Letters of introduction from influential Americans and representatives of American companies doing business in countries along the route were furnished to the advance officers and members of the flight. Eighteen supply and repair depots were designated along the route. At seven of these, major overhauls could be given; at the others, minor repairs could be made. The distribution of engines to the depots was made on the basis of replacing each engine on an aircraft after sixty hours of flight.

Spare parts would be packed in boxes made from spruce, ash, and plywood that could be used to make structural parts when needed. Gasoline would be procured from the Vacuum Oil Company (Mobil Oil) in five-gallon cans. The cans had to be lifted by hand from the ground or bobbing boats and the gasoline strained through a chamois skin before being poured into the tanks. This proved to be a back-breaking job and often required hours of effort.

Engines for the World Cruisers were selected from government stocks and, after overhaul, sent to the Douglas plant and the designated depots along the flight route. Two types of propellers were made at McCook: oak for use with pontoons, walnut when the planes were on wheels.

It was recommended by the group that the crew members selected should be sent to McCook Field for an intensified course of instruction involving the use of the earth inductor compass and the sextant and as much transition time as possible in the prototype aircraft. Maj. William R. Blair, an Army Signal Corps meteorology officer, would be assigned to study the weather in all the areas to be flown and provide instruction on weather reporting. Bradley Jones, a civilian employee and an outstanding navigator, would prepare a course on aerial navigation. Following these courses, the crews would be sent to Langley Field, Virginia, for navigation practice and operation of the aircraft on pontoons.[3] It was decided later, however, that all ground instruction for the crews would be given at Langley.

Approval of the plan was granted by Secretary of War John W. Weeks on 16 November 1923 and formally relayed to the Air Service by the Army Adjutant General on 3 December 1923.

Secretary of the Navy Edwin Denby heard about the Air Service plans and graciously offered the U.S. Navy's help to Secretary of War Weeks if it "does not involve too large operations or too much expense on our part. . . . You will understand of course that I do not mean I think for a moment of copartnership or reflected glory. I merely want to be of use to you if possible."[4]

Weeks responded and noted that the U.S. Navy had already rendered valuable help and advice during the initial planning and that he would probably call for assistance from naval vessels during the Pacific and Atlantic crossings. He said that the Atlantic portion of the route "is particularly hazardous because of weather conditions, long flights over water, and flights over uninhabited areas. In view of the fact that facilities for communication in this region do not exist, it may be necessary to call upon you for assistance in those waters."[5]

The next requirement was to choose the personnel for the flight. Word had been passed to Air Service units that application letters would be accepted through channels from pilots and mechanics. The general feeling was that those pilots who had already participated in record-making flights stood little chance of being selected. Commanders of Air Service bases in the United States were asked to forward to General Patrick for consideration their nominees from among the volunteers. One hundred and ten flying officers applied: fourteen majors, two captains, and the rest lieutenants. The total was whittled to fifty, then twenty-five, then fifteen. After carefully reviewing their service and flying records and recommendations from their superiors, General Patrick chose five lieutenants, three to pilot the World

Cruisers and two alternate pilots in case one of the others fell ill. He felt that, in addition, an experienced pilot of higher rank should command the flight and chose Maj. Frederick L. Martin. The lieutenants selected were Lts. Lowell H. Smith, Leigh Wade, and Erik H. Nelson. The two alternate pilots were Lts. Leslie P. Arnold and LeClaire D. Schulze. The mechanics for the flight would be chosen by each pilot from among eight who had been nominated after observing their work on the prototype plane at Langley Field.

Martin, 41, was a 1908 graduate of Purdue University with a bachelor's degree in mechanical engineering. He received a regular commission as a second lieutenant in the Coast Artillery that year and served in Washington, D.C., and in France with the Army of Occupation, American Expeditionary Forces (AEF), before transferring to the Army Air Service in 1920. He entered flying training, completed advanced training as a bombardment pilot, and received his wings at Kelly Field, San Antonio, on 4 August 1921. He became commanding officer of the Air Service Technical School at Chanute Field, Illinois, in 1922. He had approximately 700 hours flying time, of which about 300 hours were flying cross-country. He also was the only married officer in the group.

First Lt. Lowell H. Smith, 32, learned to fly in Mexico in 1915 while maintaining Pancho Villa's fleet of five aircraft. He enlisted as a private in the Aviation Section of the Signal Corps in April 1917 and completed flying training the following October at Rockwell Field, San Diego, where he was retained as a flying instructor. Smith, described as "sensitive and quiet, quick to think, but slow to speak" was commissioned a first lieutenant, then a temporary captain, and received heavy bombardment training in England during 1918 but did not get into combat. He decided to remain in uniform after the war and was given the permanent rank of first lieutenant; he was assigned to Rockwell Field as an engineering officer and later pioneered basic techniques for fighting forest fires with aircraft in the Pacific Northwest for four years. This experience gave him valuable seasoning in cross-country flying. He earned the Mackay Trophy for his part in the 1919 Transcontinental Reliability and Endurance Contest from San Francisco to New York and return in fifty-four hours. He finished third flying one of the U.S. Army's planes in the Liberty Engine Builders' Race at St. Louis in 1923.

In June 1923 Smith and Lt. John P. Richter conceived the idea of refueling an airplane in midair. They made the world's first complete pipeline refueling between two aircraft in flight. The following August the duo set an endurance record of more than thirty-seven hours with aerial refueling and established sixteen world records for distance, speed, and duration. The two gained more fame on a nonstop, twelve-hour "dawn-to-dusk" flight from Sumas on the Canadian-Washington border to the Mexican border at Tijuana with two aerial refuelings during the 1,280-mile flight. By the time of his selection for the World Flight he had 1,700 hours flying time of which nearly 1,000 hours were cross country.

First Lt. Leigh Wade, 27, enlisted in the Michigan National Guard in 1916. He served on the Mexican border during the search for Pancho Villa, volunteered for the Air Service, and took training as a pilot with the Royal Flying Corps at Toronto in 1917. He went to England that year and to France in 1918 where he was assigned to test the planes being purchased from the French and British for the Americans. He was eventually made commanding officer of the 120th Aero Squadron which gave advanced combat training to new pilots arriving from the United States. When the war ended, he was assigned to the Technical Information Service in Paris and was responsible for evaluating captured enemy aircraft. Upon return to the States, he was assigned to McCook Field as a test pilot flying all types of American and foreign planes. He made many high altitude flights and set an altitude record of 27,120 feet in a multiengine plane. (This record was soon broken by other McCook pilots.) Typically, as with most test pilots then, he had a number of mishaps caused by engine and propeller failures. He had extensive experience in photographic expeditions, the most noteworthy being high-altitude aerial photography of the White Mountains in New Hampshire and Vermont during 1921. He participated in the bombing maneuvers that resulted in the sinking of captured German ships off the Virginia coast in 1921 and had 1,500 total flying hours, 800 of them on cross-country flights.

First Lt. Erik H. Nelson, 36, was born in Stockholm, Sweden. He served five years on several merchant vessels and made two voyages around the world before coming to the United States in 1909 to work as a racing yacht captain. Nelson started a small automobile shop with a cousin but it failed, and he became a mechanic for an exhibition pilot who went broke and did not pay him his final month's wages. He wandered around New York City seeking various jobs as an actor in an opera, a Swedish massager, and a swimming instructor in a men's club. He became a mechanic for two automobile companies and then was hired as an aircraft mechanic by Curtiss Aeroplane Company. He tried to enlist in the Lafayette Escadrille of the French Air Service but was turned down. He finally managed to enlist as a mechanic in the U.S. Army Signal Corps—which then included the air arm—in October 1917. He applied for flight training and completed it in April 1918 but did not go overseas. He garnered extensive cross-country flying experience. His most notable flights were the Gulf to the Pacific flight of 1919; the Air Service flight from Mitchel Field, New York, to Nome, Alaska, and return in 1920; and the San Antonio to Puerto Rico flight of 1923. The year before, he had won the *Detroit News* Aerial Mail Trophy Race in a Martin MB-2 bomber. With a firm reputation established as an excellent mechanic as well as a pilot, he was stationed at McCook Field with his primary duty as maintenance liaison officer for all Air Service activities in the United States. He was very enthusiastic about the World Flight and when he became involved in selecting the aircraft, he requested that he be allowed to participate. He had 1,600 hours flying time with 800 hours flying cross country.

First Lt. Leslie P. Arnold, 30, was chosen as one of two alternate pilots but replaced Sgt. Arthur H. Turner as a mechanic when the latter became ill at Seattle before the flight departed. A native of New Haven, Connecticut, Arnold once toured New England as an actor in summer stock and later sold pianos to farmers' wives. He enlisted in the Signal Corps in 1917 and was graduated from the Military School of Aeronautics at Princeton University where he had studied aeromechanics, aerodynamics, and gunnery. Qualified as a mechanic, he was accepted for pilot training and after graduation was sent to Issoudun, France, where he served as a flying instructor until sent to the front with the 1st Observation Squadron in the Zone of the Advance just as the Armistice was signed. He remained in France until July 1919 ferrying and salvaging aircraft. Upon his return to the States, he ferried Martin bombers and participated in the 1921 bombing tests organized by Gen. Billy Mitchell to prove that airplanes could sink battleships. He participated in air shows, took special training in aerial photography, and was graduated from the Air Service Photographic School in 1922. By 1924 he had over one thousand hours of cross-country flying.

Lt. LeClair D. Schulze, 32, the other alternate pilot, held a bachelor of arts degree from the University of California and a doctor of jurisprudence degree from Stanford University before enlisting as a private in the Aviation Section of the Army Signal Corps in 1917. He received initial flying training in Tours, France, and qualified as a pilot in 1918 before proceeding to Furbara, Italy, for monoplane pursuit training. He then transferred to Issoudun, France, as an instructor, test pilot, and engineering officer. He left the service briefly after coming home from France but returned to duty as a test pilot and participated in several air races, including the Pulitzer races in 1922. Designated as an alternate pilot for the world flight, he later served as an assistant advance man for the leg across the North Atlantic, by which time he had more than 850 flying hours.

A few days before Christmas 1923, Martin, Wade, Smith, and Nelson received orders to report for six weeks of training at Langley Field during the first week of January 1924. This instruction consisted of a concentrated course in aerial navigation, meteorology, and first aid. The mornings were dedicated to these subjects while the afternoons were spent going over the maps and the pilot books containing information that Lts. St. Claire Streett and Robert J. Brown Jr. had collected. Major William H. Blair, the Signal Corps meteorologist; Bradley Jones, civilian employee from McCook Field; and Major Herbert C. Neblett, Medical Corps, were also sent to Langley on temporary duty to lecture respectively on world weather conditions, navigation, and emergency medicine. Navy Lt. Logan C. Ramsey at the Naval Air Station, Hampton Roads, Virginia, volunteered to provide instruction on operation of pontoon-equipped aircraft carrying various loads. Instruction was provided by the Navy in operating the World Cruiser prototype on floats. Two twin-engine Curtiss F-5L seaplanes were made available to give the pilots dead reckoning practice over the Atlantic Ocean out of sight of land.

Each of the pilots also made practice flights in the Douglas prototype with heavy loads up to 8,300 pounds with several types of pontoons and propellers to determine the best types for the heavy-duty work expected. Nelson, now officially designated as engineering officer for the flight, reported the results of the changes he wanted on the four production aircraft to McCook and the Douglas Company.

General Patrick had determined earlier that the pilots could select their own mechanics on the flight. Eight enlisted mechanics were chosen to proceed to Langley Field on 28 January 1924 to work on the prototype plane and assist in making any modifications that Nelson wanted, plus practice changing the landing gear from wheels to pontoons and performing routine maintenance. Of those eight, Martin selected as his mechanic Staff Sgt. Alva L. Harvey, 23, a tall Texan who had enlisted in the Air Service in May 1919 and completed the Mechanics' School at Kelly Field, San Antonio. He transferred to Chanute Field, Rantoul, Illinois, in 1921 and made a number of flights with Major Martin, then the mechanics' school commander, who was impressed with Harvey's initiative and willingness to work long hours to accomplish the necessary tasks. Harvey had taken up parachute jumping and made a number of exhibition jumps throughout the country at air fairs in 1922 and 1923.

Smith selected Tech. Sgt. Arthur H. Turner, 26, who had worked and flown with him on the Pacific Coast. Turner was stationed with the 91st Observation Squadron at Crissy Field, San Francisco, and had been recommended highly by his commanding officer. Smith had been impressed with his mechanical knowledge during the forest patrol operations and his efficiency at getting difficult tasks completed.

Wade selected Staff Sgt. Henry H. Ogden, 23, youngest of the World Fliers, who had enlisted in 1919 and had experience as a mechanic and instructor at Air Service repair depots in Alabama, Texas, Michigan, and Illinois. Shy, modest, and studious, his specialty was trouble-shooting and he spent his leisure time experimenting with aircraft engines and performing plane-to-plane transfers in midair at county affairs. After he passed a stiff oral examination by Lts. Smith and Nelson, he was recommended to Wade.[6]

Patrick authorized the selection of one officer with experience as a mechanic and Nelson selected Lt. John T. Harding, 27, a talented son of an inventor and chemical engineer. He had prior experience as a locksmith, road tester for automobiles at the Chalmers and Dodge auto factories, and auto mechanic. He had completed a course in mechanical engineering at Vanderbilt University and another at the University of Tennessee before enlisting as a private in the Aviation Section of the Signal Corps in August 1917. His mechanical skills quickly became well-known when he repaired the officers' personal and staff cars; as a result, he was sent to the Aviation Mechanics Training School in St. Paul, Minnesota. He transferred as a sergeant to Wilbur Wright Field, Dayton, and earned ratings as a Master Signal Electrician and Aviation Mechanician. He was selected as the main mechanic on a Martin bomber that made a flight around the rim of the United States in 1919, the first time the nation had been circumnavigated by air. When his enlistment was up in 1921, he remained with the Air Service as a civilian mechanic at McCook Field and accepted a reserve commission as a second lieutenant. Nelson had worked with him at McCook and selected him "on account of his exceptional qualifications as an engineer officer and to give representation to the Officers' Reserve Corps."[7] A gregarious individual, Harding had a singular physical distinction: one brown eye and the other blue, which people apparently found fascinating. He also wore a perpetual smile for which he was nicknamed "Smiling Jack."

Many decisions about the flight were being made as the requirements became clearer while the crews were at Langley. It was at this time that the decision was made to omit radios being installed in any of the planes. Other decisions included specifications for batteries, instruments, special tools and wrenches, spare parts, sea anchors, tail skid assemblies, geared hand pumps, winter flying suits and sleeping bags, all to be procured and delivered to Santa Monica by March 1 or to Seattle before April 1, and to designated depots around the world.

Propellers on the prototype World Cruiser proved to be unsatisfactory during tests at Langley and the solution was to provide two types, one like those on the Martin bombers for use when a Cruiser was used as a land plane and the other for operations from water where more takeoff power was needed. All were manufactured at McCook Field and shipped to Santa Monica and the various world stops.

The pontoons were especially vulnerable to damage with the many water landings anticipated. The crews and advance officers were cautioned about the handling of the planes after they landed. "Great stress must be laid upon the fact that the material from which the pontoons are constructed is very fragile," Maj. Oscar Westover wrote to General Patrick, enclosing photographs of the correct and dangerous positions for boats to approach the planes on the water. "No boats of any kind, or of any size, should come so near that they could by any chance touch any part of the plane," Westover said. "It must be impressed upon all boatmen . . . that they will not approach the boat near enough even to cast a line until the mechanic is in position to receive it. After the line has been received by the mechanic, they will 'weigh off' or hold the boat in such position as to keep the line fairly well extended."[8]

After the training was completed at Langley, all of the maps for the entire route were then studied and the lines of flight connecting the intended landing points marked on them. The distances and compass courses were filled in, along with notes on harbor facilities and emergency landing fields. These were sent to Washington to be supplemented with any new information, shipped to the main supply bases of each division, and given to the crews upon arrival at the various stops.

On 15 February 1924, the flight crews, including the two alternate pilots, Arnold and Schulze, reported to General Patrick in Washington for final instructions. While there they met Secretary of War John W. Weeks and President Coolidge. They waited for more than an hour in the White House while the president greeted a group of farmers, then some American Indians who had been promised a chance to meet the president. When the flight crews entered the Oval Office, it was obvious from the mountain of papers piled on his desk that the president had much work to do. He stood by the door, shook hands with each flier and his body language suggested that they should leave immediately. When someone suggested that the president should have his picture taken in the rose garden with the men who were going to show the American flag around the world, Coolidge hesitated, then followed, saying "Hurry up! Hurry up!" The fliers were disappointed at this reaction but Wade shrugged it off, saying the president, not known to have any real interest in aviation, at least smiled for the picture.

The eight fliers and two alternates also met with Maj. Gen. John L. Hines, Army Deputy Chief of Staff, and General Hatsutaro Haraguchi, Japanese military attaché at the Japanese embassy, to discuss their planned route through Japanese territory. They then departed for Santa Monica; each was given a few days' delay en route to visit their families before reporting to the factory on 25 February. None of the planes was as yet completed upon their arrival so they familiarized themselves with the installation of instruments and general shop practices at the Douglas factory.

By this time the flight was gaining considerable publicity and the crew members received numerous invitations from civic organizations in the Los Angeles area for luncheons and dinners where Martin was called upon to give short talks. "In this way a great amount of interest was developed in our undertaking among the citizens of Los Angeles, and through the newspapers the people of the United States were becoming familiar with the purpose, the detailed preparations, and the type of equipment used in making the flight," according to Martin.[9]

They also visited the movie studios where producers, stars, and especially starlets took full advantage of their presence to have photographs taken with the fliers to publicize themselves and their films. Free lodging was provided at the Hotel Hollywood in the famous movie city, and they were loaned two Wills–Sinclaire touring cars and a Rickenbacker limousine for local transportation.

The crews held frequent conferences at the factory to discuss details of the flight. At one such meeting it was agreed that Very pistols were to be fired when a plane had to make a forced landing. A green flare would indicate that the trouble could be easily corrected and the plane would follow soon. A red flare would mean that more time was required to correct the trouble and help was not needed. A white rocket would indicate that the plane was in distress and prompt assistance was needed. It was further agreed that the other planes would circle over the one forced down and only one of them would land to render assistance if conditions were favorable. Otherwise, aid was to be summoned from the nearest possible source.

At another conference, it was decided that as the planes were completed and test-flown, they would be assigned to the pilots in accordance with their rank and date of rank in the case of the first lieutenants. On 29 February, Number One was completed and Nelson flew it on a local test flight from the factory at Santa Monica to nearby Clover Field. He found that it was extremely tail-heavy, even with the stabilizer full forward. After test flights by the other pilots, the fittings were all changed to give the stabilizers two degrees more of incidence. This solved the problem.

By now the Air Service had revealed specifications of the planes that would attempt to reinforce world leadership in aviation for the United States. Press releases stated they were built under the leadership of Donald W. Douglas, whose factory at Santa Monica had turned out long-distance torpedo planes for the U.S. Navy. The challenge for Douglas was to build a plane heavy enough to carry all the fuel necessary for the long legs of the world flight, yet fast enough and with sufficient climbing ability to meet unforeseen emergencies. It also had to be rugged enough to withstand the pounding of heavy seas, ice floes, and hard landings, and take the punishment of the bitter cold of the Arctic, the fiery heat of the deserts, and the dampness of the tropics. And it had to be easily changeable from a land plane to a sea plane—from wheels to pontoons—with a minimum of ground equipment.

The end product was a two-cockpit, dual-controlled, single- engine aircraft that as a land plane weighed 4,380 pounds empty; or as a sea plane, 5,180 pounds empty. Each carried 450 gallons of fuel weighing 2,700 pounds and its maximum load with two crew members, fuel, food, clothing, tools, personal effects, and supplies was an additional 3,000 pounds. The engine was a twelve-cylinder, water-cooled 420 h.p. Liberty. The estimated landing speed with either wheels or pontoons was 53 mph. Top speed was estimated at 103 mph. The cruising speed expected under normal flight conditions was 83 mph. Maximum range was 2,300 miles.

The wing span of a Cruiser was 50 feet; length, 35 feet, 6 inches. The fuselage was made in three detachable sections—engine, midsection, and empennage. The wings could be folded back to save space while storing aircraft and for easier ground handling. As a seaplane, twin wooden pontoons were manufactured by the Douglas Company; the top was a thin veneer and the bottom planking was made of two plies of mahogany. The wings and fuselage were covered with fabric and veneered.

When the first plane was ready, Nelson test-flew it again and suggested some minor changes to increase stability. Changes were promptly made on the other three planes that were then flown to the Rockwell Air Intermediate Depot at San Diego for the purpose of swinging the magnetic compasses and checking the earth inductor compasses. Engines on all the Cruisers, however, developed problems after less than three hours of flight and were hurriedly replaced with reconditioned engines. Two of the planes were put on exhibition at Rockwell Field for the Army Relief on 9 March. Three of the planes were returned to Clover Field on 15 March, while the fourth, Nelson's plane, remained at Rockwell Field and would follow two days later.

Time was growing short now for a planned 1 April departure. Martin decided that the three planes at Santa Monica, to be piloted by himself, Smith, and Wade, would proceed to Seattle by way of Sacramento and Portland on 17 March and start replacing the landing gear with pontoons. The flight would be a further test of the performance of the Cruisers on long hops. The equipment and supplies for the depots were meantime being assembled and readied for shipment. Seattle was the destination for supplies for the first three divisions. The shipments to Alaskan points were carried by the Alaska Shipping Company, while those to the Orient were shipped on 10 March on the Providence Lines' *President Jackson.* Those destined for the Fourth and Fifth Divisions were sent to Europe on 2 March aboard the *Cambrai,* a U.S. Army transport. Supplies for the Sixth Division were shipped on vessels operating from New York. It was emphasized to the press that all supply shipments for the flight were being made on American ships.

In Washington, the cooperation of the U.S. Navy and Coast Guard was assured at this time by letters from the Secretary of the Navy and the Commandant of the Coast Guard. General Patrick wrote confirming letters of thanks and noted that their assistance was essential for the success of the flight.

The planning thus far had been extensive but there were still many unknowns. Would the supplies for the many stops arrive on time? Would the promised fuel and oil be available? Would the advance officers be able to visit their assigned areas and obtain the required information? Would any of the governments involved, especially those of Japan and possibly Turkey, suddenly refuse permission to land or over-fly portions of their respective domains? Would the weather in areas where advance information was not available prevent the flight's ultimate success? How reliable were the maps? Would the planes and the men themselves be able to withstand the extremes of temperature to be encountered?

The answers to these questions would all be supplied in time.

# 3. The Adventure Begins

While the crews had been training at Langley Field, Lt. Clayton L. Bissell, advance officer for the First Division, was gathering data to prepare for the flight down the Aleutians and found out how difficult his job would be. He received a seventeen-page set of instructions outlining what he would have to do before leaving for Alaska. He was to confer in Washington with U.S. Coast Guard and Bureau of Fisheries personnel and also obtain suggestions from the eight fliers about what would be needed to expedite their passage through the Aleutians. He would next proceed to the Fairfield Air Intermediate Depot, near Dayton, Ohio, to discuss shipments of supplies. Afterward, he was instructed to visit Oakland, California, to interview Capt. C. E. Lindquist, a trading-ship skipper who had sailed the Aleutian and Kurile islands for many years. This was an important meeting because "this section of the route is far removed from the regular route of travel and, on account of its barrenness, very little information is available on these islands from any of the sources which have heretofore been searched."[1]

Bissell and all the other advance officers were instructed to arrange for their own transportation to cover the flight's scheduled stops through their respective divisions. This would be especially difficult for Bissell. He was to go to Seattle and then to the Aleutians to make arrangements at all the planned stops for the flight: from changing the wheels to pontoons at Seattle, lodging for the fliers at each planned stop, and locating emergency stops, to investigating personally the harbors where landings were planned and arrange for the placement of 500-pound anchors and buoys in the harbors. He was also to have emergency rafts made at each location, arrange for small boats to be available, clear the harbor of small craft for the landings, and have ramps constructed on the beaches so the planes could be pulled up to allow the wooden pontoons to dry out. Fueling facilities had to be arranged, local representatives, guards, and interpreters interviewed and selected, and communications set up. Bissell was further instructed "not to overload the flight commander with information until he needs it."[2]

Lt. W. E. Gillmore in Washington wrote Bissell a personal letter with detailed information about steamships on which he could book passage. The trip from Seattle to Seward and Unalaska, he wrote, was relatively easy but the rest was a different story. The distance from Unalaska to Attu, the last island in the Aleutian chain, is about 1,000 miles, through heavy seas, Gillmore said, and "there are three or four revenue cutters that cruise around the Alaskan Peninsula and the Bering Sea that make their headquarters at Unalaska. Perhaps you might persuade one of these boats to take you and your supplies to Attu." He continued, "You undoubtedly know that Attu is wholly without means of communication with the outside world. The last station you will find with radio facilities is Unalaska."[3]

Bissell learned that the population of Attu was thirty-five native-borns and that Frederick Schroeder, a trapper of blue foxes, was the only white man there and the only person with a house–-and he might not be there when the fliers reached the island. He ran a store "but cannot be depended upon to furnish provisions in other than very small quantities, and only the necessities at that, so it might be well for you to take as many provisions as possible with you."[4]

Before Lt. Clifford Nutt left the Philippines for Japan, he learned that Lt. Col. L. E. Broome, the advance officer for the anticipated flight of British Royal Air Force Squad. Ldr. A. Stuart MacLaren, had been visiting facilities in the Far East in March and had provided much information about Japan and the Kurile Islands to the American embassy. The availability of fuel and oil would be a vital requirement where landings were anticipated and the Vacuum Oil Company agreed to have its representatives around the world cooperate wherever they had facilities. Petroleum supplies would be shipped on coastal steamers to Alaskan stops and, when necessary, on a U.S. Coast Guard cutter.[5]

Lieutenant Nutt was in Tokyo by mid-January 1924 and was sent instructions similar to Bissell's but with special information about the Japanese stops. He learned that the Japanese military leaders did not want the fliers to make as many landings as had been planned. Since the political situation in Japan was still sensitive, Lieutenant Colonel Fechet's letter informed Nutt to "make clear that we have no military motive in making this round-the-world flight other than the training of personnel, testing of equipment, and such incidental motives."[6]

"The point to bear in mind," Fechet noted, "is that we must land as soon as we reach Japanese territory in view of the long hop from Attu Island and the fact that we cannot land in Russian territory. The selection of the stops should be made with the important consideration in mind that flights of over 500 miles are very undesirable and, in fact, impossible for continuous flying on consecutive days, due to the fact that 500 miles is nearly seven hours' flying, at the end of which time three or four hours must be consumed in servicing the airplanes. All of this work must be done during daylight. Such a continuous strain on the personnel would obviously be very detrimental to the success of the flight; furthermore, it will be practically impossible for the flight to obtain accurate reports of weather conditions 500 miles in advance, which means it desirable that the hops be shorter than this and that, in any case, emergency landing harbors be provided so that, in case of running into bad weather, it will not be necessary for the flight to return to the last main stop, thus losing important time, not to speak of the strain on the personnel and the wear on the equipment."[7]

Nutt was also reminded that the time element in making his arrangements was urgent and that the flight should pass through his division to India as rapidly as possible to avoid the typhoon season. He was instructed, as were all advance officers, to "take steps to curtail entertainment, explaining to the local authorities that it is absolutely essential that the flight be expedited and entertainment which would tire the personnel, should be dispensed with."[8]

Fechet cautioned Nutt not to spend too much time checking out emergency harbors. One of them was Akkeshi, which the Japanese strenuously objected to as a possible emergency field. Fechet said, "This objection might be removed if it were understood that we were using pontoons entirely through Japan and making no land landings."[9]

Lieutenant Nutt later informed Washington that the Japanese were going to station a destroyer at Kashiwabara Bay on Paramushiru Island in the Kuriles and would have fuel and oil on board. They would not allow Nutt to be on board, however, so he would have to hire a boat to take him to Kashiwabara at great expense. The U.S. Navy meanwhile completed plans to assign two ships to the Yellow Sea during the passage of the flight through Nutt's division to "guard passage and furnish a radio chain." They would patrol and be available for rescue purposes and communications from the initial landing in Japan to Shanghai; two other ships would be placed on patrol at points farther west.[10] The Navy also agreed to have four vessels assigned to patrol the North Atlantic for that portion of the trip. All patrolling Navy ships would have on board aviation fuel and oil for the Cruisers.

The advance officers were advised to use discretion in answering inquiries from the news media involving diplomatic, military, or commercial relations between the United States and foreign countries. The Japanese at this time were still hedging about allowing the flight to land on the route that had been requested through Japan and it was feared that they might renege and refuse any landings at all.

"Just bear in mind the importance of getting the flight through Japan in as few days as possible," Nutt was instructed by committee chairman Brown. "It will probably devolve upon you to negotiate with the Japanese authorities that flights of over 500 miles are very hazardous and undesirable. All important matters should be handled by cable to this office. Anything you recommend will receive serious consideration and immediate action as we want you to know we are behind you in everything you do."[11]

Brown added, "the British are pretty well worked up over our flight and are planning to beat us if possible, making a race of it. They intend to leave the same time we leave Seattle." Brown said there were two prizes at stake: one, the crossing of the Pacific first and the other, the completion of the World Flight.[12]

While the world's newspapers were calling the preparations for world-girdling flights then being made in England, Argentina, Italy, and France a race, the urgency to make the schedule of a departure by 1 April from Seattle was being felt by the American planners. The U.S. Navy was also planning to upstage the Army Air Service publicity-wise by sending the dirigible *Shenandoah* to the North Pole to capture that much-prized aviation "first." Flown on her maiden voyage on 4 September 1923, the Navy airship was touted as the latest proof that its air arm was worth the high appropriations requested and that powered lighter-than-air ships had a potential far superior to its rival service. Obsessed with the need for publicity, Rear Admiral William A. Moffett, first chief of the U.S. Navy Bureau of Aeronautics, boasted six months before the *Shenandoah* flew that this untried lighter-than-air behemoth would cruise over all of America's principal cities and fly around the world, as well as over both poles.[13]

A preliminary Navy expedition was to sail from Seattle for Alaska on 16 February 1924 to prepare a mast and ground facilities for that flight. A Navy pilot named Ben H. Wyatt bragged to St. Claire Streett that soon after their arrival at Nome, he intended to hop from there to Russia and thereby be the first aviator to fly across the Pacific, bringing that honor to the United States Navy.[14] But President Coolidge canceled the *Shenandoah* flight as not worth the cost.

Maj. William R. Blair, the meteorological officer, was given orders to proceed with his equipment from McCook Field to Seattle and on to Unalaska on board the U.S. Coast Guard cutter *Haida.* The cutter would provide a valuable communications link with Nutt in Japan, stations in Alaska, and headquarters in Washington. Companion ships, *Algonquin* and *Eider,* would join the effort. When it was learned that the commercial coastal steamer *Starr* on which supplies and extra pontoons were to be shipped to Seward and Unalaska was too small, the Coast Guard volunteered to take them on one of their cutters. General Patrick immediately acknowledged this gesture, saying, "Due to the utter lack of transportation facilities of any kind over a great part of this section of the route . . . it would have been highly impossible to attempt this flight without assistance of the U.S. Coast Guard."[15]

The U.S. Navy was also gearing up to assist the flight. The commander of the Asiatic Fleet radioed Naval Operations in Washington that the destroyers USS *Pope* and USS *Ford* would arrive in Yokohama on 6 April 1924 and proceed to the Kurile Islands. In addition the USS *Truxton,* USS *Perry,* USS *Paul Jones,* and USS *Pillsbury* would patrol the Japanese area of flight and arrive in Yokohama on 15 April 1924.[16]

While the logistic and government arrangements for their arrival were being made around the world, the crews flew the four planes individually over a ten-day period beginning on 5 March to the Rockwell Intermediate Air Depot at San Diego to have their compasses swung. Each pilot had difficulty with the engine during the flight and immediately requested that new engines be installed. Nelson was especially concerned that he would not make it all the way. He flew the 125 miles at

8,000 feet in order to look continually for landing fields. The engines were changed because of valve clearance problems and the pilots were extremely concerned about their chances of completing a flight of more than a hundred miles. If the rest of the 35 engines that had been overhauled at McCook Field had the same difficulties, the flight would end sooner or later in disaster.

Major Martin sent a short progress report to General Patrick when he arrived at Clover Field from San Diego. He told about the engine problems and forecast that the first three ships would leave Clover Field, Santa Monica, on 17 March for the flight north to Seattle; the fourth (Nelson's) would follow later.

Possibly fearing criticism from Patrick about any stories in the press about his seven bachelor crewmen having a wild time, Martin explained: "It has been impossible to control publicity excepting to a limited extent. Every effort has been made to limit the amount of entertainment but we find that it has been much less a strain to accept the appointments which had been made for us by Lt. [C. C.] Moseley prior to our arrival, than to attempt to refuse all engagements. Being in the atmosphere of Hollywood, we have had some rather unusual experiences forced upon us, some of which have been rather embarrassing at times. They savored of a lack of appreciation of the dignity of the service. It is hoped that if some of the pictures which have been made when screen stars have been asked to be guests with us at some of the luncheons and dinners given in our honor, they will be accepted as not detracting from the dignity or seriousness of the mission to which we have been assigned, as it was felt by those planning these entertainments that this was a distinct compliment to the members of the flight. Of course, the cameramen have taken full advantage of these opportunities. The people of Los Angeles are wildly enthusiastic about our mission and have extended to us every possible courtesy. The Wills-Sinclaire automobiles and one Rickenbacker have been at the disposal of the members of the flight while in the city. These have been most useful as without motor transportation, we would have been quite helpless on account of the great distances to be covered in the performance of our duties. I am writing a letter of appreciation for these services. Every effort is being made to discourage prearranged entertainment in Sacramento, Portland, and Seattle. As to how successful this may be I am unable to say. We will be very thankful and happy when the flight leaves Seattle, with the nose of the planes ever pointed westward."[17]

Many airmen of those early days about to embark on an adventurous flight carried some lucky charms with them. On the day they were to leave Santa Monica, two stuffed monkeys were presented to each of the fliers. "If, after the flight, the monkeys are safely delivered to their California owners, the aviators will be paid $50 each for their trophies," Martin told a reporter.

"The owners expect to raffle the pair, the money to be donated to charity. Another unique gift was presented by a Los Angeles man. It was a $5 bill, with his name written on it. He said he would also pay $50 for its safe return. A chap from Chicago gave me a little bronze image that he said he had carried for good luck. After I took it I noticed good luck had not prevented the fellow from losing an eye."[18]

The three planes departed Santa Monica on 17 March as scheduled but ran into low clouds over the Tehachapi Mountains so they had to zigzag through the passes. "I signaled to Lt. Smith to take the lead of the formation which he did," Martin reported later, "and with his accurate knowledge of the mountain formations, he led us safely through the passes."[19]

They arrived at Mather Field, Sacramento, after 4 hours, 30 minutes of flying. They were met by the mayor and a crowd of several hundred. The crews immediately serviced their planes and were taken to town where they were guests of honor at a dinner sponsored by the Chamber of Commerce. They intended to fly to Portland, Oregon, next morning but the head winds were so strong that Martin decided they should fly instead to Eugene, Oregon. After an hour's flight they were only forty miles from Sacramento, but pushed on and the wind gradually lessened. Wade had to make a forced landing at Cottonwood, Oregon, to fix a water leak in the radiator and bent the plane's tail but the damage was not sufficient to prevent taking off when the leak was fixed. Martin decided not to land to risk damage to the other two planes and he and Smith continued to Eugene, a flight that took more than six hours. Wade and Ogden arrived three hours later and had to have a cross brace on the landing gear welded by a local worker. Again they were met by most of the city's prominent leaders and a larger crowd than at Sacramento, followed by a Chamber of Commerce dinner. It was a pattern they were to experience many times in the weeks ahead despite their fatigue from flying.

The three planes left late next morning for Vancouver, Washington, and were intercepted by five Curtiss JN-4s from the Vancouver Barracks Airdrome. Waiting for them was a large crowd from the cities of Portland and Vancouver. Vancouver's Mayor N. E. Allen had declared all government offices be closed to free the employees to go to the field. The Vancouver Prunarians, a civic organization that reflected the importance of the county's prune industry, were on hand in uniform.

The fliers motored across the Columbia River to Portland for a luncheon where they were all presented with bouquets of roses to remind then that they were in the City of Roses. They intended to leave that afternoon for Seattle but after an hour's flight, the ceiling dropped to less than 500 feet so Martin led the formation back to Vancouver for the night. That evening they received word that Nelson and Harding had flown for 9 hours, 45 minutes directly to Eugene from Santa Monica. Anxious to catch up, they followed a railroad at low altitude for the last 75 miles through fog and rain. Martin notified Nelson to join the flight at Vancouver if weather permitted but it did not. The other three departed Vancouver the next morning and arrived at the Air Service's Sand Point Field on the shore of Lake Washington by noon. Nelson landed there two hours later.

Once more they were met by local dignitaries including the state's lieutenant governor and Seattle's mayor and were motored into the city for a luncheon. Lt. Theodore J. Koenig, the field commander, had made arrangements for their lodging at the College Club in Seattle but the fliers did not want to waste the rest of the day. It was here that the planes would trade their wheels for pontoons and prepare for the long flight down the Aleutians. They returned to Sand Point that afternoon to begin the installation of the pontoons, and protect the metal parts with a no-oxide oil and spar varnish to protect them from the salt water and harsh weather conditions they would experience. A wharf had been constructed for the pontoon installations.

The men worked on their planes for the next three weeks. Engine and cockpit covers had to be made; propellers had to be changed to gain more power for the coming water takeoffs; maps needed to be assembled; and metal parts had to be continually oiled to prevent corrosion. Survival equipment was selected. This included a rifle, ammunition, a Very signal pistol and colored flares, fish hooks and lines, some concentrated food, a first-aid kit, a sixty-pound sea anchor with rope, and spare engine parts.

The limiting factor was that the total weight could not exceed 8,200 pounds and everything was weighed to the ounce. With this in mind, each man had to limit himself to two changes of underwear, fur-lined flying suit, cap, and gloves, two wool shirts, two pairs of breeches, one pair of hunting boots, handkerchiefs, a safety razor, toothbrush, and an automatic pistol. Although parachutes and life belts had been included on the original list of equipment, they were eliminated because of their weight and the space needed to include them. Nelson had to limit his personal items because as the flight's engineering officer, his plane also carried a variety of other items: a bridle sling for lifting a plane out of the water, bracing wire, gasoline hand pump for servicing the plane from a boat alongside pontoons, cans of clear dope and shellac, radiator no-leak compound, blow torch and soldering iron, extra pontoon port-hole wrench, waterproof glue, heavy canvas, small sheets of aluminum and plywood for patching pontoons, and a selection of bolts, nuts, cotter pins, and tape. The others joked that Nelson was ready for pleasure or shipwreck.

All the crews spent much time providing compartments and arranging the items for easy retrieval. The tools, spare parts, and standard utility supplies for the depots were specially packed and labeled at the Fairfield Intermediate Depot so that any tool or part needed could be readily located. The boxes themselves were waterproofed and made of ash, spruce, and plywood that could be used for emergency repairs. Carpenter tools for working the wood were sent in the tool chests. Tubing and other items that could not be bent readily were packed with the propellers in lengths of six feet or more. The weight, cubic contents, and dimensions of every article were carefully considered, and about 480 separate items were sent to each depot. All supplies that were being distributed to the various depots were scheduled to be in place at least a month before the Cruisers were scheduled to arrive.

The preparations took up most of their days but the citizens of Seattle would not let the fliers rest when a day's work was over. They were invited to dinners where Fred Martin usually delivered a talk about the preparations thus far and the route they were to fly after leaving Seattle. Arnold and Schulze, the alternate pilots, arrived from Washington and filled some of the speaking engagements.

General Patrick forwarded instructions that the planes were to be christened on 27 March in formal ceremonies and be named after four important American cities located on the four points of the compass. The pilots could select these cities and the planes were to be referred to by these names for the rest of the flight. The pilots drew names out of a hat in the order of their rank and date of rank. Martin named his plane *Seattle* out of sentiment for his home state of Washington and it was christened by Mrs. David Whitcomb Jr., wife of the Seattle Chamber of Commerce president. Mrs. Auwilda Connell, wife of Air Service Capt. Carl W. Connell, christened Smith's plane *Chicago.* Wade's plane was christened *Boston* by Mrs. Millard F. Harmon, wife of Major Harmon of the Air Service, while Nelson's was christened *New Orleans* by Mrs. Theodore J. Koenig, wife of the Sand Point Airfield commander. Martin assured Patrick that the beverage used for the christening was pure water from Lake Washington "in accordance with the spirits of the times."[20] The names were promptly painted in four-inch letters on the nose of each aircraft.

On the night of 2 April, President Coolidge sent a message to the fliers:

> More than 400 years ago men first navigated the world. Two years were required, in which many hardships were encountered. Now men travel around the earth by land and water in twenty-eight days. You are going to demonstrate the practicability of making such a voyage by air. Before another 400 years this may be the safest and most comfortable way. Your countrymen will watch your progress with hope and record your success with pride.

As the crews had been getting ready to depart, Tech. Sgt. Arthur H. Turner developed a severe cold and lung trouble and felt too weak to continue. Lowell Smith immediately chose Lt. Leslie Arnold, one of the two alternate pilots, to replace him as the mechanic on the *Chicago.*

"No man was ever more astonished than I when I found that I was to go along," Arnold said. "For months I had been assigned to the World Flight, but merely as an alternate pilot. I never dreamed that there would be the remotest chance of my actually going, because I thought that none of the pilots was likely to fall ill."[21]

Takeoff was planned for 4 April 1924 and a large crowd had gathered. The weather, however, was reported stormy all the way to Prince Rupert, Canada, the first stop, and did not clear up until the next day. There were cheers as Major Martin taxied away from the mooring marker, faced into the wind, and pushed the throttle forward. The others waited patiently for their leader to become airborne. As he gathered speed, there was a loud noise and the propeller began to vibrate. Martin immediately cut the throttle and taxied back to his buoy. The others cut their engines and waited to see if the problem would be solved quickly. It was not.

The tip of the *Seattle*'s propeller had been damaged from the water spray and was removed, repaired in the shops of the Boeing Aircraft Company and reinstalled. The next day at 8:45 A.M., Martin taxied out and took off, followed by the *Chicago* and the *New Orleans*. They made a climbing turn to gain altitude, then flew down the lake, across the narrows, and out over Puget Sound. The planes were full with the maximum load of gasoline, but the *Boston* was too tail-heavy and couldn't break the surface tension of the water. While the others continued, Wade taxied back and helped Ogden unload their rifle, a small anchor, and extra clothing.

They adjusted the stabilizer slightly, taxied out hurriedly and made a smooth takeoff, an hour after the others.

Wade flew solo to Prince Rupert through thick fog and a dead calm. "I flew right down on the water so glassy that I was constantly fearful of slapping the surface," Wade said. "I used the tree line on my left as a guide and followed it for a long way. In skimming over Johnstone Strait, we almost collided with ships twice. Later I learned that the three planes ahead of us had experienced the same floating hazard."[22]

The four planes were finally headed on one of aviation history's most daring flights. No one had crossed the Pacific Ocean before and some critics predicted that no one ever would, especially the eight who chose to fly down the Aleutian chain in frail machines of wood, wire, and cloth into the teeth of the infamous williwaws that brought heavy fog, face-stinging sleet, and extremely high winds. The fliers were aware from their contacts with the public that there were some who did not believe they had even a remote chance for success. Others were wagering that not more than one of the four planes would get all around the world when it seemed that the delays before they had all departed was only the beginning of the kinds of problems they would face as they headed down the treacherous string of islands noted for their unpredictable storms. But the eight men who volunteered for this epic flight were on a mission for their country and felt duty-bound to do their best to complete it.

Lt. Leslie Arnold recorded his impressions in a notebook after the takeoff of the *Chicago:*

As I look down on Lake Washington and Seattle and see them growing smaller and smaller behind us, I keep wondering what the people in the streets are thinking. . . . I wonder how many of us will get all the way around. . . .

Visibility is only fair this morning, but above the haze that half veils the earth the summit of Rainier stands out as clear as crystal. No wonder the Indians call it Iahuma, the mountain that is God. I saw Lowell glance back over his shoulder at it several times, and I'm sure the memory of its grandeur will inspire us all the way around the world. This undertaking somehow makes you feel the presence of the Ruler of the Universe as you have never felt it before.[23]

Lt. L. D. Schulze, the other alternate pilot, returned to Washington after the planes were airborne and made a report of his observations and recommendations to General Patrick. He noted the type of pontoon installed on the planes was very vulnerable to leaks and recommended future ones be made with two layers of plywood separated by a layer of waterproof canvas and then the whole wrapped in canvas. He was particularly critical about the condition of the four engines that had been removed at San Diego. They were "certainly not of a quality demanded by a venture of this importance, even though intended for a short flight, or even a test flight, for to subject the safety of any of these planes to the dangers involved in a forced landing, even for a minor cause, is, in my opinion, inexcusable where it is humanly

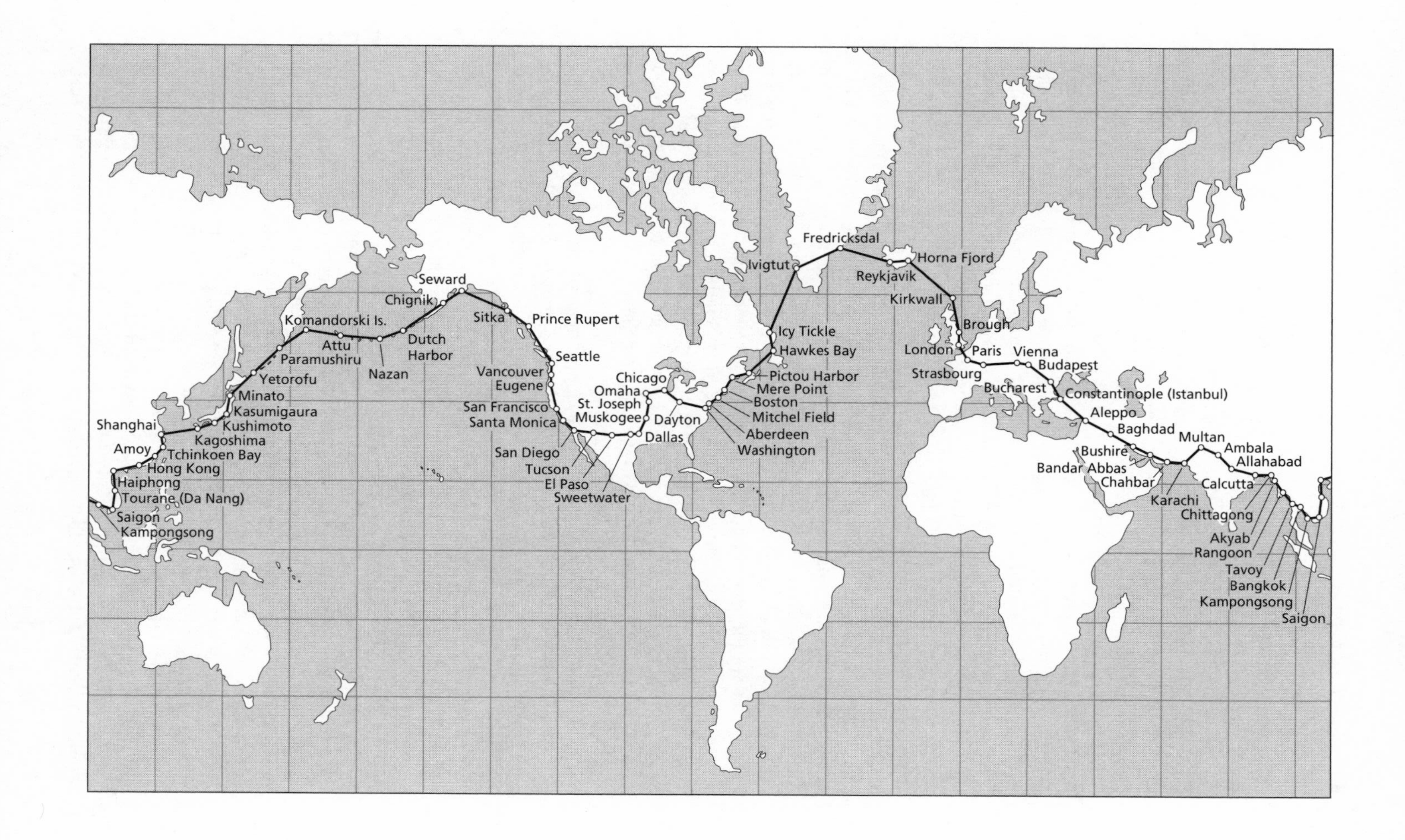
Shanghai
Amoy
Tchinkoen Bay
Hong Kong
Haiphong
Tourane (Da Nang)
Saigon
Kampongsong
Kagoshima
Kushimoto
Kasumigaura
Minato
Yetorofu
Paramushiru
Komandorski Is.
Attu
Nazan
Dutch
Harbor
Chignik
Seward
Sitka
Prince Rupert
Seattle
Vancouver
Eugene
San Francisco
Santa Monica
San Diego
Tucson
El Paso
Sweetwater
Dallas
Muskogee
St. Joseph
Omaha
Chicago
Dayton
Washington
Aberdeen
Mitchel Field
Boston
Mere Point
Pictou Harbor
Hawkes Bay
Icy Tickle
Ivigtut
Fredricksdal
Reykjavik
Horna Fjord
Kirkwall
Brough
London
Paris
Strasbourg
Vienna
Budapest
Bucharest
Constantinople (Istanbul)
Aleppo
Baghdad
Bushire
Bandar Abbas
Chahbar
Karachi
Multan
Ambala
Allahabad
Calcutta
Chittagong
Akyab
Rangoon
Tavoy
Bangkok
Kampongsong
Saigon

possible to prevent this danger. In this regard it was discovered, according to a report of several officers, that one of the motors shipped to Seattle and intended for use on the long over-water hops to Japan was faulty in one of the shaft assemblies, which would undoubtedly have caused damage before reaching Japan and this would have seriously endangered the success of the venture had this motor been used."[24]

Schulze, based on the experience on Lake Washington, reported that the crews must be vigilant about mooring their planes at an ample distance between them to avoid fouling one another in swinging with the tide and wind, as well as to obviate the possibility of collisions with the other planes and buoys when taxiing. He also recommended a safe way to moor to the buoys. This information was passed on to the advance officers for transmission to the crews.

Two days after the Cruisers departed Seattle, an article appeared in a San Diego newspaper headlined "Military Fliers Foresee Failure of World Trip." The subhead stated: "Martin's Squadron 10 Days Behind Schedule With 28,000 Miles Yet To Go." Anonymous military aviators were reported as saying that the flight would fail because the fliers were already a thousand miles behind their original schedule and thus would not be able to escape storms in Iceland and Greenland. "Many aviators believe that the war department would have achieved better results if orders had been issued for the world fliers to 'go on their own' after leaving Rockwell Field," the article stated. "At least two of the fliers, it is believed, would have been well along the Aleutian Island airway by this time, whereas the present finds the squadron limping along with a 'lame duck' and the flight to the next stop postponed indefinitely."[25] An investigation by the Air Service reported that the information originated from U.S. Navy sources.

On the diplomatic front, a communication had been received from the Japanese War Department that permission had finally been approved for the fliers to pass through Japanese waters. Most of Lieutenant Nutt's requests had been granted in his discussions with a special committee composed of eleven Japanese Army Air Service officers, seven naval officers, and representatives of the Japanese foreign office. The Japanese planned to have warships in all the harbors where the Americans intended to stop and would stand by along the route for the purpose of rendering aid in the event of forced landings or emergencies.

The Japanese Navy Department also authorized two American destroyers to proceed within the fortified zone of the Kurile Islands to carry supplies for the World Flight. Two Japanese officers would be on board each of the American destroyers to assist in guiding them through the straits between the islands. Two Japanese destroyers would accompany these American vessels. The decision to send destroyers arose when it was found that no private shipping company would risk its ships going into those waters at that time of year.

The Japanese expressed concern for all the vessels making the expedition because of the ice floes and fog prevalent during the month of April. It was presumed that there would be snow in the islands when the fliers arrived and the temperatures would be freezing. Ice would have begun to move in floes and would be a serious menace to the ships at night, as well as dangerous for the planes to land for servicing. While the Aleutians normally have a warming trend in April and May because of the warm current from the Philippines and southern Japan, the Kuriles do not benefit from this current and the fliers could expect a sudden, bitter change in temperatures during the 860-mile flight between Attu and Paramushiru.

The eight Americans were well aware of the risks. They had their orders and were determined to carry them out.

# 4. Daring the Aleutians

Martin in the *Seattle* slowed briefly after the takeoff from Lake Washington and noted that three planes were following as he headed north on the 650-mile course toward Prince Rupert usually used by steamships. Two of them were the *Chicago* and the *New Orleans.* But the third was a photographic plane that was pursuing them. Martin mistakenly identified it as the *Boston.* "As every effort had been made to have all four airplanes leave as a complete unit," Martin reported later, "it was a great disappointment to learn of this mistake, but it was considered a better policy to continue than to return again to Lake Washington, thus delaying the progress of the flight and creating an unfavorable reaction on the public."[1]

The photo plane soon dropped out and the three Cruisers headed over Puget Sound and Georgia Strait where they ran into a thick haze that seemed like smoke from a forest fire. It was the beginning of a fog that grew thicker and thicker, forcing Martin and the others to drop down to less than 100 feet above the water. They picked their way between and around small, heavily wooded islands and over an increasingly rough sea. They passed over the Discovery and Johnstone Straits and then emerged out of the fog into clear air. An excursion steamer suddenly loomed ahead and Martin banked quickly up and away from it with the others following. It had been a close encounter which could have been disastrous if they had still been hugging the water. The visibility was clear for only a few minutes before they plunged into heavy rain, which turned into sleet, then snow. Martin describes the rest of the flight:

"Along the route between the Vancouver and Queen Charlotte Islands, where the coast was exposed to the open sea, very strong quarterly winds were encountered. The sea beneath us was extremely rough. The swells were approximately twenty feet high, and breaking badly on their crest. A forced landing at this time would have spelled disaster for both the airplane and its personnel. Intermittent snow squalls continued until we were off Princess Royal Island; here the atmosphere cleared until we had a ceiling of about a thousand feet.

"Following Grenville Channel, we arrived off the entrance to Prince Rupert Harbor. Immediately after turning in toward Prince Rupert, we encountered a blinding snowstorm. The snow was so thick that it was very difficult to see. Lieutenant Nelson in the *New Orleans* stated that from his position in the formation he could not see the *Chicago* on the opposite side. As we approached Seal Cove, the yellow buoys were visible. We were then at an altitude of about four hundred feet. Knowing that the bay terminated in the mountains directly ahead and due to the poor visibility, there seemed to be ample room to glide down, turning into the wind and land near the buoys. This I did. When the *Seattle* was almost ready to touch the water, it was very evident that the forward motion would carry her against the rocks on the beach. The first impulse was to open the throttle and attempt to extricate myself from this position. A point of land jutted out to my right on which was a sawmill. Directly in front were hills whose tops were not visible on account of the storm; to the left and rear were high mountains. Realizing that on account of the weight of the airplane and its slow rate of climb, this action would result in complete disaster, I pulled back the throttle, elevated the nose of the airplane, and made a stalled landing. The plane settled slowly until about ten feet from the water when, on account of losing its forward speed, it dropped with considerable force."[2]

The impact of the *Seattle*'s hard landing damaged the left outer wing struts and some vertical brace wires on the left side causing the upper wing to sag. The *Chicago* and *New Orleans* landed safely but Smith in the *Chicago* had a very close call. On the approach to a landing its pontoons barely missed some high-tension wires stretched between poles along the beach. He just did not see them.

It had been a very hard first day. They had been in the air for 8 hours, 10 minutes. Arnold noted in his diary: "125 miles in fog, 275 in rain and snow, hell of a day."[3] While the *Seattle* was being hauled to a nearby Prince Rupert shipyard dry dock for repairs, Sergeant Harvey took out of his knee pocket a rabbit's foot that he had been given in Sacramento by a spectator and threw it overboard in disgust.

Wade and Ogden landed an hour later. Their total flying time had been forty-five minutes less than the other three because Wade had chosen a different route. He never did see the other three planes after he took off and was doing his own navigation where the weather was better than the others had experienced. All were so tired that they made no effort to service their planes that night as they had agreed they would always do. They were taken ashore in small motor boats and were greeted at first by a few spectators on the dock.

The crowd grew as the word spread that the fliers had landed. The weather had been so bad that no one thought they could make it and the reporters had returned to their hotel. The mayor greeted them, saying, "Gentlemen, you have arrived on the worst day we've had in ten years!" That evening they were hosted at a civic dinner by the townspeople and given welcoming souvenirs and good luck charms to add to those they had already received at Seattle. "Went to bed early as possible, next to exhausted," Harding noted in his diary.[4]

Martin and Harvey were downcast over the accident and their gloom spread to the rest of the fliers. Everyone was quiet and retired early at the hotel that Bissell had arranged for them. Next morning, 7 April, the *Seattle* was hoisted out of the water and it was found that the damage could be repaired by replacing the struts and brace wires. Struts were fashioned out of seasoned cypress by skilled carpenters at the Canadian Pacific Dry Dock Company and the brace wires were replaced by a set that Nelson had carried in the *New Orleans.* Martin and Harvey worked on their plane in freezing rain and snow; the others inspected their own. While handling the bottom cowling on the *Boston*'s engine, it slipped out of Ogden's hands and dropped in the cold water. It could not be retrieved so a new cowling was hammered by hand from a sheet of copper by a local tinsmith.

On the afternoon of 9 April, Martin flight-tested the *Seattle* and announced they would leave early the next day for Sitka nearly three hundred miles away. It was raining when they arose at 5:30 A.M. on the tenth but the reports from Sitka, located on Baranof Island, and points in between were encouraging so Martin decided they would go. He had previously announced that each of the pilots should have an opportunity to lead the formation. Smith was designated leader for the 282-mile hop to Alaska's first capital.[5]

For the first time all four planes left together. They took off at 9:25 A.M. and passed Ketchikan an hour later where below they could see several hundred townspeople waving on shore and on boats as they passed by at low altitude. It was raining lightly. When they were passing through Clarence Strait about sixty miles from Sitka, a thick haze cut down on forward visibility. Smith led the flight down low to about twenty feet over the water and swung south around the tip of Baranof Island to avoid the high hills that were covered with clouds. Harding noted that the water below had thirty-foot swells and visibility ahead was only about 100 yards. Then "a happy sight popped into view. That was two small fishing smacks tugging over and through the heavy sea with all hands waving frantically to us. Their friendly salutations were quickly returned, although the rain drops felt like lead shot being thrown into our faces and against our hands."[6]

Bissell, the advance officer, had reported that the harbor at Sitka was excellent—about three miles in one direction and three thousand in the other. "Coming in from the sea," Wade recalled years later, "the harbor sight was exhilarating: mirrorlike water, a tiny city back-dropped with snow-capped peaks, and a sky full of soaring seagulls."[7]

The three planes landed in the Sitka harbor at 1:35 P.M. Eilor Hansen, the local representative, had a small scow anchored in the bay waiting for them with gas and oil. They were also met on the scow by local townspeople. Waiting on the beach was a band and a large crowd; that night they were treated to a dinner at the residence of a Mr. Mills and stayed at a local hotel.

The landing approach had been a scary one for Wade and Ogden. The *Boston* got into the propeller wash of the *Chicago* and barely avoided the rocks on the side of the narrow channel. "The propeller wash from another plane is a veritable miniature cyclone," Wade explained. "It shakes you and throws your ship about and puts you through a series of crazy maneuvers that will turn your hair gray."[8]

The crews decided that henceforth they would follow a ritual for the rest of the flight: prepare the planes for the next leg before going ashore. Harding explained what they had to do: "Check gas, oil, and water. Fill gas and oil tanks to desired amount for next jump. Wash down engine and plane with kerosene to remove oil, soot, and dirt before they get cold and set. Select personal baggage to go ashore, including thermos bottles, hand ax, films, maps, etc. Cover engine section and cockpits. Check ignition leads, rigging wires, pontoons for water leakage. Fill radiator with desired alcohol, glycerin, and water mixture. Flush gasoline strainers and clean voltage regulator and reverse current relay coil-breaker gaps. In other words, get the plane all OK for early start next day, weather permitting. [It's about] three to five hours real honest-to-goodness manual labor. Every move on the plane or near the pontoons had to be done carefully for fear of falling into the water, or breaking something."[9]

They did not get off on the morning of the eleventh because of heavy rain. That afternoon a raging sleet storm developed and someone noticed the *Boston* was dragging its anchor and heading toward a barge and flat rocks near the *New Orleans.* Everyone rushed to the shore and a number of small boats were engaged to prevent its drifting until additional anchors could be found and attached to all the planes. There was another near disaster when Harding accidentally released the *New Orleans* from its moorings and the wind carried it rapidly toward the *Boston.* Ogden saw the danger and shouted to H. E. Smith, a forest ranger in a nearby boat, who hurriedly maneuvered to stop the plane's drift when it was only two feet away from a collision that would have severely damaged both planes. Arnold, in his diary, noted, "Without him we would have lost two of the planes right then."[10]

When the day was over, Arnold wrote, "Everyone was soaking wet, cold, tired, and hungry, and in spite of Prohibition we cracked the medical supply and all had a good stiff drink. And we needed it, too."[11]

It rained, hailed, and snowed on the twelfth and there was another incident that could also have spoiled the flight. While Harding was checking the *New Orleans* in the evening, it slipped its moorings and started to drift toward the rocks on shore. In desperation, he frantically removed the engine and cockpit covers, jumped into the cockpit, primed the engine and started it. He held it in position with the power on until a boat got a line to the plane and he was able to taxi it back to its position and moor it securely. "Such circumstances as these kept all of us under a tremendous strain as to the safety of our planes, both day and night," Martin reported later.[12]

The morning of 13 April was clear and calm so Martin decided they would take on 325 gallons of fuel in anticipation of flying to Seward instead of stopping at Cordova if the weather were clear when they approached. With Wade leading, they took off but the clear weather soon dissipated and they flew into violent snowstorms.

To be able to navigate, Wade flew over the shoreline at about 100 feet while the others flew in echelon formation offshore. Nelson describes the danger they faced:

> We had to descend to the edge of the water and crawl along the beach to keep from getting lost. Leigh [Wade] suddenly turned the *Boston* sharp to the left as though he had seen a mountain up ahead. The rest of us were so close to him that it was all we could do to bank steeply enough to avoid crashing into each other. By the time we flattened out again, we were separated and out of sight of each other in the snow. But luck was with us and we got together again in a few minutes.[13]

The planes continued on to Yakutat Bay at about ten feet above the breakers. "The beach was covered with snow and the air around us was filled with it," Nelson recalled. "Everything was one color and we might have almost been flying in total darkness. Sometimes we flew so low that our pontoons almost dragged on the water. Occasionally we passed over wrecked boats half buried in the sand, or over piles of logs washed up by the sea, and I kept wondering if we would hit them. Most of the time I flew standing up in the cockpit braced against the back of the seat with my feet on the rudder bar so that I could look out over the front of the plane as well as over the side."[14] Arnold noted in his diary, "I hope we never have to fly through such thick weather again."[15]

The weather suddenly broke into completely clear skies and unlimited visibility as they approached Cordova. They decided not to land as they thought they would if the weather ahead were intolerable. They proceeded instead to a landing in Resurrection Bay at Seward. They learned later the citizens of Cordova were disappointed because they had arranged a reception and dinner, and had even sent all the way to the States for decorative bunting. Martin radioed apologies to the mayor later when he found out how much the town had done to honor them.

In Seward they taxied to the prearranged buoys and met the mayor, H. B. Ellsworth, the local representative, and arranged for servicing of the planes for the flight to Chignik. They stayed that night in the Hotel Van Gilden and awoke on the morning of 14 April to find it snowing and blowing hard. Extra anchors were put out to guard against heavy winds when the fishermen told them the harbor gets so rough that they can't bring their boats into the docks. They relaxed that day and were entertained for several hours as the fishermen taught them to tie knots. Martin had lost his glasses somewhere and purchased reading glasses in town so he could read his maps. The weather improved that night and the moon came out bright and clear. "The effect it had upon the mountains was beyond description," Arnold wrote. "The most wonderful scenic effects in the world are right here in Alaska, I claim."[16]

Up at 5 A.M. on 15 April, the pilots checked the weather while the mechanics went to the planes after warming some oil over a bonfire onshore. The planes left for Chignik at 11 A.M. in exceptionally clear weather for the 425-mile flight with Nelson leading in the *New Orleans*. The *Seattle* had difficulty getting off so the other three planes circled and took photographs of each other as Martin taxied back and tried again; he succeeded on his third attempt. For the next four hours, the flight was uneventful and even enjoyable, although stiff head winds slowed them down considerably. Harding remarked, "The clear deep blue water below, clear sky above, and snow-covered peaks and glaciers on our right were beyond description in beauty and splendor."[17]

Three crews of the planes, all flying into extremely strong winds, noticed that the *Seattle* had dropped down to a lower altitude than they were and had been staying to the rear of the formation. All but Martin climbed over a mountain while he chose to go around it. When they reached Cape Igvak at 2:30 P.M., the *Seattle* could not be seen through the thick haze and everyone was uncertain as to whether Martin and Harvey were really in difficulty or still just lagging in the rear. With such fierce head winds, they did not have enough fuel to return and search and still reach Chignik. Reluctantly they sped on to reach Chignik as soon as possible. They landed on Anchorage Bay in a poorly protected harbor at 4:22 P.M. They had logged 6 hours 38 minutes flying time.

The mechanics tied their planes to prearranged buoys while Wade and Nelson hurried ashore to radio the information to Unalaska that their leader was missing and believed down on Portage Bay. When he did not arrive by dark, they requested that the U.S. Navy immediately send the *Corey* and *Hull* to that area. Both ships, about twelve hours away, proceeded at full steam and estimated they would reach the bay the next morning. Radio messages were broadcast requesting any vessel in the vicinity to assist in the search. The Alaskan mail steamer *Starr* responded immediately and headed for the area while relaying radio messages to other stations telling of the missing plane.

It was to be another unforgettable day for Martin and Harvey. After about four hours of flying, Harvey, looking over Martin's shoulder at the oil-pressure gauge, suddenly yelled at Martin that the pressure had dropped to zero. There was no alternative but to seek a landing immediately. They were at about 500 feet over Portage Bay off Cape Igvak where the sea was reputed to be the roughest body of water along the Alaskan coast. Martin had enough power left to maneuver into the shelter of a cove and made a safe landing in smooth water. He warily taxied parallel to the beach and shut the engine down.

As soon as Martin slowed the *Seattle* sufficiently, Harvey leaped out on the pontoons to look at the engine and found a three-inch hole in the left side of the crankcase. Both men looked skyward to see if the others had noticed they had dropped out but no planes appeared. They were alone and helpless and there were no signs of habitation onshore.

Martin could not explain why the other planes had not seen him head to Portage Bay. In a letter he wrote to General Patrick, he said, "Our arrangements are that the last ship will fly over the ship in distress until they get a Very pistol signal indicating the seriousness of the trouble. Why this was not done I have not had an opportunity to learn. The seriousness of this oversight will be impressed upon all."[18]

Martin and Harvey were so sure that assistance would come soon that they decided to sleep in their cockpit that night, rather than wade ashore and build a fire to dry out their clothes. They ate a few malted milk tablets and divided the night into watches of four hours each, with Martin taking the first watch. Still, despite their heavy winter flying suits, gauntlets, and fleece-lined moccasins, neither could sleep because of the bone-chilling cold. They pulled the canvas cockpit cover over their heads and sat slumped shivering in their seats. The wind began to pick up ominously, followed by icy rain and snow showers.

At 5 A.M. Martin saw thin wisps of smoke on the horizon, which soon magnified into two U.S. Navy destroyers heading in their direction. Harvey fired three flares at one-minute intervals with the Very pistol. Both ships stopped briefly and then seemed to move on, so Harvey fired three more shots. One of the ships approached cautiously to within a mile of the plane and a small launch was sent with the executive officer of the USS *Hull* on board. The launch towed the plane to the destroyer and the men were treated to a hearty breakfast. They learned that the other ship was the USS *Corey* and both had been making soundings for the U.S. Army Signal Corps that was laying a cable that summer. They had completed their work and were returning to Seattle. They had heard the broadcast asking for help to locate the World Cruiser and had proceeded full speed to Portage Bay, a distance of 312 miles. The *Corey* radioed that Martin and Harvey had been located and that a replacement engine as well as gas and oil were needed.

Others had begun searching on land when they heard the radio reports. Phil B. Reed, superintendent of an oil-drilling operation for Standard Oil Company at Pearl Creek, had left on horseback for Kanatak to board the company ship *Pilgrim,* and was then en route from Kodiak to aid in the search. The snow in the pass was eight to ten feet deep as he tried to follow a tractor path through the mountain range. He did not arrive until the next afternoon. When he learned what Reed had done, Martin promptly wrote a letter of thanks for his efforts to Reed's headquarters in San Francisco.

The weather continued to worsen. Martin and Harvey were advised that it would be nearly impossible to anchor the plane offshore because of the extremely high winds on the bay. They were towed in the plane ten miles to the village of Kanatak where they were greeted by the entire population of forty. They floated the plane carefully into a narrow creek and then into a small pond with the help of men from the village. They slept that night in the living room of Charles Madsen, proprietor of the general store.

It was the next day that the two men first experienced the destructive winds called the williwaws that sweep down from the mountain passes at tremendous velocity. They were told stories about how they would tear boats from their moorings and toss them up on the beach in pieces and even rip life boats from their fastenings on large ships and smash them into bits. "We labored under constant dread that the *Seattle* might be destroyed at any time, night and day," Martin wrote. "It is believed that only due to the constant vigilance, assisted by men from the village of Kanatak accustomed to lightering supplies from the boats that come into the harbor, that the *Seattle* was protected from destruction."[19]

Martin told of an incident when he and Harvey had returned to Madsen's house after checking the lines holding the plane. They suddenly heard the howling of a williwaw passing through the village and rushed to the window in time to see the *Seattle* lifted completely out of the pond and dropped heavily on its right pontoon. They rushed out to check the damage and tighten the lines. Fortunately, no damage had been done.

Smith and the others had meanwhile landed at Chignik and learned of the *Seattle*'s plight. They radioed Bissell at Dutch Harbor to rush a new engine to Martin on the U.S. Coast Guard cutter *Algonquin*. At the same time Martin radioed Smith to proceed to Dutch Harbor and he would meet them there as soon as the engine was installed and weather permitted.

Martin and Harvey worked for three days in the high wind and blowing snow disconnecting the damaged engine. The new engine arrived on 19 April. A whale boat brought the engine ashore and placed it on a motor launch with a boom that was towed into the pond at high tide. But high winds prevented them from working for two days. Martin developed a severe cold and stayed in bed. A watchman was hired to keep an eye on the plane. When the wind calmed down on 21 April, Harvey and sailors from the *Algonquin*, with some townspeople handling the lines, worked from 7:30 P.M. until 6 A.M. next morning in blowing snow, using gasoline lanterns for light, and installed the new engine.

Another williwaw hit on the twenty-third and ice formed around the plane. Men from the village helped Martin and Harvey break it up to prevent the wood veneer pontoons from being crushed. It was decided to make skids and place them under the pontoons. Then they could drag the plane down the creek to the bay where it had become sufficiently calm to take off. This was done and early on the morning of the twenty-fifth, the plane was dragged to the bay just as it began to snow; high waves were developing and visibility was extremely poor. Favorable radio reports from Chignik had come through that morning and Martin decided to take off, hoping that the storm was local and they would soon fly out of it. He lifted off without difficulty and realized immediately that he should not even attempt to take a direct heading to Chignik.

"It was too dangerous to fly a compass course on account of the limited visibility," Martin said, "making it impossible to check our position except that we were within a few hundred feet of the shoreline on account of the danger of flying directly into some of the projecting head lands along the route. This made it necessary to fly directly over the shoreline. Such an emergency had been considered and under such circumstances, Sergeant Harvey was always to watch for obstructions on the opposite side of the plane from which I might be looking. It was necessary that I keep my eyes constantly on the shoreline which was on the starboard side and, when the shore was visible on the port side, Sergeant Harvey would kick the rudder and I was forced at times to bank the plane vertical to escape disaster as danger was always near at hand. Under these conditions, we followed the shoreline for two hours, fifteen minutes without an opportunity to look at my map."[20]

The snow continued as they came across a bay and Martin considered landing on a quiet stretch of water. They plunged on briefly but when the snow increased, he turned around and landed. Harvey dropped the anchor while Martin checked his maps and decided that they were on Kujulik Bay, east of Chignik. After they waited an hour and a half, the storm abated; they took off and landed smoothly on Anchorage Bay where the village of Chignik sat at the foot of mile-high mountains rising abruptly out of the sea. It consisted of a few dozen huts, two canneries, a hundred Aleuts, and twenty whites whose job was to get the canneries ready for the annual salmon run.

After learning that their leader was safe, the other fliers spent the time tending to their planes, visiting the radio station that Bissell had arranged to handle their messages, listening to the amusing bear, deer, and fish stories told by the local fishermen, and resting in a cannery bunkhouse. The fliers were all impressed with a Sergeant Rogers and his ability to "talk" in code on the radio. He was able to communicate with the station at Dutch Harbor, with the ship that brought mail and provisions, and with other stations many miles away. "Thanks a million times for radio in such places," Harding jotted in his diary.[21]

On 19 April, a message was received from Martin that the *Seattle* was being towed to Kanatak and it would take several days to replace the engine. He felt it would be best for the group to push on to Unalaska Island and wait for him there. Unalaska was a major supply point with better facilities for taking care of the planes, changing the engine on the *Boston* (Wade reported it was failing), taking on supplies, and preparing for the long flight-legs to Japan.

"About that time a radio message came through from a thousand miles to the southwest with the news that all the harbors in the Kurile Islands were filled with ice and that it was doubtful if we could get through and on to Japan," Smith said. "But we didn't let that disturb us, and we decided that we were going to get to Japan, even if we had to put the planes on skis and slide there!"[22]

A stiff wind was blowing when the men untied their planes from the buoys. They took off from Chignik and experienced what a williwaw was like in the air. "The old wheel was fairly spinning in both directions and Wade and Erik and I had to keep kicking the rudder bar to stay right side up," Smith said. "This condition continued and the 'willies' threatened us until we reached Dutch Harbor."[23]

After leaving Chignik, the crews repeated most of the experiences of their previous flights, going around, under or over snow squalls, looking down on rocky islands and volcanoes and upward at ice-capped mountains. Smith was leading and took a shortcut over Kuiukta Bay and Fox Cape, along the southern edge of the Alaska Peninsula and over Umnak and Akutan Islands, into the waters off Dutch Harbor on Unalaska Island where the *Haida* was waiting patiently. The 390-mile flight had taken 7 hours, 26 minutes. "To buck strong, gusty head winds for this length of time to only get 390 miles is no easy or pleasant task," Harding recalled. "Both of us were tired, cold, disagreeable, and hungry. The men of the *Haida,* with their trained crew of blue-clad sailors in their boat, was certainly a pretty and welcome sight."[24]

The crews landed and tied up to the moorings in the harbor that had been prepared as requested and a guard was hired to watch the planes at night. They were greeted on shore by Bissell and Maj. William R. Blair, the weather officer, Capt. J. F. Hottell, and eighty men of the U.S. Coast Guard cutter *Haida.* A Pathé News cameraman named Hudson was also there and filmed their arrival. Exhausted, the fliers were given a Thanksgiving-like dinner of turkey with the usual trimmings, and escorted to the quarters given up for the night by the *Haida*'s men. The *Haida*'s searchlight was flashed on the planes every five minutes during the hours of darkness so guards could check on their condition.

At 3 A.M. the guard roused Smith and Nelson out of a sound sleep and said a williwaw had blown one of the planes loose and another was drifting dangerously. The two were rushed out by motor launch and reinforced the moorings. That day it was decided that wooden ramps would be built on the beach and the planes towed up on them. Runways were constructed of 3″ × 12″ planks that were weighed down with bags of sand to hold them steady. The planes were winched up on them and tied down so the crews had an opportunity to go over their planes more thoroughly than if they were in the water. The engine exhaust manifolds on all the planes were badly burned and cracked and had to be removed. They were rewelded aboard the *Haida.*

An engine change was required on the *Boston* because of bad bearings; this work presented a problem. There was no hoist available to lift the engine out and replace it with the new one. The skipper of the *Brookdale,* a large freighter tied up at the Dutch Harbor pier, volunteered the ship's crane and the help of his crew. The plane was lifted fifty feet out of the water, then across the deck onto the dock on the other side; the ship's boom was used to make the engine exchange.

Radio communications were proving to be imperative for the success of the flight down the Aleutians. It was necessary for the crews to know the weather conditions ahead of them in a timely manner. If a plane had to drop out during a hop, the other planes were to proceed to the nearest radio station and drop a note reporting the plane's probable position and condition so help could be sent as soon as possible. And there was a third reason: publicity. The world press and the public wanted to be kept informed about the flight's progress and radio was the only way to spread the news.

Most of the radio work was performed through the Aleutians by the Coast Guard cutter *Haida* and radio traffic reached its height between April 18 and May 18. Bissell and Blair, the weather officer, were on board and were the vital links for official messages that flowed to Washington via the Dutch Harbor Naval Radio Station. Press stories were sent to the Estavan Radio Station on Vancouver Island, British Columbia. Bissell had arranged for each cannery along the route to send messages to Dutch Harbor giving the time that the planes passed over.

After their arrival at Dutch Harbor, there was nothing the three crews could do but continually check their planes, keep a radio watch on word about Martin, wander around the area, which included an Aleut settlement called Illiiliyook, play bridge, and write letters in time for them to be put on the *Brookdale* before it left for Seattle. They had their meals aboard the *Haida* but were given quarters in the home of a Mr. Strauss, a manager for the Alaska Commercial Company that bought fox skins from the Aleuts in exchange for food necessities. It was here that the crews had their first real experience with the power of the "willies" on the ground. Smith's diary entry for 21 April is a classic example of the sudden fury:

> It had been perfectly calm for hours when, all of a sudden, a wild and wooly williwaw rushed down the mountains at fifty to seventy-five miles an hour. After it had blown for a few minutes, another came along from an entirely different direction. This one picked up big sheets of water and carried them across the bay. A boat lying on shore went rolling end over end. Some iron barrels on the dock were scattered in every direction. Arnold and I happened to be walking down the street when we heard a clanking. A big iron drum came bounding along. We jumped out of the way and let it crash into a fence. Then the "willie" hit a pile of lumber on the dock that had recently been unloaded and hadn't yet been lashed down. The boards went scaling off the top of the pile just like a deck of cards.[25]

Les Arnold recalled his experience on the night of 24 April. He and the others were sitting in the *Haida*'s wardroom when a guard rushed in and said the planes were afloat:

"We thought they were surely safe," he said, "even at high tide. But a gale suddenly swept in from the Arctic Ocean and the waves dashed so high up [on the beach] that they tore the planes loose. It was a night that none of us will ever forget. Not only was it as dark as the nethermost pit, but it was snowing like the dickens, the wind was howling, and the waves were booming on the beach. Of course, every able-bodied man rushed out with us to the rescue, including sailors and officers on the *Haida*. We had no lights except our pocket flashes. But the searchlight from the cutter would reach its long finger of light into the gloom and help us. We were all rushing about wildly and wading around in the water trying to get hold of the planes before they were swept into the bay. Some of us floundered in that icy water right up to our necks, and worked for two hours and a half. It was after midnight, with the weather near zero, before we managed to pull the planes higher on the beach, away from the threatening seas, and had them safely secured. One of the sailors from the *Haida* proved himself a hero by diving into the icy water to prevent a large plank off of the broken runway from smashing one of the pontoons. When we got back to the trader's house that night, we were so cold that we couldn't even unbutton our coats."[26]

It was on 30 April that Martin at Chignik received favorable weather reports from Dutch Harbor. It was still snowing, but not knowing when they might have a better day, Martin decided to take off. At the suggestion of James Osborne, the cannery superintendent, he planned to take a shortcut over the portage northwest of Chignik that Osborne said the other planes had taken. This was in the opposite direction from that originally planned.

Word was received that day at Dutch Harbor that Martin and Harvey had left Chignik. It was the only report sent. For hours the *Haida* listened in for messages from the canneries along the route; none had seen the plane. When no report was received from King Cove, the first reporting station, the cutter *Algonquin,* which was in the vicinity, started a search, calling for assistance from cannery vessels nearby. At the same time, the *Haida,* with Bissell aboard, left Dutch Harbor to aid in the search, leaving Blair there.

Radio traffic was intense as messages flowed to and from the *Haida.* The search was organized by Bissell and divided into sections with the U.S. Coast Guard in charge of vessels searching the Bering Sea side of the peninsula near Port Moller. The *Algonquin* and the *Haida* became the focal points for news; many false reports were received and had to be checked out. None was substantiated.

In the days that followed, messages flashed back and forth telling what efforts were being made to search for the *Seattle.* The *Pioneer,* a U.S. Coast and Geodetic Survey ship, was detached from a survey and began to search along the south shore of the Alaskan Peninsula; the *Discoverer,* another survey ship, followed an easterly route toward Chignik. Two dog-team parties were organized at Chignik and worked inland from there. Small motorboats were sent out from the canneries on both sides of the Alaskan Peninsula to check out the coastal areas for the missing fliers.

There was intense press interest in the States. A message for the Associated Press in Seattle was sent by a reporter named Nichols located at a cannery at False Pass, Unimak Island. He related that the residents there said they had just passed through the worst five days of storm they had ever known and added, "The Pacific Ocean has been lashed by terrific gales, the wind frequently reaching 100 miles per hour. The air at the wireless station has been filled all day with snow blown from the mountain sides and neighboring peaks. Even the sea gulls making their home here did not fly today. The temperature has ranged from zero to 16 degrees above zero during the storm. If Major Martin succeeded in reaching Dutch Harbor he will be fully qualified for any bad weather that might arise later. The residents believe that a mistake was made in attempting the 400-mile flight from Chignik to Dutch Harbor during the gale."[27]

After a week had passed with no news about the *Seattle,* the North American Newspaper Alliance (NANA) offered a thousand dollar reward to "the person or persons first to furnish definite information resulting in the discovery of the actual fate of either aviator or the plane *Seattle.*"[28] Instructions were sent to Evan J. David, the NANA correspondent aboard the *Algonquin,* to take immediate steps to have the notice broadcast to all Alaskan canneries, ships, and trading posts, and to hire Indian runners to spread the word among the Aleutian villages.[29]

General Patrick responded in a letter of appreciation that the Air Service would use every facility at its command to broadcast the notice of the reward offered by the newspaper alliance.[30] On 10 May, the Coast Guard cutter *Bear* left San Francisco carrying Lt. E. S. Tomkin, pilot, and Sgt. I. C. Cooper, observer, with a Curtiss seaplane and supplies to Chignik so a thorough air search could be conducted along the Alaskan Peninsula.

As the days passed and no word was received that Martin and Harvey had been located, the fliers at Dutch Harbor were anxious to continue. They wrote letters to their families to be left for the next freighter leaving for Seattle because they knew it would be their last chance before arriving in Japan. Reading, sleeping, and bridge games helped to pass the time. A couple of the men shoveled snow off the tennis court and played a few sets for exercise. A temporary laboratory was set up and films taken en route were developed. The williwaws came and went frequently without warning and bad days turned into fair ones when they could have departed, but then quickly changed back into short periods when it snowed and blew too heavily for flying.

One of the interesting experiences they had was on 27 April, Easter Sunday, when they attended a four-hour church service in the Russian church in the village of Illiiliyook with the entire village of white people: twenty-one men and six women. They checked on the condition of their planes daily to be sure they were ready when the word came that they could continue. This was not to come until five days later.

# 5. *Seattle* Is Lost!

The portage Martin had been told was low ground and could be easily traversed after takeoff did not appear after he left Chignik on the morning of 30 April. He suddenly saw a mountain loom ahead out of the mist. Thinking he might have turned too quickly toward the north after taking off from the Chignik lagoon, he turned back to get his bearings and tried again, this time in a westerly direction. He was concerned about flying over land with pontoons but when he saw blue water ahead, he headed for it.

"Our ceiling now was about 200 feet," Martin recounted. "But somehow that body of water never got any nearer. Instead we were approaching fog. I was now strongly inclined to turn back to Chignik and start all over again. But as we had come this far and the water seemed so near, we kept on. The fog grew so dense that it drove us down within a few feet of the ground. Still we found no water. But feeling certain that we had left the mountains behind us, I thought it would be safest to climb over the fog, which I felt sure would only extend for a short distance.

"In order to make sure of getting all the way to Dutch Harbor, we had taken on board two hundred gallons of gasoline and oil. We had been gaining altitude for several minutes when, suddenly, another mountain loomed up ahead. I caught a glimpse of several dark patches, bare spots where the snow had blown way. A moment later we crashed."[1]

The plane was climbing slightly when it hit the ground. This was fortunate. The right pontoon had struck the incline of the mountain at a gentle slope and the plane crunched to rest on the snow without much of a jolt. The two men were stunned briefly and climbed stiffly out of their cockpits to check on each other. Harvey was not hurt but Martin had broken his goggles and had a small cut over his left eye and a bloody nose. They walked around the wreckage to assess the damage and found the right pontoon was under the left side of the fuselage with the left pontoon near by. The pontoon struts were crushed and torn loose from the fuselage. The lower right wing was completely demolished. The upper right wing was pulled back about halfway between its original position and the tail of the plane. The lower left wing was slightly damaged while the upper left wing was intact. The propeller was broken but the fuselage and tail surfaces were not damaged.

"Our despair was a terrible experience," Martin recalled. "Further participation in the round-the-world flight was at an end. We thoroughly appreciated our plight as we knew this part of the western [Alaska] peninsula to be uninhabited, excepting by a few people at considerable distance apart along the shoreline."[2]

The two assessed their equipment and food and realized they could be in deep trouble. They had only two sandwiches each, which had been prepared by Mrs. Osborne at Chignik, along with a thermos of coffee, but that had been broken. The only other food they had between them was a dozen malted milk tablets and two thermos bottles of concentrated food in liquid form that Martin had purchased in Los Angeles. This contained parts of raisins, figs, walnuts, peanuts, barley, wheat, and celery. As they prepared their knapsacks for hiking, Martin found that his compass was broken, but Harvey had been given a small card compass by a friend before he left Chanute Field. It was very inaccurate but they started out at 2 P.M. heading southward, estimating they were about ten miles from the coastline on the Pacific side of the peninsula separated from the ocean by a mountain range that they would have to climb over. They both soon experienced snow blindness from the relentless white glare. Martin explained:

"The fog was very dense and was so white as to blend completely with the snow. The snow was deep and smooth, leaving practically no objects visible. This experience was very peculiar as the vision was limited to a few feet. It was found to be impossible to walk in a straight line as our sense of balance seemed to be affected. It was necessary to stop frequently and check our course on the compass. Invariably we found that we were walking other than in the desired direction. The slope of the mountain varied but probably was rising at an angle of about thirty degrees.

"After walking until about 4 o'clock the same conditions prevailed so we returned to the airplane as it did not seem likely we would find a place where shelter and wood could be found before darkness fell. We followed our footsteps in the snow . . . and by walking rapidly we returned to the airplane in seventeen minutes. Here we prepared for the night by picking up broken parts of the airplane for fuel, put on our heavy flying suits, and waited for darkness."[3]

They crawled into the plane's baggage compartment, which was about 2½ feet wide, too small for either to rest comfortably.

The fog was still very thick the next morning, and they stayed with the plane all day and all night, meantime making themselves as comfortable as possible. They started a fire that melted and formed a pit. They placed the metal cowling from the engine under the fire. With a small spade they cut some ice into one-foot square chunks and built a wall under the wings to shield them from the icy wind. Harvey recalled:

"The following day, with the fog still persistent and with our having been forewarned that the spring fogs prevailed for days, we realized our situation was perilous. To expect outside rescue efforts was pure folly. The matter of survival was entirely up to us, so we made an agreement and shook hands on it. We would start for the coast, never to return to the airplane again. Saying, 'Farewell, *Seattle,* we regret leaving you here wrecked and battered,' we walked away. . . .

"Our maps failed to show the rugged mountain area on the Peninsula. After reaching the coast, and having the opportunity to review our experience, we found we had followed a westerly course, working our way along the north slope, the Bering Sea side, always searching for a pass to the Pacific."[4]

With one leading and the other following about 100 feet behind, they were able to progress in a nearly straight line up the slope, over the crest, and down the south side to a small creek. Pushing on southward, they climbed to the top of a steep mountain and the fog lifted slightly, just in time to save them from a serious accident. Four or five paces ahead, the mountain dropped so abruptly that the person in the lead could have slipped down into a canyon about 1500 feet deep.

"Realizing the futility of trying to find a passage through the mountains in the fog," Martin reported, "we returned to the creek we had just crossed knowing that this would eventually take us to the shoreline of the Bering Sea if followed. As we were not forced to climb any hills, we made excellent progress over comparatively level ground."[5]

Harvey was having trouble with his eyes, which were badly inflamed due partly to the smoke from their fire and partly to snow blindness. After walking for nearly six hours, they located an alder thicket for firewood and made camp on the snow by cutting small green branches to lie on. They took turns keeping the fire going while the other slept.

They talked at length that night and decided that it would be foolish to continue to try to reach the coast on the Bering Sea side of the mountain range because their maps showed no villages or canneries on that side and they had been told no driftwood could be found there.

"Sergeant Harvey's eyes were now in a serious condition," Martin said, "and he could hardly see despite the fact that he was wearing amber goggles. But by using boric acid from our first aid kit the inflammation was reduced, and by the following morning his eyes were nearly back to normal. The fog had now lifted and we climbed the mountain to about 2,500 feet. From its summit we looked off to the southward and could see nothing but a sheer wall of rock, and more mountains, the tops of which were hidden in the clouds. But off to the southwest, through our field glasses, we saw a lake. Hoping that there might be a trapper somewhere on its shores, we set out about 11 A.M., but at 4:30 we were still three or four miles from it. Once more we camped for the night in an alder thicket. During the daylight hours, we succeeded in killing two ptarmigans with an Army pistol. We cooked one in the meat can of my mess outfit and had it for supper."[6]

They started out again on the morning of 4 May and reached the lake about noon. They scanned the lake but saw no signs of humanity. Now Martin was having difficulty with his eyes and their plight was beginning to grow more serious. Their best chance for finding signs of habitation now seemed to depend on finding a pass through the mountains to the south. They sought a stream at the southernmost end of the lake, thinking that it would come out on Ivanof Bay. When they found it, it was flowing northward but they followed it anyway, hoping to find it running through a pass in the mountains.

Harvey took the lead and they kept going as they both knew they were getting very weak. Their only food supply had been a quart of concentrated beef that they consumed a teaspoonful at a time in a cup of water. They arrived at low, marshy land and made camp at 2 o'clock in the afternoon. There was plenty of wood for a fire and grass for a bed. These gave them the first good rest they had had since the crash. They each slept about four hours while the other posted guard. Then on 5 May they continued their trek through the swampy area. After about three miles, they came upon some dry creek beds that made the going easier. They halted at 3 P.M., exhausted and hungry, and again camped in an alder thicket. While Martin rested, Harvey made a reconnaissance of the area and reported that he saw a large body of water he estimated to be about three miles farther to the south.

They arose early and by 7:30 A.M. arrived at the shore of the water Harvey had seen and found a small cabin only half a mile away. Refreshed by the welcome sight, they hurried to it and found evidence that it might have been occupied within the past twenty-four hours. They found a small cache of food including flour, salted salmon, bacon fat, baking powder, dried peaches, condensed milk, syrup, and coffee. There was also a small stove with some wood and a pint of oil for an oil heater. They built a fire and prepared some pancakes but found they could eat only two each because their stomachs would not accept any more. There was no furniture so they made themselves as comfortable as possible on the floor and slept until they were awakened by the cold. The fire had died out. They got up, started the fire, ate again, put some salmon aside to soak, and went back to sleep.

It was snowing heavily the next morning and all day. Then on May 9 the snow turned into rain. They took a walk to try to establish their location on a map and, to their surprise, determined that they were on the Bering Sea side of the peninsula. That afternoon, Harvey bagged two snow shoe rabbits that they cooked for dinner. This helped them regain their strength. When they rummaged some more around the cabin, they found some mail and a carton that had contained cans of condensed milk addressed to the Port Moller Cannery. They located Port Moller on their map. They estimated it to be about twenty-five miles away and decided to hike in that direction next day.

They arose feeling much stronger the next morning, 10 May, and ate a hearty breakfast of rabbit, pancakes, and gravy. They cleaned up the cabin and started out in clear, calm weather.

"We made excellent progress along the beach," Martin said, "with the exception of three or four miles where the rocks from the cliffs, as large as ordinary dwellings, extended down to the water's edge. It was easier to climb over these than to pass them by climbing through the snow over the tops of the mountains. This impeded our progress a great deal. We arrived at the narrowest spit which extends well out into the bay near Port Moller at 4 P.M. From this point we could see the wireless mast and smoke stack at the camp. While we were wondering whether we would find [the place] inhabited, smoke came from the cannery. After crossing the spit which was about a mile wide, we were approached by a motor launch coming from the cannery."[7]

There were two Aleut men and three women in the launch who were on their way from the cannery to a village on the western side of Moller Bay. Martin and Harvey waved and yelled and the launch steered toward them. Jake Oroloff, leader of the group, quickly took them aboard and hurried to the cannery where they arrived at 6 P.M. to be greeted happily by the superintendent and employees. After a hearty meal, Martin sent a message to the Chief of Air Service: CRASHED AGAINST MOUNTAIN IN FOG 30TH 12:30 NEITHER HURT SHIP TOTAL WRECK EXISTENCE DUE TO CONCENTRATED FOOD AND NERVE ARRIVED CAMPER'S CABIN SOUTHERNMOST POINT PORT MOLLER BAY MORNING 7TH EXHAUSTED FOUND FOOD RESTED THREE DAYS WALKED BEACH AWAITING INSTRUCTIONS HERE.[8]

"We were safe at last and could completely relax," Martin wrote after he reached Washington. "We never will forget the joy of that night's sleep in a comfortable bed protected from the cold."[9]

The word of their rescue spread quickly around the world while the two men feasted and rested. They learned that all vessels at points along the shores of the Alaskan Peninsula had been searching daily since their departure from Chignik. This included about a dozen boats from the canneries, the U.S. Coast and Geodetic Survey, and the U.S. Coast Guard. Dog teams and ground search parties had also been sent inland from Chignik.

On 12 May, Martin and Harvey received a message from the vice president of the Pacific American Fisheries Company inviting them to be guests aboard the *Catherine D,* a company steamer that was to leave Port Moller on 14 May and take them to Bellingham, Washington. The ship departed on schedule and after several stops at other canneries arrived offshore at Bellingham on 21 May. A company motor launch came out to meet them; aboard were Mrs. Martin and their son, Robert. When they arrived at the wharf, a band began playing, and they were surprised to find more than a thousand people there to welcome them back to the United States. The great crowd included the mayor, government officials from Seattle, and Air Service officers.

Harvey reflected on this episode in his memoirs. "The experience gained, the hazards faced, and the few hardships endured proved invaluable in the years since," he wrote. "I have always cherished the memory of those few months. A strong bond of friendship and mutual respect was formed between Major Martin and me which has endured throughout the years."[10]

When it was affirmed that Martin and Harvey were safe, General Patrick sent a radiogram to Martin: WE REJOICE AND THANK GOD THAT YOU ARE BOTH SAFE CONFIDENCE IN YOU UNABATED YOU HAVE PROVED YOURSELF STILL WANT YOU TO COMMAND FLIGHT CANNOT ARRANGE YOU TO OVERTAKE OTHERS BY GOING WEST YOU AND SERGEANT HARVEY WILL REPORT TO ME HERE WITHOUT DELAY PLAN TO SEND YOU EAST TO REJOIN FLIGHT AT FURTHER CONVENIENT POINT FROM WHICH YOU CAN COMPLETE THE JOURNEY WITH THE REST OF YOUR COMMAND.[11]

General Patrick asked Lt. Col. James E. Fechet, chief of Training and War Plans, to determine the farthest point east that the prototype plane then at Langley Field, Virginia, might be available for Martin and Harvey so that they could join the World Flight. Fechet responded that it could be sent to Constantinople, Turkey, by ship with an estimate of ninety-one days for preparing the plane and shipping it from New York, plus about two weeks to get it assembled and flight-tested. This would be after the other three planes should have passed that point. Fechet noted that the Turkish government had been troublesome in allowing free customs for the shipments of supplies for the flight to Turkey and implied they might impound the substitute plane. If the plane were shipped to London, Fechet estimated it would take forty days to get there and another fourteen days to get it to Brough, England, and make it ready for flight. He recommended that this course of action be taken.[12]

Martin was grateful that the Air Service chief wanted him to join the flight later but reminded Patrick that they had all agreed before the flight that if any had to pull out, the flight would go on. "The success of this great undertaking is the essential thing and not the wishes or desires of any of the fliers. . . . While there is nothing I should like better than to rejoin the flight and again take command, by that time a considerable part of it will have been accomplished without me. In fairness to Lieutenant Smith, who succeeded me in command, I think he should so continue and himself bring the flight back to the United States."[13]

The prototype was worked on at Langley but in rethinking the situation after Martin's letter, Patrick decided that no effort should be made to have Martin and Harvey rejoin the flight. The plane itself, however, would still play a future role not yet contemplated.

After Martin and Harvey had been delayed with engine failure at Kanatak, Fechet as chief of the Training and War Plans Division, wrote a memorandum to General Patrick that showed the competitive urgency to continue the mission:

"The English Round-the-World Expedition has reached Karachi, India, after having covered a distance of 4,921 miles within one month after starting from Croydon Airdrome, London, England," he wrote. "The United States Army Air Service flight has covered 3,375 miles in 39 days [since they left San Diego]. If the British Expedition succeeds in completing the flight around the world with one ship and their comparatively meager preparations, it will greatly detract from the prestige of American aviation, even if the Air Service flight is successful.

"Policy involved—What is the paramount consideration: to get the American flight around the world first, either intact, or in part; or to get the four airplanes around the world as a flight? If this last policy is adopted, a survey of the situation would indicate that though the American expedition was successful, it would complete the flight after it had already been accomplished by the British. The expedition has been repeatedly delayed because of the misfortune of one plane, and from present indications, will suffer similarly in the future, so that if the first policy is favored, instructions must be immediately issued to provide against serious delays from the same cause in the future. It is recommended that every effort be made to get the American flight around the world first. If this recommendation is approved, it is further recommended that the following be sent to Major Martin: "VITAL THAT FURTHER ACCIDENT TO ANY ONE PLANE DOES NOT DELAY PROGRESS OF OTHER PLANES."[14]

There was another element of urgency in getting the three planes in the air as soon as possible. Fechet stated on 30 April in a follow-up memorandum to General Patrick that the U.S. Navy vessels waiting in the Kurile Islands for the fliers had only between two and three weeks of fuel remaining. The planes so far had only progressed an average of one stop every five days and had five more stops over the most difficult portion before reaching the Kuriles. They could not make it at that rate to Japanese waters while the American vessels were still there to assist. Fechet recommended that the two men aboard the *Seattle* "be definitely withdrawn from the flight unless this airplane is now at Dutch Harbor and ready to proceed at once."[15]

There was still another note of urgency for the flight to push on. The start of the American flight had given impetus to the attempts of other nations to pursue their world-flight plans. In addition to the British flight of RAF Squad. Ldr. A. Stuart MacLaren, the Portuguese flight of Capt. Sacadura Cabrál and Adm. Gago Coutinho, and the Argentine flight of Maj. D. Pedro Zanni were announced.

Also entering the competition was Lt. Pelletier d'Oisy and his mechanic, Sgt. Bernard Vesin, both of the French air service, flying a Breguet 19A2 two-seater observation plane. Since France could not afford to organize and support a World Flight, however, d'Oisy intended to go only halfway and do it in record time. His planned route was from Paris to Tokyo via Bucharest, Romania; Aleppo, Turkey; Baghdad, Iraq; Bandar Abbas, Persia; India, Rangoon, Burma; Saigon and Hanoi, Indochina; Hong Kong; Shanghai and Peking, China; and Seoul, Korea. They departed on 24 April 1924 and successfully completed their flight at Tokyo on 9 June.

MacLaren was flying a Vickers Vulture with Flight Officer W. N. Plenberlieth, navigator, and Engineer Sergeant Andrews, mechanic. They left Calshot near Southampton on 25 March and made the first stop at Le Havre. They then planned to fly to Lyons, Brindisi, Athens, Cairo, Baghdad, Basra, Karachi, Calcutta, Rangoon, Hong Kong, Tokyo, and across the Pacific by way of the Aleutians to Vancouver, Toronto, and Newfoundland. They would then cross the Atlantic by way of the Azores and Lisbon. Lt. Col. L. E. Broome was the advance man for the MacLaren flight.

MacLaren had landed at Rome and after leaving there on 31 March en route to Athens and Cairo; he had a forced landing at Lake St. Mathews on the Island of Corfu. There was considerable damage to the plane and a new engine was requested from London. Only two spare engines had been provided for the flight; one was at Tokyo and the other at Vancouver. He intended to continue the flight when he could solve his logistics problems.

The Portuguese flight proposed to follow nearly the same route as the British but starting at Lisbon. The flight was divided into three sections: Lisbon to Yokohama, Yokohama to St. John's, Newfoundland, and Newfoundland to Lisbon. They were to use a Fokker TW3 single-engine amphibian. They arrived at Shamahun near Macao on 20 June but the aircraft was damaged in landing and they were slightly injured.

The Argentine world flight of Maj. D. Pedro Zanni began from Amsterdam, Holland, on 22 July 1924. With him were Lt. Nelson T. Page, Argentine naval air service, as navigator, and Felipe Beltrame as mechanic. Zanni intended to use three Fokker C-IV planes, two amphibians, and one fitted with wheels, over approximately the same route as MacLaren. A special "mystery" plane, later identified as a Fokker TW3 monoplane, was to be used for the Atlantic flight. The attempt ended on 19 August 1924 when Zanni crashed while taking off from Hanoi, French Indochina. No one was hurt but the aircraft was destroyed. One of the other Fokkers was rushed to him from Japan and he flew on to Tokyo. Zanni later abandoned the attempt to fly farther via the Aleutians because by that time the ports in the northern Pacific were reportedly icebound.

There was yet another reason to attempt to speed up the Army Air Service attempt. The U.S. Navy was planning to make its first serious effort to cross the Pacific with a flight across its widest span—California to Hawaii. The flight was to be made by three flying-boats especially designed with metal hulls. One was built by Boeing in Seattle and designated PB-1; two others were built at the Philadelphia Naval Aircraft Factory and designated PN-9. Just as with the crossing of the Atlantic by the Curtiss NCs in 1919, the plan was to station ships along the course to guide the planes using smoke and search lights and be ready to assist in an emergency. Two planes started on the World Flight in August 1925; both failed.[16]

While the other crews had been waiting at Dutch Harbor for news about Martin and Harvey, Lt. Lowell Smith, the ranking lieutenant of the group, was designated the leader on 2 May and received the following message: DO NOT DELAY LONGER WAITING FOR MAJOR MARTIN TO JOIN YOU STOP SEE EVERYTHING DONE POSSIBLE TO FIND HIM STOP PLANES NUMBER 2, 3, AND 4 TO PROCEED TO JAPAN AT EARLIEST POSSIBLE MOMENT PATRICK.[17]

This was the signal they had been waiting for. The crews got their planes ready for takeoff on 3 May. Their target was Nazan on Atka Island, 365 miles farther out the Aleutian chain. The wind was light, the air very cold, and the visibility was excellent. Local Aleuts helped them push the planes into the water and a small boat towed them out to their moorings. They taxied through a narrow space between the dock and shore, down the boat channel and around a large red buoy to be ready for the "go" signal from Smith. The entire population of Unalaska was on the dock waving at them.

The route took them along the northern edge of Unalaska and Umnak Islands, through the Islands of the Four Mountains, past Yunasaka, Chugul, and Seguam islands into Nazan Bay. Although they flew through rain and snow showers, it proved to be an easy flight; they accomplished it in 4 hours, 19 minutes. Waiting in the harbor was the *Eider,* a small U.S. Bureau of Fisheries boat. Its crew had prepared excellent moorings for the planes in a well-protected part of the harbor. The *Haida,* with Major Blair on board, was withdrawn from the search for the *Seattle* and proceeded to Atka, while the *Algonquin* continued looking for Martin and Harvey.

The *Eider*'s radio was the only means of communication to let the world know of their arrival. On shore was a radio set installed years before by the Bureau of Education that had long been silent. The Aleuts had used the power plant for a chicken coop and the antenna was used as a clothesline and a rack to dry fish. When the *Haida* arrived, its radiomen placed the station into temporary operation while Blair set up a weather station to furnish reports from Atka. He then reboarded the *Eider* and headed for Attu, the next stop, where the ship's crew would establish moorings and he would radio weather reports to Atka.

The town of Nazan was populated with seventy-nine Aleuts and one white schoolteacher named Nye. The crews were put up in a local trading store owned by A. C. Goss of Dutch Harbor who had invited them to use it when they got there. There were some army wool blankets on hand but no beds so they slept on the floor. No food had been stocked so the *Eider* provided them with eggs and canned goods. Smith turned out to be an excellent cook and served a much-welcomed breakfast of ham, eggs, and coffee. For lunch, they made a deal with the village elder that they would fix the magneto for his boat engine if he would get them two chickens to eat. Smith showed his considerable culinary skills again with stewed chicken, to which were added sweet potatoes, coffee, bread, crackers, and pickles.

The *Haida* arrived on 5 May. The crews spent the day fueling their planes. This proved to be a tough job. "The drums had been placed on the beach some time ago," Arnold wrote in his diary that day. "And there being no dock we brought the boat as close to shore as it would come, put out a couple of planks, and then rolled the drums aboard. But to reach the planks it was necessary to wade knee-deep in the water, then row the boat alongside the plane, and pump the gas aboard. Today there was a stiff northwest wind making a choppy sea which frequently broke over the boat so that long before the task was finished all hands were wet and cold."[18]

Although the planes and crews were ready to go on the sixth, the weather reports from Blair were unfavorable. Smith seriously considered flying to Kiska where a base had been established for the British flight. They could meet the *Eider* there and at least advance some of the distance to Attu. But Smith fortunately changed his mind. The next day, a heavy, wet, driving snow kept them earthbound, causing Arnold to comment, "The Aleutians have but two kinds of weather it seems, bad and worse, and today's was of the latter variety."[19] Wade asked an old trapper when the seasons changed and his answer was, "We have only two seasons here. This winter and next winter."[20]

The eighth was better than they had experienced for a long time but the weather westward and at Attu was reported extremely unfavorable with fog and high winds. They spent the day on a sailboat hunting ducks, fishing, and shooting at eagles with an Army rifle. They never seemed to hit until one of them (they never knew which one) brought down a large bald eagle with a wing spread that measured 7 feet, 3 inches.

The weather reports from Blair were good on the ninth so Nelson lined up with the others following into the wind and took off at 9:00 A.M. Just as he was starting a turn, a williwaw hit from a different direction and he was forced down heavily on the water. Only his skillful piloting prevented a crash and he was airborne again. When the others saw what had happened, they changed their takeoff direction and caught up with him. It was a long, cold 555-mile trip with occasional snow squalls as they passed the southern end of Great Sitkin Island, skirted the edge of the next few islands, touched the southern edge of Semisopochnoi Island, passed over Kiska and Buldir islands, then made the over-water jump to Chichagof Harbor at Attu. The only life seen during the nearly seven hours, fifty-two minutes of flying were birds and a large number of whales.

The *Eider*'s seven-man crew under Captain Beck had made excellent arrangements for mooring in the harbor and took the planes' crews aboard for warm meals and rest. The *Haida* arrived on the eleventh and confirmed the good news that Martin and Harvey had been found and were not injured. "It was heartening news to all of us at Attu," Wade said, "but the flight was hardly started. Who might be next? I shut my mind to the thought, tried to start each new day with yesterday wiped from the slate."[21] Harding wrote in his journal that the news was "great to hear. It seemed hard-hearted to proceed and leave them lost but every one of us and headquarters in D.C. were doing all possible to find them. Boats, vessels, canoes, dog teams, etc. had been combing the Alaska Peninsular coasts and mountains since their disappearance."[22]

Serious discussions were held that night about the next leg that would take them across the Pacific Ocean. If successful, it would be one of the most significant flights in aviation history, comparable to the 1919 one-way Atlantic crossings by British pilots John Alcock and Arthur Whitten Brown in a Vickers Vimy; the flight of U.S. Navy Lt. Cmdr. Albert Read in the Curtiss NC-4; and the round trip by the British airship R-34.

There was a concern among the U.S. Air Service crews that there was a high likelihood of encountering strong, very rough weather if they were to set course for the 870-mile flight directly to Paramushiru, Japan. That length of flight even at normal cruising speed would take more than ten hours. In closed-door sessions on the *Eider* they discussed whether or not they should deliberately head for the Komandorskis for fuel. Since no arrangements had been made to land anywhere in Russian territory, they had been warned before they left Washington that to do so might have serious consequences, implying that the Russians would arrest them and impound the planes. The fliers agreed among themselves that they would take their chances with the Russians. Smith ordered that no hint of this possibility would be released to the press so the world would not know their intentions. The *Eider* was to be stationed off the shore of Bering Island, one of the Komandorski group, and was steaming in that direction with moorings, gasoline, and oil. Lieutenant Bissell would be on board, and the *Eider* would relay messages through the *Haida,* which would remain about fifty miles off Attu.

The possibility of the *Haida* proceeding to Russian waters had already been considered in Washington; the *Eider* was able to haul more gasoline for the planes so it was chosen to proceed all the way to Japan if necessary. The commander of the Coast Guard's Bering Sea Patrol had asked a month earlier "under what circumstances may cutter enter territorial waters of Russia to assist or refuel an airplane? Also convoy destroyer Division No. 38 to Japan provided cutter required to extend cooperation to Japan. Request headquarters make necessary provisions obtain fuel, oil Hakodate [Japan]."[23]

Rear Adm. Frederick C. Billard, the Coast Guard commandant, quickly replied: "Headquarters sees no objection cutter entering territorial waters Russia to assist Army airplanes. Understand Coast Guard mission convoy planes until contact made with destroyers Asiatic Fleet. Use your discretion re further cooperation. If necessary, radio American Embassy, Tokyo, relative fuel.[24]

Shortly after the fliers left Seattle, the U.S. Navy destroyers *John D. Ford* and *Pope* had gone to positions off the Kurile Islands with a Japanese escort and expected to remain no longer than two weeks. When it appeared that the flight was delayed, the *Ford* and the *Pope* exchanged places several times when they needed fuel and supplies. The Japanese had agreed to let them proceed there but only with Japanese army and navy officers aboard and the stipulation that no photographs were to be taken by anyone on board showing any of the Japanese coastline. Several severe storms were encountered during this period and the ships' supplies ran low.

While the fliers were still at Attu, Smith had radioed the *Ford* requesting that it reconnoiter Kronotski for possible landing places along the coast. Lt. Cmdr. Holloway H. Frost, skipper of the *Ford,* was exasperated—from fighting the storms and floating ice—waiting for the planes to appear and replied: WILL NOT ENTER RUSSIAN WATERS UNDER ANY CIRCUMSTANCES EXCEPT TO RESCUE A PLANE.[25]

The fliers wanted to leave Attu as soon as possible but an especially strong williwaw prevented fueling the planes for early departure. They decided to go ashore despite freezing rain and fog to see what America's farthest west village was like. They found it consisted of only a Russian Orthodox church for the fifty-nine Aleuts; a number of *baraboras,* 8 × 10–foot huts of grass and sod in which six to eight people lived; a small wooden shack owned by a trader named Frederick Schroeder who used it as a trading post during the summer months; and a hut used by the Coast Guard where shore parties from the cutters stayed briefly during their infrequent visits. Harding and Ogden decided to explore the area. They did some rock climbing to pass the time but decided not to climb higher when they reached the foot of the 4,500-foot snow-covered mountain.

The weather was better on 12 May and the day was spent oiling, gassing, and checking the planes with the help of crew members from the *Haida.* The fliers and

Bissell went ashore again and stayed in Schroeder's shack. There were only two beds so most slept on the floor on mattresses and bedding furnished by the ship; food was also provided by the ship. Two radiomen and a cook from the ship joined them to set up a radio station on shore that they would man to relay weather reports from the the *Haida* after it left for its offshore location.

The condition of the planes was a major consideration and Arnold's diary entry for 13 May describes the difficulty they had with them:

"In the morning some of us went aboard the planes and attended to various odd jobs, but the afternoon was spent getting thawed and dried out. Mr. Schroeder has a number of novels here and all hands are busy most of the time reading some wild tale.

"It is the custom to hang lanterns aboard the planes at night so we can easily keep track of their positions but tonight for the first time we were unable to hang them on. Harding and Ogden started out in a dory but the wind was so great they were blown past the planes and on across the bay in spite of their efforts to row against the wind, finally abandoning the dory and walking back to the hut via the beach — and for the second time today being soaked through."[26]

It snowed all day 14 May and winds reached about 40 mph but not enough to prevent the men from amusing themselves by fishing for mackerel, black bass, and cod. They went aboard the *Haida* for dinner and each took a bath. "I don't dare mention when we had our last one," Arnold wrote as a final diary entry for that day.[27]

They arose at 5 A.M. on 15 May and Major Blair on the *Eider* reported fairly favorable weather to the Komandorskis as far as he could determine. The Cruisers taxied out of Chichagof Harbor and were off at 11:25 A.M. with Lowell Smith in the lead.

"At 12:20 we passed the *Haida* and circled low to wave to our Coast Guard friends who had worked so enthusiastically for us," Smith said. "Bering Sea is one of the roughest bodies of water in the world, as we had long since discovered, and right here where it joins the North Pacific is the roughest part. So the *Haida* was rolling and tossing along like a cork, yet every man on board was hanging on with one hand and waving good-bye to us with the other."[28]

The three planes circled the ship once to observe some deck signals and then turned west. This leg of the flight would take them into the next day when they crossed the international date line.

While the U.S. Army pilots were struggling to get the planes through the Aleutians, the U.S. Navy ships operating out of Yokohama had been having their difficulties with the fierce winter weather. Aboard the *Ford* was Linton O. Wells, an aggressive reporter for the Associated Press based in Tokyo. He had persuaded Lt. Cmdr. Frost, leader of the task force assigned to assist the fliers, to take him aboard so he could report firsthand on the Pacific crossing. Also aboard were Captain S. Isoda, Japanese army officer, and Lieutenant M. Yamada, naval officer. A naturalized American citizen of Japanese parentage, J. S. Kanematz, was also aboard as an International News Service photographer.

The Japanese officers were not cooperative and would not allow the Americans to go ashore at Hitokappu, an unfortified bay on a deserted strip of the coast sparsely inhabited by fishermen. It was not a restricted zone and could not be fortified for ten years after signing at the Washington Conference, provided that the Japanese were adhering to the agreement. Further, there were no troops or fortifications on the entire island of Yetorofu. The American ships were prevented from radioing between the ships by the Japanese blocking the transmissions every time they were attempted, even during the hours that had been agreed would be reserved for their messages. "This was only the beginning of a series of petty and pusillanimous near-persecutions and sly affronts offered American dignity and prestige by the Japanese with whom we had official relations," reported Major R. S. Bratton, an American Army officer attached to the embassy in Tokyo.[29]

After much discussion, the Japanese finally allowed the *Ford* to drop anchor at Hitokappu to await the Cruisers. Watching were three Japanese destroyers—the *Tokitsukaze, Isokaze,* and *Amatsukaze.* The *Pope* was also there and Frost decided to leave it at Hitokappu while he took the *Ford* to Kashiwabara Bay at Paramushiru Island. There was little information available about the World Fliers' progress at this time and a long wait ensued. With time on his hands after sending daily dispatches to his office in Tokyo through the ship's radio, Wells began publication of the *Paramushiru Breeze,* a six-page newspaper in which he wrote stories based on the fragmentary radio reports he received about the fliers. He had followed reports of Martin's forced landing at Kanatak, the delay for repairs, and the *Seattle*'s subsequent disappearance. The *Ford* meantime battled fog, snow, icy winds, and riptides which kept the ship swaying continuously like a pendulum. The ship had to go on reduced rations so Wells went ashore with a party of sailors and shot some birds (they proved to be inedible). On a later hunt in a whaleboat with sailors from the *Tokitsukaze* to hunt bears, he narrowly escaped drowning when the boat leaked and they had to be rescued by a motor launch from the ship.

The *Pope,* accompanied by its escorting Japanese warship, replaced the *Ford* while it steamed to Hakodate to replenish fuel and provisions. Wells transferred to it and described the typhoon that hit Kashiwabara Bay on the morning of 8 May—an example of the risks the U.S. Navy ships were taking to support the round-the-world flight:

> Picture the scene: Three destroyers—two Japanese, one American—are anchored in a shallow bight off a narrows which flows between two adjacent headlands into an ocean of mountainous waves. The wind strikes at these vessels with a velocity of more than one hundred miles an hour and shrieks with fury when it fails to destroy them. Their anchors drag. They roll steadily from side to side: twenty, twenty-five, thirty degrees each way from the vertical. To put to sea would probably mean disaster, so their skippers attempt to keep them where they are.
>
> By the night of May 9, the storm was so violent it was like a bad dream. Captain [J. W.] McClaren would allow the wind to push the *Pope,* time and again, as far across the

bay as he thought it safe to go, then maneuver her into the wind, put on speed, and regain his position. On 10 May, a Japanese steamer, the *Hokushin Maru,* was driven ashore by the gale-force winds and the captain and eight crew members drowned.

There came a moment when disaster seemed inevitable. Pushed relentlessly by the wind, the *Pope* bore down on the *Tokitsukaze* with appalling speed. Captain McClaren issued commands sharply. There was a jangle of bells in the engine-room, and as the powerful engines responded to the Master's orders, the helmsman threw the wheel hard over. A few seconds later the *Pope*'s bow crashed into the *Tokitsukaze*'s side, slid aft along it, and drifted into the darkness. From the forecastle the officer-on-watch reported a dented prow. The *Pope*'s searchlight revealed a deep impression in the *Tokitsukaze*'s side and all the paint scraped off her to the stern. An exchange of radio messages revealed that no serious damage had been caused.

The gray light of day was welcome, but it brought no relief. In fact, the intensity of the storm increased. As it entered its third day, everyone on board the *Pope* abandoned hope of ever seeing any member of the Army World Flight.

About eight o'clock that evening Captain McClaren entered the wardroom and leaned his weary, parka-covered back against the hot, shiny radiator.

"Better put on life preservers," he said. "This is worse than last night and I don't see how we can pull through."[30]

Yet somehow the ship did pull through and the weather improved as it always did eventually. The *Pope* and *Ford* exchanged places again and Wells rejoined his former shipmates. They were standing off the Kurile Islands by this time when word was received that Martin and Harvey had found their way out to safety and were unhurt. The other planes were at Attu also battling the Pacific typhoon. When the weather calmed, Lieutenant Commander Frost radioed appeals to Smith to take advantage of this respite. On 17 May, as wet snow was falling, Wells walked out on deck and looked morosely at the bleak, gray scene. Suddenly he heard aircraft engines, looked up, and there were the three Cruisers. He immediately went to the radio room and asked that the following message be sent: " 'Three planes arrived at 171135,' meaning 11:35 A.M., Saturday, May 17, 1924." He returned to the deck and shot some photographs of the planes circling and landing. His report sent later that day stated:

"The first flight in aviation history was made in this ice-fenced and remotely situated bay bordering the Arctic when six United States airmen landed here (Kurile Island) at 11:30 this morning, completing the most perilous undertaking ever attempted and winning to America the honor of being the first to cross the Pacific by air.

"Fighting their way through a world of obstructions, bucking cold, blustering Arctic winds, thick, almost impenetrable fogs, blinding snowstorms, icy rains, receiving as a result lacerated skins, all of which they beat and retard in every turn, the six airmen in landing here added another laurel wreath to the long list of America's accomplishment."[31]

Journalist Wells's report was in sharp contrast to the brief and less colorful message sent by Smith from the *Ford* at Kurile Island:

Left Attu yesterday at 11 A.M. Snowstorms over Pacific forced us to land offshore at Komandorski at 4:30 P.M. Did not go ashore. Left there at 8 A.M. today and landed here at 2:35 P.M. 180 meridian time. Flight over fog twenty-five percent of time, snow ten percent, and excellent weather the rest. Planes and personnel okay. Severe storm upon landing. Leave next good weather.[32]

Wells's zealous devotion to his job had paid off. When the fliers came aboard the *Ford* after refueling, he was able to interview them and scored a news exclusive with his follow-up stories of which he was justifiably proud.

Wells remained on the *Ford* and spent more time with the fliers when they were at Kasumigaura. He followed their progress after they left and wangled a bunk on the destroyer USS *John Paul Jones* with orders from his Tokyo office to cover the American flight as far as Calcutta. He transferred to the USS *William B. Preston* at Hong Kong and headed by way of Singapore for Akyab to await the Americans there.

The American fliers would meet Wells again and a popular myth would be born.

# 6. First across the Pacific

"The weather was most peculiar," Arnold noted in his diary for what was now 16 May, after they had crossed the International Date Line. "To the south we could always see snow and squalls while to the north it was clear."[1]

When the sky to the south looked ominous, Smith was glad he had not planned to risk confronting a serious snowstorm over this long stretch away from land. "So we headed toward the Komandorskis, deciding to take our chances with the Bolsheviks rather than face the wrath of a storm," he wrote later, not mentioning that they had actually planned to do so. "For three hours we flew out of sight of land, wondering all the time what the Russians would think when they saw three giant planes swoop down out of the sky in this remote region where even ships only come about once a year.

"After we had changed our course to avoid the storm and headed for the Komandorskis, our nearest land was Copper Island, two hundred and seventy miles away. This island is nine miles long and one mile wide—not a very large object, and one that could easily be missed in an ocean, had our navigation been at fault. This was our first long water flight and consequently our first real test, so that, after straining our eyes for hours in an effort to sight Copper Island, it was rather a triumph to see it eventually dead ahead over our radiator caps.

"At 3:05 we arrived at Copper Island, the most easterly of the Komandorski group. That bleak bit of land out there in the Bering Sea sure looked good to us. From a promontory marked Polatka Point on my map, I headed northwest toward Bering Island, the largest of the group, and at five o'clock saw a dent in the coast and the wireless towers of the Soviets looming above the village of Nikolski. About the same moment I spotted the *Eider* five miles offshore. But it was too rough for us to come down away out there, and [the *Eider*'s] officers, realizing this, steamed to three miles from Nikolski and dropped buoys while we circled the island."[2]

Smith and the other two planes landed at 2:35 P.M. and taxied to the buoys that the *Eider* had hurriedly and secretly dropped on the lee side of the ship out of sight of land. A boat immediately started out from shore with five bearded men aboard; two were in uniform carrying rifles and three in civilian clothes. The crews decided to remain in their cockpits in case they had to take off in a hurry. The *Eider* launched three boats and went to the side of each plane but the Russians showed no signs of hostility. Smith and the others climbed down from their cockpits and got into the boats, motioning for the Russians to follow them to the ship and go aboard with them.

There was a sailor of Lithuanian heritage on board from Chicago who was able to communicate with the Russians. He found them courteous but firm in their right to challenge the fliers' presence. They apologized for not being able to invite anyone ashore but said they needed permission from Moscow. The Americans assured them they were airmen on a flight around the world; they would only stay long enough for the weather to settle and then be on their way. The Russians made it clear that everyone would have to stay on the ship until they communicated with their government to determine what they should do. They returned to shore and a while later sent out a boat with a flagon of vodka as a gesture of good will.

The crews inspected and refueled their planes that night from the fuel stock the *Eider* had brought and found that the mooring bridles on the *Boston* and the *New Orleans* had been chafed almost in two by the mooring buoys. When the work was done to reinforce the bridles, the crews returned to the *Eider* for a brief night's rest.

When Capt. Johannssen Beck in the *Haida,* still anchored off Attu, received the *Eider*'s message, he immediately headed his ship under full steam to intercede if the Russians started any trouble. He had already received authorization to proceed within the territorial Soviet waters "for the purpose of rendering assistance to or rescuing the planes and personnel in distress, but will not effect a landing on shore with the cutter's boats or crew, nor engage in any commercial transaction with the subjects of Russia, unless circumstances are most urgent and clearly demand such action in the cause of humanity."[3]

The crews awoke at 4:30 A.M. and prepared for takeoff. Just as they were getting ready to depart, the bearded men returned with the message that the Americans would not be permitted to land. Smith waved to thank them, signaled to the others to start engines, and all three took off together into what Smith called "an ideal spring morning."

The route to Paramushiru took them over the Gulf of Kronotski, the village of Patropavloski, and the mountains of Kamchatka. They crossed the mainland at Cape Shipunski two hours after takeoff, a significant landmark in their world-girdling quest. They had reached the Asian continent and thus had scored a historic "first"—the first aerial crossing of the Pacific Ocean.

When it was known in Washington how much the U.S. Coast Guard had helped the fliers during the flight to Attu, General Patrick wrote a long letter of appreciation to the Coast Guard commandant. He acknowledged that the plans for the North Pacific portion of the flight were based almost entirely on information furnished by the cutter's personnel. The crews of the *Haida* and the *Algonquin* were especially commended. "Whenever an emergency has arisen," Patrick said, "they immediately arose to the occasion and cooperated to the full extent of their ability. At several times during the carrying out of our plans over this section of the route we have been faced with barriers apparently insurmountable. In each case the Coast Guard vessel and personnel have entered the breach and enabled us to carry on."[4]

Patrick noted that the two vessels were required to enter Alaskan waters earlier than usual and when it was found that commercial vessels were too small to carry the large wing boxes and supplies needed at Dutch Harbor, "it was a Coast Guard vessel that enabled us to get these spares to Unalaska on time. When Major Martin needed assurance at Kanatak, 500 miles from Dutch Harbor, the Coast Guard cutter *Algonquin* immediately rushed to his assistance with a new engine."[5]

Patrick also noted that both cutters had carried on an untiring day and night search for Martin and Harvey along the shoreline of the Alaskan Peninsula. The cutters had additionally provided invaluable assistance by maintaining communications when no other means was available for a great part of the time. "In recording one of the most interesting and thrilling aeronautical exploits of contemporary history," Patrick concluded, "your well-organized and efficient force, both in your headquarters and in the Bering Sea Patrol, have played a major part."[6]

The 585-mile leg from the Komandorskis to Paramushiru in the Kurile Islands of Japan was covered in seven hours. The course Smith followed was due west toward the Kamchatka Peninsula, then down its coast to Paramushiru. The first half of the flight had been made in occasional fog and light snow squalls. These forced them to fly lower and lower until they were barely skimming the waves. The second half was made through fog and heavy snow which changed to rain and strong winds by the time they approached Paramushiru. Shortly before 3 P.M., local time, they rounded a point of land and saw the U.S. Navy destroyer *John D. Ford* and two Japanese destroyers, the *Tokitsukaze* and the *Amatsukaze,* waiting for them in Kashiwabara Bay. They circled the area several times and could see the sailors on the decks of all three ships waving in the drenching rain.

The crews had difficulty mooring the planes to buoys laid by the *Ford* because of the strong currents, riptides, and fierce winds. Afterwards boats were sent from the destroyer that took them to the ship. Here, thoroughly wet and cold, they were welcomed by Lt. Cmdr. H. H. Frost and his crew along with representatives of the Japanese Army and Navy. Also present was Linton Wells, the aggressive American newspaper reporter for the Associated Press. He immediately persuaded the ship's radio operator to send an urgent message to his office in San Francisco: FLIERS ARRIVED KASHIWABARA BAY PARAMUSHIRU 17TH AT 11:35. Wells had scored a major world news "beat."

A number of messages of congratulations were received, one from General Patrick for their "epoch-making" flight and another from Secretary of War Weeks who said: YOURS IS THE HONOR OF BEING THE FIRST TO CROSS THE PACIFIC BY AIR

THROUGH ITS ARMY AND NAVY OUR COUNTRY HAS THE HONOR OF HAVING LED IN THE CROSSING OF BOTH GREAT OCEANS THE ARMY HAS EVERY FAITH IN YOUR ABILITY TO ADD THE CIRCUMNAVIGATION OF THE GLOBE TO ITS ACHIEVEMENTS.[7]

General Ugaki, the Japanese Minister of War, sent a message to Weeks congratulating the United States for the accomplishment. Any fear that the Japanese would not welcome the fliers was put aside. The distance covered by the fliers in the six weeks since they had left Seattle was 4,150 miles; they had covered it in 59 hours of flight time for an average speed of just a little over 70 mph. "We are all greatly relieved to have the Aleutian Islands and the Pacific behind us," Arnold commented in his diary, "for these we have considered the most difficult part of the entire trip—and from the time we left Seattle it has been a daily battle to keep the planes from being wrecked."[8]

Because of the 45-mph wind that night that rocked the ship roughly from side to side, the fliers did not get much sound sleep as they rolled back and forth in their narrow bunks. The next day was more of the same strong wind, making the water too rough to refuel the planes and check them over. The men sat around all day on the *Ford* chatting with their hosts, playing bridge, and getting their hair cut which, according to Arnold, they badly needed.[9]

They were invited aboard one of the Japanese destroyers that afternoon and were treated to a dinner in their honor with strong libations. The Japanese were pleasant hosts and there was no discussion of the anti-Asian legislation then being signed into law in the United States. Smith and the others were restless. They were also concerned about their planes, which had been taking a beating. As the engineering officer, Nelson was especially concerned when he saw the planes tossing wildly from side to side, their wings and pontoons slamming into the waves. At 2 A.M., they took lanterns, rowed out to them, checked for any damage, and refueled. The quarter-inch bridles that tethered the planes to the moorings were badly chafed and had almost worn through. They were immediately replaced.

They were off at 7:30 A.M. for Hitokappu Bay on Yetorofu Island, into a biting wind and fog. When word was received on the *Haida* that they had departed, she rendezvoused with the *Eider*, and headed back to Dutch Harbor after taking Bissell aboard. Bissell must have felt great relief. He had not only managed to get three of the planes through his division but had rallied the effort to find Martin and Harvey. He, for one, could write off the experience as "mission accomplished."

The Cruisers were airborne on 19 May for more than seven hours on the 595-mile flight to Yetorofu. This proved to be one of the coldest days of flying they had experienced since leaving Seattle. Wade recalled that "now and then we would stamp our feet just to see if they were still with us. We kept plunging in and out of snow squalls and hopping over one Japanese island after another. We were later amazed to discover that there are more than four thousand islands belonging to the Empire of Japan, extending all the way from the latitude of Alaska to the latitude of Madeira [350 miles off Morocco] and Cuba."[10]

The route took them over many volcanic islands where they could see people, boats, and villages, a distinct change from the Aleutians. When they arrived at Hitokappu Bay, the destroyer *Pope* and the Japanese destroyer *Tokitsukaze* were there to meet them. On shore were several hundred Japanese, many of them school children who had walked nine miles from the town of Furebetsu on three successive days to witness the arrival. The crews did not go ashore that night and hoped to depart the next morning. They refueled the planes and, dead tired, spent the night aboard the *Pope*.

The landing at Hitokappu Bay on the Pacific side of Yetorofu Island had not been planned originally by Lieutenant Nutt as advance officer. When the *Pope* had arrived in the Kuriles in April with fuel and supplies for the flight, she found that the waters between the islands of the Kuriles were blocked with ice and that the floes extended nearly fifty miles into the Pacific. For these reasons Nutt persuaded the Japanese to permit a landing at Yetorofu which was then clear of ice.

Smith hoped the group could get off early the next morning but their old enemy, fog, boiled into the bay and he canceled flying for that day. They went ashore and visited the village of Yanketo and were invited into a house by an elderly gentleman. None had ever had any exposure to Japanese customs and etiquette. They were truly embarrassed as they shuffled inside, leaving their shoes outside, sipping tea, and observing their host's living conditions. "We were fascinated with the village with its tiny houses that looked like eggshells," Wade commented. "Here for the first time since leaving Sitka, Alaska, we saw trees. But they were squatty, stunted ones, flat on top as you see in old Japanese prints and fans. Here, too, for the first time we saw horses, shaggy-haired little animals no bigger than a Shetland pony."[11]

The second Japanese destroyer arrived and the fliers were invited to witness sumo wrestling matches on board. Following the bouts, the Japanese officers served wine and cakes. Then the Americans invited them aboard the *Pope* to see an American motion picture.

The weather remained unfavorable and the flight was not able to depart until 22 May for Minato, a fishing village on the northeast coast of the main island of Honshu, 485 miles away. They had breakfast at midnight and prepared to leave shortly thereafter but were delayed--again by fog—until 5:30 A.M. They encountered light fog conditions as they plodded along a series of mountainous, volcanic islands. The city of Minato, the largest city they had seen since leaving Seattle, was first seen at 10:30 A.M. and the *Ford* was sighted in the bay; Lieutenant Nutt was on board. The three planes circled the city, then landed in the bay while hundreds of people ran down the streets to the waterfront. Although Smith had wired ahead to Nutt that he did not want any party arranged, a "welcome" arch and reception tents had been erected and large crowds lined the beach and wharves. Hundreds of school children waved American flags and a giant fireworks display suddenly lit up the sky.

It was obvious a large celebration had been planned; sadly it was not to be attended by the fliers. Nutt greeted the public and had arranged for sampans to carry gas, oil, and water to each plane. They were behind schedule and, after a brief consultation, Smith decided they would not go ashore and asked Nutt to convey their regrets. At 1:00 P.M., they took off for Kasumigaura in large rolling ocean swells they had not before experienced. The *Chicago* developed an engine problem, and Smith returned to the bay while the other planes circled. Arnold found the trouble was related to a short in the battery, quickly repaired it, and joined up with the other two.

They plunged into fog and rain for the first two and a half hours. Then it cleared and the weather turned "balmy," according to Wade. They were all fascinated by the interesting scenery dotted with rice paddies, sampans, and fishing smacks and junks bobbing up and down in the ocean. They could see many small villages tucked away in the valleys, along with some private estates with well-kept grounds. The number of people rushing out of their houses to look upward, watching from the beaches and hills, increased as they came down the eastern edge of Honshu, Japan's main island. Shortly after 5 P.M., they swung ashore and landed on Lake Kasumigaura. This was the home of the Japanese Naval Air Base, located about fifty miles north of Tokyo. The distance they had flown that day was equivalent to the distance from Chicago to New York. By this time they had flown 5,657 miles and had spent 75 hours, 55 minutes in the air. Most significant, they had pioneered the last gap of an air circumnavigation of the globe between continents, as the Atlantic had already been flown and others had flown between Europe and the Far East. About twenty thousand Japanese were waiting to see them land and come ashore. Arnold described the scene:

> Long concrete runways extended into the lake and led up to a stone pier where the throng waited to give us the first big reception we had encountered since leaving Seattle. There were three of these runways, and motorboats came out to tow a plane alongside each. As we approached the pier at the Japanese Naval Air Base, the people waved thousands of American and Japanese flags and shouted 'Banzai!' There were photographers to the front of us, photographers to the left of us, photographers to the right of us, on platforms, on poles, and even on the roofs. There were newspaper correspondents from all parts of the world—French scribes with beards, Englishmen with monocles, and Americans with straw hats and horn-rimmed glasses.[12]

The fliers received a cordial welcome from the Japanese admiral in command of the base and were assured they would receive all the help they needed. After they made their planes safe for the night, they were taken to the Naval Air Service Club where the local officers hosted a dinner and showed them to their separate rooms. Orderlies were assigned and the men received their first mail from home.

Although the fliers were anxious to see Tokyo, there was much work to be done the next day. Kasumigaura was one of the major supply bases for the flight. The planes were to be overhauled with changes of engines and pontoons and the installation of larger radiators for warmer climates ahead, as well as new propellers and manifolds. While Smith and Arnold were working on the *Chicago,* it was rammed by a small boat and one pontoon was damaged. After the pontoons were replaced, Arnold barely saved the plane from being rammed by an unmanned drifting boat. He crawled out to the edge of one wing and held it off by sheer strength until he was relieved by a fisherman in another boat.

That evening, the admiral hosted them to a typical Japanese dinner in the nearby town of Tsuchiura. Arnold described it:

Having heard often of the geishas and wondering just who they really were, although tired we all looked forward to this party. Nor were we one whit disappointed. When we stepped from our limousines to the veranda of the tea house, checked our shoes, and were welcomed by a crowd of Japanese maids in flowered kimonos, it seemed as though we had stepped into the pages of a storybook.

We entered a room with a floor covered with straw mats and with walls that were mere screens made of wood and paper. The admiral invited us to kneel on silk cushions. Then a tiny table of lacquer was placed in front of each of us by the pretty geisha girls who were there to serve and entertain us—demure, delightful, laughing-eyed, sixteen-year-olds. Each time one of them brought in another course she would kneel and touch her forehead to the matting. Each geisha devotes herself exclusively to the man she is waiting on, removes the various courses, brings others, lights his cigarettes as he reclines on his cushion, fills his little cup with warm sake, and initiates him into the mystery of using chopsticks.[13]

The uniforms for everyone that had been sent ahead arrived from Tokyo on the third day. The fliers could then dress in regulation Air Service uniforms for the first time since leaving Seattle. The citizens of the town gave them fans and paintings as souvenirs and they were taken to the Imperial Hotel in Tokyo where they were greeted by thousands of curious Japanese waving hats, hands, and American and Japanese flags. They spent the next two days attending receptions, luncheons, dinners, teas, and dances. Many of the speeches by Japanese officials were translated by aides, although subsequent conversations with high-ranking Japanese were usually in English.

They were welcomed by American ambassador Cyrus E. Woods, the Japanese ministers of war and navy, members of the Imperial Aviation Association, the entire foreign diplomatic corps, and were rewarded in the Imperial Palace by Prince Kuni of the royal family. They each also received a medal from the *Jiji Shimpo* newspaper "for those who display exceptional talent and skill and a useful profession." General Ugaki, Japanese Minister of War, presented each of the them with a solid silver saki cup with their names engraved inside and a silver bowl engraved with the image of a Cruiser, their route of flight, and the crossed flags of the two nations.

During a visit to the Tokyo Imperial University, the president, Dr. Yoshinao Kozai, addressed them in English at a dinner in their honor. He praised them for their achievement and added, "At the same time we envy you, for your daring is backed by science. Indeed it is the happy union of courage and knowledge that has gained you your success and this honor of being the first of men to connect the shores of the Pacific Ocean through the sky."[14]

The reconditioning of the three planes for the tropical portion of the flight took a week and they were now thirty-one days behind their planned schedule. Two of those days had been spent making dollies for the Cruisers and tracks for them so the planes could be hauled out of the water and towed to a hangar for the work.

When they learned that the number of events, always elaborate, planned for them was to last two weeks, Smith begged the Japanese to compress them all into forty-eight hours. There was too much work to be done on the planes and no one could do it but themselves, although the Japanese mechanics were always poised to help. The Americans noted that the Japanese made precise drawings of every visible part of the planes, took many photographs, and even carefully measured the size of the rivets and cotter pins that the Americans used.

In the few hours when they weren't working, the fliers went shopping or wrote letters. They turned in their heavy flying equipment and packed for the next legs of the journey southward. Everywhere they went, crowds followed them. In stores they visited, proprietors welcomed them with frequent bows, honored by their visit.

"With the realization of the significance of the flight, our sense of responsibility increased," Wade said. "It was no longer just a personal adventure. The United States could not be let down. We started watching ourselves and our actions on the ground. Diplomatic correctness became as important as our aerial skills. Sergeant Ogden, my mechanic, was the only enlisted man left on the flight, and his lack of rank posed embarrassing problems. The difficulty was explained to Washington by cable and when we arrived in Shanghai, an order was waiting from General Patrick making him a second lieutenant. For the rest of the flight we never stopped kidding him about his 'social commission.'"[15]

While they had been in Tokyo, Squadron Leader MacLaren had been winging his way from England toward Japan. Lt. Col. L. E. Broome, his advance officer, met with the Americans at breakfast on 23 May when they were interrupted by a messenger with a telegram: MACLAREN CRASHED AT AKYAB PLANE COMPLETELY WRECKED CONTINUANCE OF FLIGHT DOUBTFUL.[16]

What followed showed the spirit of brotherhood that then existed among fliers regardless of nationality. The spare Vickers Vulture that MacLaren had arranged to have waiting for him in Japan had arrived by ship at Hakodate harbor, five hundred miles north of Tokyo. Broome wired the British naval commander-in-chief of the China Station to see if he could help; he replied that he had no vessel available for such a purpose. The British flight was a private venture and had no government assistance or financial backing. When Smith heard this, he asked Broome to go with him to meet Capt. John S. Abbot, commander of the Forty-fifth Division of the U.S. Asiatic Fleet in Japanese waters, to see what he might suggest. Abbot immediately volunteered to place a destroyer at Broome's disposal to get the spare plane to MacLaren if his superior in Washington, D.C., would approve. Approval was promptly granted and Broome was dumbfounded. All he could say was "That's the finest bit of sportsmanship I've ever heard of!"[17]

At 7 A.M. next morning the American destroyer *John Paul Jones* left Yokohama Harbor with orders to take the plane in three large boxes from Hakodate to Hong Kong. Also aboard was Linton Wells, ever the intrepid reporter. On 3 June, the *Jones* arrived at Hong Kong and transferred its load and Wells to the *William B. Preston,* commanded by Lt. Cmdr. Willis A. Lee Jr. On 11 June, the spare plane was delivered to MacLaren to be reassembled. The American Navy and the Air Service were in the unusual position of assisting a foreign rival who might circle the globe first. But at the same time, they heard that Lt. Pelletier d'Oisy had survived an accident near Shanghai but his plane was completely wrecked. He was out of the race.

The Cruisers meanwhile were towed out to their mooring spots on the fifteen-mile-long lake and each made at least two test hops on 30 May. While the men worked on their planes, a Japanese fighter performing a test flight over the lake disintegrated in midair. Pieces of the plane hit the water about 100 yards from the *Chicago.* "Fortunate that another Cruiser was not put out of the race," Harding commented.[18]

Smith, concerned that they were losing valuable time, met with Captain Abbot and finalized plans for the assistance of the Asiatic squadron for the entire distance to Calcutta, India. They scheduled the departure for Kushimoto for the morning of 1 June and were surprised to see that a special train had arrived from Tokyo with the chief of the Japanese Air Service and a host of other officials. "We were much surprised to see them," Arnold wrote, "but they replied that they looked upon the circumnavigation of the world by air as an event sure to usher in a new age, and an age in which they intended Japan to play a leading part. As we all shook hands, their last words were: 'Keep a lookout for Fujiyama off to the right.' "[19]

The fliers were off at 5:30 A.M. in ideal weather with Smith in the lead and old Fuji was there in all its storied glory. The route of flight was by way of Inuboye Point to Iro Point and directly from there to Kushimoto, a distance of 305 miles. Soon after leaving Iro Point, the flight plunged into a severe rainstorm which became a mild typhoon that turned more severe as they landed at Kushimoto after 4½ hours of rough going. The moorings proved to be unsatisfactory as each plane immediately began drifting to shore after being made fast to the buoys. All three planes taxied to the opposite side of the bay and waited until the *Pope* came near and furnished them with new anchors. They refueled and went aboard the ship for the night, exhausted from fighting the rain and waves. A greeting party from the town planned to come out to the ship but the sea was so rough they couldn't get a boat safely near the *Pope* and had to return to shore. While the others slept soundly, Smith was told by a lookout that the *Chicago* was drifting. He and a group of sailors went out to his plane in the driving rain and attached another anchor to the bridle.

The next day, 2 June, after the storm had subsided, they went ashore where they were presented with decorations and souvenirs, "enough to start an Oriental museum," according to Arnold. "Among the decorations we received were three [for the pilots] presented the day we landed at Kasumiguara. Smith begged the Japanese to make up three more for Jack, Hank, and myself, and to present all six at once, since they were so kind as to honor us. He explained that we were simply six American airmen flying around the world together, and that we were all on an equal footing. This was mighty decent of Lowell and we all appreciated it, but none more so than Ogden."[20]

They were off for Kagoshima into a stiff head wind shortly after noon that day and it took them six and a quarter hours to span the 360-mile distance. The route of flight was past Muroto Point and Cape Ashizuri to Aritake Bay, and across the peninsula to Kagoshima, the southernmost city of Japan proper, located on a bay featuring the Sakurajima volcano in its midst.

During the flight from island to island they passed safely through two complete storm centers of considerable intensity. They saw many steamers, junks, and fishing vessels and were pleased to see two American destroyers, *Perry* and *Stewart,* patrolling the ocean route for them. While over Bungo Channel, the *Boston*'s engine began overheating from loss of water and Wade landed in a well-protected harbor on the coast of Kyushu Island. Ogden filled the radiator with salt water while the other two planes circled. Wade soon rejoined the others and the flight landed at Kagoshima after sundown at 7 P.M. and were met by the U.S. Navy repair ship *Black Hawk.* Lieutenant Nutt was aboard and had made excellent arrangements for buoys and refueling. A large crowd made up of at least two thousand school children was waiting on the beach waving flags they had made in school. The fliers went ashore briefly where a few short speeches were made and souvenirs handed out.

The fliers stayed aboard the *Black Hawk* that night and the next day to await word that the U.S. Navy ships were in position for the flight across the Yellow Sea to Shanghai. Each Cruiser crew had difficulty keeping small boats away from the planes, a problem that was to be repeated many times until they reached Calcutta and exchanged the pontoons for wheels.

They awoke on 4 June to excellent weather and hoped to make an early takeoff. Each had a heavy load of fuel for the 550-mile flight. But the water was so smooth and the wind so light that they had to do what seaplanes often have to do. They taxied around to disturb the water and make ripples so the pontoons could break the suction of the water, a problem each experienced at one time or another during water operations. Wade and Nelson finally got off but Smith did not after making several tries. When the others circled to look for signals, Smith didn't want them to have to try a takeoff again in the calm water and waved them on toward China.

"Suspecting that there was something wrong with our pontoons," Smith explained, "we taxied back to our moorings, donned the bathing suits that had been presented to us by the people of Portland, Oregon, and spent the rest of the day swimming about under the pontoons. We discovered that a metal strip had been torn away by the force of the water, so that there had been just enough resistance to prevent us from getting off as we should.

"Swimming around under the pontoons was a job for a mermaid, not for an airman, and we swallowed quarts of water. But we finally got it fixed, and the following morning the *Black Hawk* sent two fast motorboats in front of us to kick up the surface of Kagoshima Bay, enabling us to follow the others toward China."[21]

# 7. To China and the "Paris of the Orient"

The original schedule called for the world fliers to reach Shanghai on 5 May. Yet it was not until 5 June that the *Boston* and *New Orleans* were en route on the long flight across the junction of the Yellow and China seas to make that first stop in China. After wagging their wings to show that they understood Smith's desire that they continue without him, Nelson and Wade headed southwest in the best weather on the longest sea journey of the trip so far. The engine was purring soundly so Nelson let his mind "browse" while Harding took the wheel. He commented to historian Lowell Thomas that he "seemed to see dozens of giant planes passing me in the sky with passengers making weekend trips between Shanghai and San Francisco, just as they now do between Paris and London. It seemed to me that the airplane was destined to be the agency that would bring the races of the world into such intimate contact with each other that they would no more feel inclined to wage wars than the people of Oregon feel like fighting the inhabitants of Florida.

"If our flight helps in any way to hasten this era, we shall be repaid a million times over for our efforts. Just what significance it will have to our fellow countrymen, we do not know. But there is one thing we do know, that it has done much to stimulate enthusiasm for aviation in Japan!"[1]

The two planes droned on in the best weather they had experienced since leaving Seattle. A serious problem developed for Nelson and Harding. As they reached the flight's midpoint over the sea, the exhaust stack on the right side of the engine of the *New Orleans* became so hot that it began to burn the rubber off the ignition wires. Nelson throttled back to try to cool the metal and the engine kept purring satisfactorily. He later admitted, though, that if they had more than about two hours to go, they would have had to ditch.[2]

The *Boston* and *New Orleans* passed the USS *Ford* about seventy miles off the Chinese shore; it was the first of the several destroyers assigned to monitor their progress southward. They knew they were approaching the entrance to one of the great rivers of the world when the sea below changed from deep blue to green and then a muddy gold, the latter caused by the eroding silt upstream. It was the Yangtze-Kiang River, China's chief commercial artery and the longest river in Asia. Millions of people live along its shores.

As the two crews flew across the mouth of the river, they saw thousands of junks, sampans, river boats, and large steamships, all trying to avoid each other. Anticipating their arrival, the harbormaster at Shanghai had cleared several miles of waterfront for their landing space. The river's drop from the sea's entrance is so slight that the ocean tide is very swift and runs upriver for two hundred miles. This rapid tide made it difficult for both crews to tie their planes to the buoys.

When they finally completed the tie-ups, they boarded an excursion boat containing hundreds of Americans and Europeans who had rented the boat to give them a historic reception. A delegation led by a General Lee, chief of the Chinese Air Force, and other high officials welcomed them to China and congratulated them for their achievement. Their arrival marked the first time that aircraft had linked America and China by air.

After meeting and shaking hands with the welcoming crowd, the four fliers excused themselves and rowed back to their planes rather than go ashore to meet a huge throng and a large force of uniformed militia that were clamoring to welcome them. They apologized to the hosts on the boat but hoped they would understand that their work on their flying machines came first.

Nelson felt strongly that the long exhaust manifolds on all the planes' engines should be replaced with short, straight stacks to avoid overheating the engines as he had experienced. Since none was available in the advance supplies placed there, he arranged for a machine shop in downtown Shanghai to make three sets of stacks out of boiler tubing.

It was dark when they finished their work and were taken to the luxurious Hotel Astor in downtown Shanghai. They bathed, put on their wrinkled uniforms, and were taken by limousine to the home of a merchant prince. To their surprise, they were ushered into a huge ballroom where a large crowd with women in evening gowns and men in formal dress and others in military uniforms greeted them. The fliers made their way along a reception line while an orchestra played American music. Little girls walked ahead of them singing and spreading roses.

Smith and Arnold arrived the next day and experienced the same problem tying up to their buoy as the others had. They also were given the same kind of welcoming ceremonies on the excursion boat but returned to work on the *Chicago* by lantern light until long after dark. Smith was not interested in seeing the sights and met with Lt. Malcolm Lawton, the advance officer, and American naval officers to plan the safest way to take off from the crowded river and to position the destroyers for the upcoming flight to Amoy (later Xiamen). He decided that they would not take on sufficient fuel and oil for the 600-mile flight but a lighter load of each in order to take off in a shorter distance and avoid hitting any of the hundreds of sampans that were always scurrying on their self-absorbed excursions. Smith worked out a plan with the U.S. Navy destroyer captains to proceed down the coast and refuel at Tchinkoen Bay, three hundred and fifty miles from Shanghai. They took on sufficient fuel for only five hours of flight. Nelson found meanwhile that the pontoons on the *Chicago* were out of alignment and may have contributed to Smith's difficulty in getting off the water at Kagoshima. He helped Smith and Arnold straighten them.

All was ready on 7 June and the takeoffs were as dangerous as the pilots had feared. The harbormaster was not able to clear a wide path and the river traffic was worse than when they had landed. All three planes nearly collided with some unheeding sampans and had to abort their first takeoff attempts. The water was also very rough because of swells from the ocean. But Smith and Wade were finally able to see a clear lane, scoot among several small junks, and depart. Nelson in the *New Orleans* had to quickly zoom right to evade a junk and went plunging up the river at a high speed, barely dodging the traffic. A large sampan suddenly loomed in front of him and he yanked back on the wheel with all his strength. He had enough speed, fortunately, to lift off and topped the mast of the wayward craft by a scant few inches.

It took four hours, thirty minutes, for the three planes to reach the destroyer off the China coast and refuel. They left at 2:45 P.M. to continue the flight along the coast to Amoy and arrived at 5:35. En route they flew very low to look at the hundreds of villages along the shore and the thousands of sampans filled with families and animals. Feeling exhilarated because the weather was excellent and the planes were responding perfectly, they played leapfrog over the junks.

At Amoy the destroyer *Preble* was waiting. It was under the command of Captain Glassford, commanding officer of the destroyer division escorting the flight through Indochina. They found that excellent arrangements for fueling and mooring had been made by the Standard Oil Company. Curious Chinese in their junks crowded around closely as soon as the fliers tied up and tried to refuel and check their engines. Much time was spent pushing them away from the pontoons. The boats with sails could not be easily controlled and repeatedly drifted into the planes. The launch from the *Preble* tried to keep them at bay and the officer in charge, frustrated by their refusal to back off, decided that the only way to drive them away was to sink a few. He headed toward a few sampans at high speed and swerved to capsize them. From then on the boatmen kept at a respectful distance.

Amoy, located in the south Fujian Province of China, sits on an island at the mouth of the Jiulong River. It was one of the earliest seats of European commerce in China. Amoy has a storied past as the major base of pirates and buccaneers who plundered the coastal villages and raided passing ships. The fliers had no desire to visit the city and stayed aboard the *Preble* for the night. The crews wanted to leave at daybreak next morning but had more difficulty preparing for departure. The curious Chinese again crowded their boats around the planes and refused to allow a clear takeoff path. Again the Navy helped, yet it took an inordinate amount of time and they were not able to take off until 10:30 A.M.

They were warned before takeoff that they might run into a typhoon on the 310-mile flight down the coast and around China Point to Hong Kong. As they plunged ahead, the skies darkened ominously with lightning streaking at frequent intervals. A strong wind with extreme turbulence estimated at about a hundred miles an hour hit them from the rear and increased their ground speed to 150 mph. It did not last long, fortunately, and they emerged over a calm sea. But they soon ran into fog and a driving rain that forced them down low, barely topping hundreds of boats of all descriptions. The increasing number of them proved that they were nearing Hong Kong, the crown colony that was ceded by the British to China in 1842, with one of the busiest seaports in the world. It prospered before and since as an east-west trading center and commercial gateway to South China.

Hundreds of boats of all descriptions and sizes filled the harbor with a faithful American destroyer anchored among them. Smith and the others circled over the scene looking for the yellow buoys that were supposed to have been anchored in a clear area. They could not find them. The instructions telling them where to tie up had not been received before they left Amoy. Smith flew low over the destroyer and was waved over to the other side of the bay. The planes finally landed at 1:35 P.M. and taxied to a small cove near the Standard Oil Company dock.

All that day and the next were spent refueling and working on the propellers of the three planes in the Standard Oil machine shop. A leaking cylinder jacket on the *Chicago*'s engine was welded with the help of the company employees. One pontoon on the *Chicago* was still causing problems and was leaking badly. J. W. Shaw, the oil company agent, arranged for a portable crane on a barge to lift the plane onto the dock. Here they installed a new pontoon that had been brought previously to Hong Kong by one of the Navy destroyers.

The morning of 10 June was extremely hot as the fliers prepared to leave for Haiphong, French Indochina (now Vietnam). The shortest distance would take the planes over a peninsula between the South China Sea and the Gulf of Tonkin, variously shown on their maps as Leih-Chew, Quant-Chaw-Wau, and Luichow where "there are more tigers and leopards than anywhere else in China," according to Smith. It would be a risky flight for a seaplane because if any of the Cruisers had engine trouble, a crash was inevitable in the rugged jungle.

"Evidently, the natives of Luichow Peninsula had never seen airplanes before," he added. "We flew only five hundred feet off the ground, and as we came roaring into view we could see the Chinese running in every direction. When we caught up with them, they would swing off either to the left or to the right to avoid the dragons that seemed about to gobble them up."[3]

Leigh Wade remembers that particular flight from a different perspective. "From Hong Kong to Haiphong, we passed over a group of islands that rival our Thousand Islands if not surpassing them in beauty," he wrote years later. "Some were mere rocks of various colors, while others were covered with a jungle forest. We were pleased to have had clear weather for a fog or storm undoubtedly would have meant disaster as the islands were so close together."[4]

The trio of planes reached the mouth of the Red River at sundown and were moored again near a Standard Oil Company pier. Several motor launches eased up to the planes and a group of French men and women wanted them to come aboard one of them for a welcoming reception. They did not seem to understand why the men had to service their planes. One particularly aggressive Frenchman tried several times to step aboard one of the pontoons of the *Chicago* to deliver a welcoming speech but Smith pushed his boat off each time. It was dark when the fliers were ready to go ashore and the man was still there. Smith was embarrassed to find out that he was the French governor-general who was trying to invite them to a formal reception. He apologized for his unintentional discourtesy and accepted the invitation for the group.

But they had a problem. Since they had discarded their clothes before the flight from Japan to China, they could not attend formal functions in their greasy flying suits. On several occasions, they borrowed suitable clothing from the officers on board the escorting destroyers. Smith explained that they would "size up" the officers they met on board and borrow white trousers and shirts, shoes, socks, ties, and sun helmets. "This would enable us to board the waiting rickshas and sally forth to the evening's festivities as snappily groomed as any cake-eater of the China coast."[5]

At the reception that night, the fliers learned that the Portuguese fliers, Brito Pais and Sarmiento Beires, had arrived in Rangoon, Burma. They had crashed in India but the British Royal Air Force had given them a new plane and they were determined to continue their quest to win the honor of being first around the globe. At the same time, MacLaren, the British pilot, was still at Akyab waiting for the American destroyer to bring him his replacement Vickers amphibian from Japan.

"This news of the progress of the Portuguese was like a tonic to us," Smith reported later. "Excusing ourselves from the reception, we hurried back to the destroyer, got a good night's sleep, and were up at dawn the next morning, June 11, hoping to reach Saigon, or at least to get halfway down the coast of French Indochina that day."[6]

The trio of planes had the same difficulty getting off the Haiphong River's smooth surface as they had experienced on previous takeoffs from quiet waters. All three planes refused to break the water's suction despite the pilots pushing the Liberty engines to full throttle and rocking back and forth on the wheel. The ubiquitous junks and sampans also seemed determined to impede their takeoffs and forced the planes to zigzag as best they could to avoid collisions. All of the planes eventually got off but it took Wade twelve miles at full throttle for him to break his pontoons loose, even though his airspeed indicator showed the normal takeoff speed of 55 miles an hour.

Once airborne, the flight to Tourane, French Indochina (later named Da Nang, South Vietnam), a seaport halfway between Haiphong and Saigon, seemed destined to be an easy one but fate intervened for Smith. They crossed a narrow peninsula and cruised low over rice fields where hundreds of men, women, and water buffaloes labored in the bleaching sun. The rice fields gave way to thick jungle and then the Gulf of Tonkin. Thirty miles off the coast, the *Chicago*'s engine began to overheat, causing Smith to look quickly for a quiet lagoon. He turned west toward the shore, found one, and landed. Arnold leaped out, grabbed a bucket, filled it with water, and handed it to Smith who poured it in the radiator. Seeing what the problem was, Wade and Nelson circled until Smith was airborne again and rejoined them.

The problem was not solved for long. Twenty minutes later, the engine temperature had risen and the engine began to pound ominously. Both men began to look for a lagoon and found one about three miles inland. Smith throttled back and glided toward it while the engine seemed to be going to pieces. Smith landed immediately and Arnold leaped out of the rear cockpit, extinguisher in hand, ready to put out a fire if necessary. A connecting rod had broken and was projecting through the crank case. Water had been lost through a cracked cylinder and an auxiliary water valve. The engine didn't erupt into flames but they were now stranded on a small lake without food or water, far from any visible habitation, with an engine that could not be repaired.

Nelson and Wade had watched the *Chicago* glide down and land safely in the lagoon. After they saw Smith and Arnold get out on the pontoons and signal that the engine was beyond their ability to repair, both landed to help out. They gave them all the drinking water and food they were carrying and promised to get a new engine to them as soon as possible. They then took off for Tourane, leaving the two stranded airmen to assess the primitive area in which they landed. The lagoon was full of fish traps, so there must have been people nearby to service these. Many tropical birds soared overhead. What caused them to exercise caution as they inspected the engine damage were the crocodiles that occasionally surfaced, looked at the strange object that had entered their domain, and slowly slithered away.

After about an hour, a dugout emerged from the jungle covering along the shore. Steering it cautiously was a nearly naked native who seemed concerned that these large birds had tied up to the bamboo stakes marking his traps. Smith and Arnold understood his concern and got out their anchor and ropes and allowed the plane to drift to another part of the lagoon before throwing the anchor overboard.

Seeing that the lone fisherman was not harmed by the white men, others paddled out to look them over. They became so chummy that they climbed on the pontoons and their weight threatened to sink them. Smith and Arnold spent the rest of the day in the hot sun shooing them off. They thought they would try to persuade one of the boatmen to take them to shore but hesitated when a man in a white robe who looked neither native-born nor European rowed out from shore and spoke in French. Although apparently a priest, he seemed to want only to buy cigarettes from them. When they were able to make him understand in their pidgin French they had no cigarettes, he refused to get them water or food and paddled off. Arnold found an empty bottle in the plane's storage compartment and followed him in a borrowed dugout hoping to get some fresh water. He had seen what looked like a small mission church hidden in the jungle foliage and found a spring behind it to fill the bottle.

The water didn't last long between the two men and their thirst became more intense. In late afternoon, a sampan arrived with three more French missionaries dressed in white robes. They seemed more sympathetic and warned both men not to drink any water offered by the natives from their dugout canoes. While Smith stayed with the plane, Arnold went ashore to the home of the priests and was treated to a welcome glass of wine. They gave him a bottle of it, some boiled rice wrapped in leaves, and several baked yams to take to Smith. It was pitch dark when he returned to the plane. He did not realize that he had been gone for more than three hours.

Smith meantime had been having difficulty keeping the natives and their dugouts away from the pontoons in the darkness; in desperation he fired a few rounds from the Very pistol over their heads to scare them off. After doing this several times, he then aimed his flashlight directly at them. They thought this meant he was going to fire at them again and they backed off. Smith had become desperately thirsty under the broiling sun while waiting for Arnold and had gulped down a few swallows of water offered from one of the dugouts. He knew better because they had all been warned before they left the States about the dangers of drinking water in the tropics, yet the urge to drink had overwhelmed him.

While Smith and Arnold were having their difficulties, Nelson and Wade had arrived at Tourane and began immediately to make arrangements to obtain a new engine. They hurriedly boarded the destroyer *Noah* that was waiting for them and met Lt. Malcolm Lawton, the advance officer who had arranged the supply bases and mooring points along the China coast. It was decided among them that Nelson would return to the lagoon while the USS *Noah* would bring a new engine from Saigon. The destroyer had been positioned there for just such an emergency and would now arrange to get a new engine as near as possible to the *Chicago*.

Also aboard the *Noah* was M. Chevalier, the Standard Oil Company representative Lawton had appointed as an agent. He took the men to his home to study a map of French Indochina in order to locate the lagoon and plan the best route to reach it. It was found that the *Chicago* was down nearest the city of Hue, capital of the Province of Annam (later incorporated into Vietnam), which could be reached by a good road in an automobile. Nelson and Chevalier would confer with French officials there and proceed then by the best means through the jungle. Wade, Ogden, and Harding meanwhile would perform maintenance on the *New Orleans* and *Boston* and wait.

It took three hours for Nelson to reach Hue. Although the road was reasonably smooth, they had to go through wild jungle country and be ferried across several streams by barges. When they arrived at Hue, they were told that it was impossible to reach the lagoon by automobile and they would have to go part of the way by barge or sampan. Nelson tells about his experience:

"At the little hotel in Hue we bought sandwiches, milk, soda water, and other things to take along for the boys, engaged a man who spoke a little French to guide us, and at 11 P.M. that night we were off in the automobile. There are many waterways through this part of Annam so we decided to make first for a place owned by a friend of Chevalier's. He owned a rice plantation on the river that ran into the lagoon we were looking for. We got within two miles of the plantation in the automobile; then we had to load our food and other supplies into a sampan and continue upriver.

"It was pitch dark, not even a star. How the natives could find their way around the bends in that stream on such an inky night was beyond me, but evidently their eyes are better trained for penetrating darkness than ours. This is a great tiger country, and the Annamites live in mortal terror of 'Master Stripes.' They also have a wholesome respect for crocodiles. Before we got into their sampan they threw a little cooked rice into the river and offered up a prayer to the spirits of the night, imploring them to protect us."[7]

They arrived at the plantation of Chevalier's friend and were advised to proceed overland through the jungle for a few miles to the home of a native-born priest who could advise them on the best way to get to the lagoon. The friend persuaded a few men to carry the food and guide them through the jungle.

"Just how far we hiked I do not know," Nelson said. "We proceeded single file, and what impressed me the most was the multitude of little shrines all along the way where the men said their prayers and left offerings for the tigers and their other forest friends. Every traveler who goes this way leaves a banana or a bit of rice on these altars. There were shrines every five minutes, and occasionally we passed a good-sized temple. On both sides of the trail there was dense jungle that could only be penetrated by cutting your way through with an ax.

"At last we arrived at the thatched house of the priest. While the local men remained outside, he invited us in, told us he had neither seen nor heard any airplanes, but would send for some of the men who had been out fishing that day. At the same time he ordered one of his servants to notify the mandarin who lived a mile or so away. The fishermen were unable to help us, but they did say they had seen two monsters flying through the air that afternoon.

"The mandarin came to the priest's bungalow dolled up in a gorgeous silk costume and followed by quite a retinue. He was most polite and offered to place sampans and men at our disposal. So we set off downriver again. Exhausted, I stretched out in the bottom of the sampan while Chevalier inspected the banks with the two flashlights we had brought along. When we passed a village, then the night would be rent by the cries of the people onshore and those paddling us who answered shout for shout.

"An hour or more went by before anyone could give us encouraging news. At last a man told us that there was an airplane in a lagoon not far away. Eureka! We knew we were on the right track. From then on, we kept the flashlight going continuously, and called out every few minutes. At last we heard an answering shout."[8]

Smith and Arnold had spent the night on the plane after drinking the wine and eating the rice and bananas. Exhausted from the heat and humidity, Smith crawled into the plane's tool compartment with his head sticking outside the opening while Arnold stretched out on the wing. It was about 3 A.M. when both men happily returned the shouts from the rescue party. The reunion was especially memorable for Erik Nelson as it was 12 June 1924, his thirty-sixth birthday. The three fliers and Chevalier partied until daylight celebrating with the food and beer Nelson had brought along for the occasion.

There was much work to be done. The three went ashore and arranged for men in the nearest village to attach three sampans in tandem to the plane and tow it twenty-five miles upriver to Hue, the old capital city of what was later South Vietnam. There they would await the arrival of the new engine. The parade of boats was led by a chieftain reclining in his royal chair under a huge umbrella, while his concubines lit his cigarettes and served him drinks. A tribesman beat a tom-tom for cadence while families and friends trailed behind in their houseboats. About halfway, Nelson and Chevalier debarked near where they had left the automobile the night before and the *Chicago* continued its spectacular tow to Hue. Arnold, stretched out on one of the plane's pontoons, kept shouting, "I'm going to quit the Army, come back here, and start a super race!"

"Our French friend had sent a courier ahead to warn the inhabitants of Hue that we were coming," Smith recounted. "So when we arrived the whole population was out to meet us. Erik and Chevalier, who had arrived ahead of us, had rounded up a company of Annamite soldiers to guard the plane, which we beached close to a bridge that looked as if it would be a good place for changing engines. And so it was; for it was much simpler to use the bridge for raising the engines than to attempt to rig up a derrick."[9]

At dawn next day, Nelson and Chevalier left for Tourane while Smith and Arnold disconnected the engine from the plane. By midmorning the heat had become so intense that both men nearly fainted. M. Bruel, a professor at a local college, had been observing them at work and invited them to his home. He had his servants give them a bath by throwing buckets of cold water on them and then loaned them clothes while their dirty coveralls were laundered. They were entertained during the evening with songs and dances by students and staff of the local college and spent that night at a small French hotel.

The spare engine had been rushed by the USS *Noah* from Saigon to Tourane where Wade had remained to watch over the *New Orleans* and *Boston.* When the engine arrived, Nelson, Harding, and Chevalier left for Hue by automobile, while Ogden and four volunteer sailors from the destroyer accompanied the crated engine in a motor lorry.

Ogden would never forget that ride as they left Tourane in the dark. "It was so dark I couldn't tell what sort of country we were going through or what pace we were making, but it must have been fully thirty miles an hour," he said later. "Traveling at that rate in a truck over a jungle road is enough to shake your toenails to your throat."

Up and up and up we went. It seemed as though we must be ascending Pikes Peak or Mount Everest. Occasionally I saw two balls of fire gleaming through the trees, and knew that it must be some wild animal. Finally we came to the top of the mountain range and started to coast down the other side. If we were making a mile an hour, we were doing between forty and fifty. . . .

Suddenly the bumping ceased and I felt as though I were riding in an airplane again. Sure enough, we were flying, and a moment later we flew into some trees. Mr. Annamite had buzzed right off the road into the jungle. It took us thirty minutes to disentangle the truck from the underbrush and get it back on the road. But even this experience taught him nothing. On we went, as if kicked by an army mule. Fifteen minutes later, we jumped off the highway again and crashed into a pile of rocks. Next day, on the return journey, I had a look at this place and noticed that on the far side of those rocks there was a thousand-foot precipice, so the good Lord was watching over us on this trip.

When we got to the bottom of the mountain, there was a place where the road went diagonally across a railroad track. Instead of continuing on the road, the fool Annamite swerved off and went bumping over the ties. It took us another half hour to drag the truck back to the road.

We crossed a second range of mountains, and on our way down the grade this time, the brake band broke. I had climbed into the seat next to my neck-or-nothing chauffeur, hoping that my presence might tend to sober him somewhat. It was lucky I had, for he had just brain enough to do what I signaled, to throw the engine in low speed. In doing so, however, he let go of the steering wheel, so we left the road again. If it hadn't been for some trees, I am sure we should be going yet, because there was a deep valley right under us. My heart stopped beating at least ten times that night.[10]

Ogden's risky adventure was still not over. They reached a lagoon when they entered the next valley and had to be transported across it on a barge poled by fishermen. When halfway, the barge began to leak and the men panicked. They immediately poled back to the beach they had left and got there just in time to off-load the truck. The crew of the sinking barge hollered for friends on the other side of the lagoon who came over with their barge. Ogden, the sailors, and the truck with the engine finally made it to Hue as dawn was breaking.

With the help of Smith and Arnold, the old engine was lifted out of the plane and the new one was dropped into place. All the engine lifelines were connected and the plane was ready to go in less than four hours in what Ogden, an experienced hand at engine changes, said was record time. Smith started it up and taxi-tested the plane before taking off for Tourane, sixty miles away.

The episode had been an extraordinary example of cooperation between the U.S. Navy, the French agent, sailors, priests, boatmen, and the fliers themselves. The entire episode had taken only seventy-one hours from the time Smith and Arnold had landed on the remote lagoon until they flew the plane away with its new engine.

Nelson and the others returned to Tourane with the truck and arrived before nightfall on 15 June. Next morning the crews arose early and the three planes were airborne for Saigon shortly after 5 A.M. The weather was favorable but the *Boston* had its troubles during the flight when the generator stopped working. The cause could not be determined. When they found that no spare generator was available,

Nelson, a master at innovation, later installed an extra storage battery with a switch so that one battery could be used for a short while, then the other.

After flying over more jungle, rice paddies, and quiet lagoons, the trio of planes arrived over the entrance to the Mekong River at 1:30 P.M. The three planes landed at the French Army Hydroplane Station on the Saigon River north of the city. They had arrived at what was then called the "Paris of the Orient," the most southern point they would reach nearest the equator.

# 8. On to Calcutta

Saigon may have been considered a friendly city to most tourists during the early 1920s yet the World Fliers found it anything but agreeable. They spent the first night as guests at the home of the manager of the Standard Oil Company and worked on their planes most of the next day. In late afternoon they borrowed white shirts and trousers from the *Noah*'s officers and went into the city to a sidewalk café. This brought back for several of them happy memories of their days in Paris during and after the Great War. The fliers found that Saigon, forty-five miles from the sea, was a modern city with many European buildings, schools, and colleges, and a heterogeneous population with about five thousand Europeans, mostly French. The intercity main means of transportation was still the time-honored rickshaw.

After sitting awhile and noting that everyone was being waited on but them, Wade called a waiter over to give him their orders. The waiter was surly and said he couldn't serve them and they would have to leave. When they asked why, he replied that no one could be served at that café who was not wearing a coat.

"We fully appreciated that it was somewhat uncommon for Europeans to be without coats," Wade explained, "and we tried to explain who we were and how, as Air Service officers, we could put on our naval friends' trousers and shirts in order to come ashore, but that it was impossible for us to wear their tunics and masquerade as members of another branch of the United States government service."[1]

It made no difference to the waiter. He said he knew who they were and they would still have to leave. "This frosty reception didn't increase our enthusiasm for Saigon," Wade added. "We voted the city a 'washout.' To make the affair all the more unpleasant, the Frenchmen sitting at adjoining tables apparently relished our embarrassment and sided with the café management."[2]

On another visit into the city, the fliers boarded two rickshaws and told the drivers to take them to the Governor General's house where they had been invited to dinner. After winding through a number of streets and alleys, they became suspicious of where they were being taken. They arrived at a house of ill repute where the madam, standing on the porch, told them she was sorry, the house was full. The fliers were late for dinner but their French host understood. He told them they looked like American sailors in their borrowed white clothes so the drivers thought they must have wanted to go to a 'sporting house.'

The airmen were glad to leave Saigon on the morning of 18 June for Kampongson Bay. This was on the eastern side of the Gulf of Siam in Cambodia. Their purpose in going there was for refueling from an American destroyer. Smith and the others had decided to make this stop after reaching Saigon because of the extreme heat that meant longer takeoff runs for the planes. They would have had difficulty getting off the water at Saigon if they had taken on a full load of fuel. It had not been contemplated originally but they had to delay an extra day in Saigon so the destroyer could proceed to that location.

After takeoff from Saigon, the three Cruisers followed the coast of the China Sea and the coast of Siam (now Thailand) for the first 430 miles around the southern extremity of Cochin China (now part of united Vietnam). This coast was low and sandy; in surprising places it was bordered by mangrove swamps. There were many lagoons where safe landings could be made in emergencies and where help could be obtained from passing vessels. At least a hundred miles could have been saved if Smith had decided to cut across the lower end of Indochina. Still, a forced landing in the mangrove swamps would have meant disaster for a downed crew because the plane would surely be wrecked and it would have been nearly impossible for the crew to make their way to safety or allow a rescue party to get to them.

The planes flew for three hundred and fifty miles along the coast until they reached the city of Kampot. Here the character of the country had changed to rugged mountains. The fliers landed at the mouth of the Kampongson River, which was sufficiently sheltered to protect the planes from high winds. They were refueled with the help of the destroyer's crew. They then took off for Bangkok, the capital, 245 miles to the northwest at the northern end of the Gulf of Siam. They landed on the Menam River and again had to dodge junks, sampans, and houseboats. Once in a while human bodies were seen floating by with no attempts being made to retrieve them. The heat and humidity were extremely debilitating as the crews began to service the planes. Right off the fliers had the same problem as before of protecting the planes from being rammed and crushed by curious boatmen. To protect them, the Siamese police strung circles of boats around each Cruiser.

It was at this time that stress began to take its toll. There were sharp words among the crews as they labored in the heat and drenching humidity on their respective planes. But when the work was finally done, harsh remarks were soon forgotten.

Minor repairs and routine inspections were made before the crews went into the city, famous for its beautiful palaces and temples. A modern city already equipped with electric street cars and electrically lighted streets, it was the gateway for the country to the outside world. Although cholera epidemics broke out frequently, it was rapidly becoming one of the more healthful cities in the Orient, despite the deplorable unsanitary water supply.

When the brief tour was completed, some of the men spent the night on the destroyer while the others decided to take advantage of the soft beds, mosquito netting, and electric fans at the Royal Hotel of Bangkok. Next morning, they all met with Mr. Dickerson, the American chargé d'affaires, who escorted them around the city. Unfortunately they could not meet King Rama VI; he had been unable to reach the city in time. They visited his palace and met a number of generals, admirals, and ministers. They were escorted to the stables of the royal white elephants and the temple of the Sleeping Buddha. When they paid their respects to the ranking Siamese prince, they were ushered into his drawing room. To their surprise, a framed picture of General Billy Mitchell, Assistant Chief of the Air Service, occupied a place of honor on the prince's table. Mitchell had visited Siam for a tiger hunt a few weeks before. The prince was deeply impressed with the man who was trying to make the world conscious of the potential of the airplane for defense and international commerce.[3]

It had been a busy sightseeing day and Smith commented later, "I imagine we saw nearly as much during our half-day ashore in Siam as many visitors see in a week."[4] Before they left, they received one invitation they could not accept. Smith explains:

"One quaint old world custom remains as popular as it ever was—decapitation. As a special honor, it was suggested that a beheading bee should be arranged for us. This event was to have taken place a fortnight later, but we were told it could easily be hastened for our benefit: no doubt it would have had we not sent our regrets at being unable to attend the 'frolic' owing to our desire to get on with the flight."[5]

By this time, the flight had covered 10,795 miles since leaving Santa Monica and had 14,536 miles to go to return there, plus the additional distance to Seattle, the official starting point. Before they departed Bangkok on 20 June, the planes had to taxi up and down the Menam River several times to ruffle the water's surface in order to take off. The next major stop where maintenance could be performed was Rangoon, Burma (now Myanmar) but Smith decided again to take on a lighter fuel load at Bangkok and make a refueling stop part of the way near a destroyer on the Tavoy River. This waterway empties into the Bay of Bengal on the east coast of Burma, 240 miles south of Rangoon, then a part of India.

But there was another command decision that Smith had to make. To go directly to Tavoy, they would have to cross the Malay Peninsula, a distance of 130 miles, or fly around it so they would be over water in case of emergency. An engine failure over the Malaysian jungle would mean almost sure disaster for a downed crew but would save more than eight hundred miles. They were behind their original schedule and the monsoon rains were about to begin. On the other hand, the engines had been operating so well and the navigation would be relatively easy. Smith decided to take the risk: he opted for the short cut that would save two days.

Although taking the risk paid off, the flight was anything but routine for Nelson and Harding as they skimmed over the jungle treetops. Harding explains:

At times our pontoons barely skimmed the jungle-covered summits of these untrodden mountains. We would shoot out over a valley and suddenly a downward current of air would catch us with such a bump that I thought we'd be impaled on the horn of one of those rhinos that live down there.

While crossing a fissure in the middle of the peninsula, we were suddenly drawn down toward the jungle just like a gnat inhaled by a green monster. The *Chicago* and *Boston* were to our right at the time and were not affected by this particular "pocket," although they too were having the bumpiest trip they had ever experienced. It just seemed as though we couldn't get over that ridge, so Erik banked to the left and we flew right back the way we came in order to get out of the depression and into a "raising" air current. But again when we started over the ridge we were drawn into that valley of vapors.

Meanwhile, the other boys were wondering what had happened. So they flew back and circled around waiting for us. At last we made the ridge, and I'll say we were the happiest airmen east of Suez when we finally succeeded in climbing out of the pocket and winding through the mountains until we reached the sea.[6]

The three planes reached Tavoy and saw the USS *Picard* waiting to refresh their fuel and oil tanks at the moorings the sailors had placed. While they were being serviced, a monsoon wind suddenly engulfed them in rain and high winds. The sea boiled up dangerously and the waves seemed too rough to allow takeoff. But there was no sheltered cove to escape to so Smith signaled the others to follow and managed to get airborne. Wade in the *Boston* bounced along on the waves and hit a big one that rode over the stay wires on his wings; one of them gave way but he continued with the wire dangling, thinking that he could make Rangoon rather than take a chance on a landing in the rough sea. The *New Orleans* followed and had two wing wires snapped by the strong waves. Nelson decided that with two wires gone, it was better to taxi back and repair them. This took a half hour and Nelson was on his way behind the others.

While Smith and Arnold had gotten off without a problem at Tavoy, the landing and its aftermath on the Irrawaddy River at Rangoon was not routine. They had flown seven and a half hours to cover the 430 miles and were dead tired. The planes were met in the harbor by the USS *Pruitt* for refueling and the crews found the river off Monkey Point as crowded with boats as at other places they had visited in the Far East. After landing and taxiing to the mooring buoy in the *Chicago,* Arnold fell in the water as he reached for it. Smith, intent on avoiding a collision with a boat coming toward him, didn't see him fall and quickly taxied away. Arnold shouted and floundered in his weighty flying clothes. When Smith finally saw that Arnold was missing, he maneuvered the plane so Arnold, sputtering and mad at himself for his predicament, could climb back onto a pontoon.

The river traffic at Rangoon nearly ended the flight for the *New Orleans* that first night. A large river boat under full sail, apparently being steered by a careless helmsman, drifted down the river and headed for all three Cruisers. Everyone else thought they were moored well out of the waterway traffic. But the U.S. Navy saved the day. Arnold relates the story:

> When the sailors from our destroyers guarding the planes saw this huge hulk with its sail silhouetted above them, it was almost too late for them to prevent her from riding down all three Cruisers. The *New Orleans* happened to be the nearest plane in line. Realizing that they had only a few instants in which to save her, one of the sailors clambered up the stern of the Burmese boat, clipped the helmsman in the jaw, and took charge.[7]

The collision was fairly gentle but extensive repairs were needed to the lower wing's leading edge and spars. Nelson arranged to have the plane towed to the beaching area used by an airplane company operating seaplanes. The plane was pulled up on a ramp with a dolly and the wing was repaired. The pontoons were also repainted and varnished. It took five days to do the work and more would be needed when they reached Calcutta, a major repair base.

It was fortuitous for Smith that they would have this delay. He was completely debilitated with an attack of dysentery which had gradually worsened ever since he drank the water he had been given on the lagoon near Hue. Thanks to an English doctor, Smith was moved to the house of a Mr. Kemp where he rested for three days and recovered sufficiently to leave. The others meantime stayed at the British Royal Engineer's clubhouse, a few miles outside of the city, where they swam in the club's pool, played water polo, and sipped cool drinks.

While the repair work was going on, the men took turns visiting the city to see the lifestyle of the native-born Burmese and the Europeans. They visited Shwe Dagon, the largest pagoda in the world. But five days was enough and when Nelson said his plane was ready and Smith said he felt better, they taxied out for takeoff. This was now 25 June. The *Boston* and *New Orleans* were able to get off by following in the waves left by an ocean steamer, while Smith in the *Chicago* took advantage of Wade's ability to make enough waves to allow his pontoons to break loose from the surface. Watching this, Arnold wrote later, "In finesse and delicacy of touch no airman has ever surpassed Leigh Wade. To take a heavy Cruiser down and daintily run its pontoons through the water so that they are barely an inch below the surface and skim along like that for a mile, is the feat of a wizard. That's Wade!"[8]

To make up for lost time and to escape the increasing monsoons as much as possible, Smith led the flight northwest across the Irrawaddy delta and copious rice fields toward Akyab, Burma, and the Bay of Bengal. En route they flew into one of the heaviest rainstorms they had ever encountered. They attempted to fly around it when they couldn't find any breaks in the downpour and managed to stay together despite the poor visibility. The route went over the Arakan Mountains.

The Cruisers landed at the Akyab seaport and hurriedly took on gas and oil. This was a stop they wanted to leave as soon as possible. The area had the dubious distinction of averaging more than four hundred inches of rainfall a year. They were preparing to take off when a message was received from the *Preston* that the moorings were not yet safe at Chittagong, their next stop, and they should delay one day. They went ashore and were entertained that night at a club by the British commissioner and other Europeans.

Stuart MacLaren, the British pilot, who had now received his second plane courtesy of the U.S. Navy, had been delayed for weeks at Akyab waiting for his replacement plane and had just left. The Americans, without knowing it, had passed over him where he had landed on a small bay to escape the storm they had just flown through. He afterwards told them he had heard but not seen them when they flew by. By this time, the French and Portuguese fliers had failed in their efforts to conquer the globe.

Despite the rain, they left at 7 A.M. next morning, 26 June, for Chittagong. Smith was leading and noticed that the rain was heaviest near the shore so he turned out about 15 miles over the Bay of Bengal. The rain lessened after about an hour and they followed the coast to the seaport of Chittagong (now in Bangladesh) at the mouth of the Chittagong River. They landed, refueled quickly from the U.S. destroyer *Preston*, and headed for Calcutta, the southern terminus of the third division. Linton Wells, in a motorboat, was able to chat with them briefly while they were tied up at the buoys for refueling and catch up on their experiences since he had last seen them.

There was now a dangerous flight ahead as they took a compass course over the deltas of the Ganges and Brahmaputra rivers. These swampy areas were known for the tigers that inhabited the jungle areas and the crocodiles in the marshes. If a plane went down, it might take months to locate it. Each crew flew with all eyes ahead looking for stretches of water where a landing could be made. As soon as one was located, they would look ahead for another and steer toward it—just in case. The weather most fortunately was clear. They spotted the Hooghly River easily and flew upstream eighty miles to the city of Calcutta, then the second largest city of the British Empire and known as the "City of Dreadful Night." They flew an additional sixteen miles to Port Canning north of the city, then followed a railroad up the river and landed in midafternoon at a mooring area where they hoped there would be fewer boats to harass them.

They were to tie up at moorings for oceangoing ships which were so large that the planes had to be towed to them. It was hot work and when the planes were finally attached and prepared for the night, each man realized how oppressive the air was. There was no breeze and all of them were soaked with perspiration. The British river police agreed to guard the planes and the crews were invited on board the launch of the governor of Bengal for a trip downstream to the city. Hundreds of people lined the riverbanks and the rails of the river steamers that thumped along nearby. When they arrived at the dock near the European quarter of the city, a number of Americans, British, and Bengali officials waved a welcome and cheered them as they debarked.

Fatigued from the work and the heat, they were taken to the Great Eastern Hotel and assigned rooms. Smith, as flight commander, was given a luxurious suite, consisting of two bedrooms, a bath, an office, and a sitting room. Uncomfortable in such posh surroundings, he asked Arnold to share it with him. While they were looking around, there was a knock on the door. A bearded man wearing a turban, long white coat, and skintight pants entered and asked if they desired a personal servant. They immediately accepted the offer and found that he had the power to order others to wash their clothes, get food and drinks, and bring anything else they desired. They named him "Bozo." When they didn't need him, he would squat on his heels outside their door. If they called out for Bozo, he would quickly open the door and comply with their wishes. The other men had similar experiences.

Everyone was so tired and hot that they spent the first evening in their rooms entertaining callers and newspapermen. Everyone realized that much hard work lay ahead of them. The ponderous pontoons were to be exchanged for wheels, and the planes were to undergo as much of an overhaul and replacement of parts as could be managed. To accomplish this, the planes should be moved to an airfield or some area where they could be worked on in close proximity to each other. The only one of any size was at Dum Dum, twenty miles outside the city. The planes would have to be hauled ashore, the wings removed, and then hauled by truck to the airdrome and reassembled. This would take an inordinate amount of time and Smith disapproved the idea. After much discussion with British harbor and street maintenance officials, arrangements were made to fly the Cruisers downstream and land in the midst of the river traffic near Fort William in the center of Calcutta. The planes were towed to a dock by a motor launch from one of the destroyers and a large crane lifted them out of the water so the pontoons could be removed and the wheels and tail skids attached. The planes were then rolled to the Maidan, a large park in the center of the city. City officials authorized the cutting of some trees, electric equipment, and telephone wires that were in the way.

After positioning their planes to work on them, the fliers were taken to the Great Eastern Hotel where Linton Wells found them and reported that they had a "damp and hilarious" reunion. He offered to help work on the planes and his offer was gladly accepted.

Before the Cruisers had departed from Seattle, Lt. Harry A. Halverson, the advance officer for the fourth division along the planned route of the flight between Calcutta and Constantinople (later Istanbul) had his own adventures. He had left Manila on 25 March 1924 and traveled by ocean vessel to Hong Kong, Singapore, Rangoon, and Akyab before going by rail to Chittagong and ten other cities in India. Subsequently he visited three cities in Persia, two in Iraq, four in Syria, and four in Turkey. These trips were by steamer, rail, automobile, and airplane which were hampered many times by infrequent and uncertain steamer and train schedules. Poor roads and washed-out bridges caused enforced layovers. Hardships were experienced with officials who did not speak English. The Turkish government's enforcement of strict passport regulations also caused him great inconvenience. By the time he had visited all the stops required and arrived in Constantinople on 27 June, he had traveled 11,000 miles in the previous three and a half months to make the preliminary arrangements. His report explained the difficulties he had at each stop and the final paragraph explained why it had taken so long to complete his assignment:

> Many conditions combine to make traveling and the completion of a mission such as mine over the route which was covered very difficult. For one thing the wheels of progress move slowly in all Eastern countries. Officials are hard to see due to their office hours and the word "expeditious" is taboo in most places. What little advance information I had received was erroneous and of little or no use. Little and in many cases no information of the desired kind was available and the means for disseminating such information as was available was practically nonexistent. In many instances I had recourse to files but needed to find and write up personally such information as was available and pertinent. Owing to the same reason and scarcity of clerks and stenographers at various consulates, it has been necessary to personally accomplish all typing and detail work.[9]

Halverson was very frank in his evaluation of the many places he visited. He summarized the territory between Karachi and Baghdad as "extremely uninviting from the standpoint of flying. Along the northern coast of the Persian Gulf, landings cannot be attempted except in the water with any degree of assurance that even the lives of the pilots could be saved." He quoted Major W. T. Blake, one of the British fliers who attempted a World Flight previously, that Chabar "is a most desolate hole, as indeed are all these stations along the Persian Gulf. There is nothing to do except fish and occasionally obtain a little shooting in the mountains nearby, though if a white man, or an Indian, ventures too far from camp he will be captured and murdered by the natives."[10]

The crews were made aware of the potential dangers and possible delays they might experience from information Halverson left behind at each stop. All were grateful for the forewarnings and mindful of the difficulties that the advance officers, all pilots, had experienced.

The Maidan proved to be an excellent location for the work that had to be done at Calcutta. A large number of supplies and spare parts had been accumulated there as planned. The planes were pushed into a grove of trees out of the sun and the disassembly and replacement of parts began. A thorough inspection of all fittings, control wires, fasteners, and fabric was made. Grease was cleaned off the planes to prevent dust from collecting on them while flying over land.

Gasoline strainers, tanks, and screens were thoroughly cleaned and the fuselage fabric was repainted. Larger engine radiators were installed to counter the extreme heat of the ruthless desert that lay ahead. They worked until long after dark for several days because the monsoon season was approaching rapidly and the fliers were anxious to get away as soon as possible. New engines were needed but it was decided to send them ahead by train to Karachi because it was beyond the monsoon belt and would probably save time that might be lost because of the rains. Hundreds of Indians gathered day and night to watch the Americans and it took fifty policemen working in shifts to hold them away from the planes.

One obstacle they had not counted on was the sacred cows that wandered the city and could not be touched. Occasionally one would stroll under a plane's wing and lie down. Ogden, tired of the interference with his work, would twist their tails until they bellowed in resentment and plodded off. The police did not notice.

A call for volunteers from the two faithful American destroyers anchored in the harbor resulted in an overwhelming demonstration of enthusiasm to help out. Every man not assigned a watch volunteered and selections for shore liberty had to be made by their respective commanders. "If the World Flight had done nothing else," Smith commented, "it would certainly have stimulated a fine spirit of comradeship between the Navy and the Air Service."[11]

The tired airmen did take some time off to see the sights of Calcutta, one of the world's most crowded cities. They went shopping, had their laundry done, and had tropical uniforms made. The American Legion Post of India gave the men a banquet; they were so tired, they left early. Next morning, as they were leaving the hotel to go to the Maidan to work, they met their hosts on their way home.

The fliers were treated to a dinner with the Standard Oil Company representative in Calcutta on 29 June and again left early. As they were leaving in the darkness, Smith stepped into a hole in the walkway and fell heavily to the ground. He was in intense pain all that night but refused to admit he was injured. Next morning a British doctor examined him and found he had broken a rib. He was taped up and although obviously in pain with every movement, said they would definitely leave on 1 July. After a day of rest while the others put the finishing touches on the planes, he was at the Maidan at daybreak, obviously in pain and still weak from the effects of diarrhea. He led the trio of planes out to the center of the park for the takeoff to Allahabad. Mysteriously, instead of six men in the three planes, there were now seven.

Linton Wells had been instructed by his office in Tokyo to return there after the fliers departed from Calcutta. He was reluctant to do so. He had been covering the story for weeks since the flight left Seattle and felt that the big story of the flight still lay ahead. He pleaded to be taken along. "We sympathized with him but gave him a flat 'No,' " Wade recalled later. "The hot, humid weather dictated that we keep the planes as light as possible. He had helped with the maintenance during the stay in Calcutta but orders were orders."[12]

Wade had been impressed with Wells's eagerness to report their story and finally gave in. Wells's argument that he could fill in on the work shift for the injured Smith made sense to him because he had indeed worked hard assisting the fliers and ran errands for them while they worked on the planes. Wade told Wells that if Smith approved, he could fly in the rear seat of the *Boston* with Ogden. Nelson, always sensitive to the performance of the aircraft, objected strenuously to the idea. Wells countered that changing from the heavy pontoons that weighed nearly half a ton to the lighter wheels weighing only about two hundred pounds would enable the planes to climb and cruise faster and the extra weight would not matter. Smith still did not like the idea but Wells was persuasive and Smith, knowing that the Air Service would probably benefit from accurate reporting of that portion of the flight, finally gave in. He cabled General Patrick in Washington asking for permission to have Wells fly to Allahabad and perhaps as far as Constantinople. Wells hurriedly packed a few belongings weighing about 25 pounds and arranged for shipment of the rest to Paris, hoping that he could go that far with the flight. Yet no answer had been received from Washington by takeoff time and Wells was ready to go. He reported what happened next:

> Appearing at the Maidan at six o'clock the next morning I was under the impression I was about to accompany the American World Flight as a representative of the Associated Press. This was an erroneous assumption. On receipt of a cable saying that I was going to Europe with it, the Associated Press fired me for disobedience of orders in not returning to Tokyo, but news of the fact didn't reach me for several days.
>
> Thousands of people had packed the Common to witness the takeoff. Just before we were to leave, Wade asked Ogden if he thought he could share the after cockpit with me and Ogden had drawled, "Suits me." When the *Boston* roared across the Maidan, Ogden and I were jammed into the cockpit like a pair of Siamese twins, and during the six hours and thirty minutes' flight to Allahabad neither of us could move an inch. Thereafter, we placed a board across the arms of the single seat, which gave us about eight inches more width, but it elevated us an equal distance, so our heads protruded over the fuselage. As a consequence our faces became badly burned. It speaks well for Hank Ogden's disposition that never once during the two thousand miles of flying did he utter a word of complaint over the discomfort by sharing his seat with me.[13]

But Ogden was miserable trying to get comfortable in the seat designed for one man. He later stated bitterly after the flight from Allahabad to Ambala near the snow-capped Himalayas, "If it hadn't been that we were flying high enough to keep fairly cool and if it hadn't been for the glorious scenery of the snow-capped Himalayas, I believe I should have thrown Wells overboard. As it was I was sorely tempted to feed him to the crocodiles in the Jumma River."[14]

For many years it has been erroneously reported that Wells was a stowaway and had hidden in the *Boston*'s baggage compartment with only his toothbrush and a pencil. Smith wrote a memorandum for the record to prevent any future misunderstandings:

"Lieutenant Leigh Wade, having given his consent to the request of Linton Wells, an American newspaper man representing the Associated Press, that the latter be permitted to accompany the American World Flight in the capacity of a passenger in Plane Number Three [the *Boston*], piloted by Lieutenant Wade, I, as Commanding Officer of the Flight, also approve the proposal.

"If in my opinion the presence of Mr. Wells in Plane Number Three, at any time or any place, is likely to endanger the success of the American World Flight, it is understood that he, Mr. Wells, shall be forthwith left behind."[15]

# 9. Paris by Bastille Day

The flight to Allahabad was long but relatively pleasant compared to the weather of the previous several days. Each pilot was pleased at how much more easily his plane handled without the weighty pontoons attached.

Smith led the trio of planes north along the Hooghly River, west across the plains of Bengal, Bihar, and Orissa, and then the United Provinces to the junction of the Ganges and Jumna rivers where the city of Benares was located. They dodged in and out of rain showers and eventually came to Allahabad for a landing at the large Royal Air Force flying field six miles from the center of the sprawling city. They had been in the air for six and a half hours and arrived under a broiling sun. Wells and Ogden climbed down stiffly from the rear seat of the *Boston* and stretched their limbs. Ogden immediately handed Wells a gas can and motioned him to fill the tank and the other two planes as well while the six fliers sat in the shade. The crews, especially Ogden, had decided that Wells would pay for his transportation.

"This meant sitting for hours in the broiling sun atop a hot metal engine cowling, emptying countless two-gallon tins of gasoline into a chamois-covered funnel," Wells wrote later. "After that I had to feed the engine oil and wipe the wings and fuselages clean of dust and grease. By the time the ships were serviced for the next jump, I was ready to drop in my tracks, but the boys had another job for me: making their speeches at the inevitable nightly banquet. And, as they sneaked quietly off to bed, I had to remain and entertain their hosts."[1]

The Royal Air Force pilots, having a good reason for a party, kept Wells up most of the night telling stories. At 7:30 the next morning, he climbed in with Ogden for another day of cramped misery. The destination was Ambala, the principal base for the British RAF on the Indian frontier 480 miles away. En route they passed near Agra, the home of the magnificent Taj Mahal, and flew over Delhi, crossroads of the ancients. Delhi was also the interim capital of British India while the modern administrative city of New Delhi was being built.

The British gave the fliers an enthusiastic welcome and offered to help in any way they could. The *New Orleans* had developed a leak in a cylinder jacket and Nelson said he did indeed need their help to find a new cylinder. The RAF quickly volunteered to have a new cylinder airlifted to Ambala from the major repair and supply depot at Lahore where they maintained a surprising stock of about 2,000 Liberty engines and parts. The plane that was bringing the part unfortunately developed engine trouble and made a forced landing at Amritsar. The pilot, uninjured and intent on completing his mission, rented a bullock cart to take him to a station where he caught a train and arrived at the base at 3 A.M.

Nelson and Harding installed the new cylinder that morning. "It was no small favor that this British airman had done for us," Nelson remarked later, "and we appreciated it more than we had words to express."[2] The RAF pilots that evening hosted the American crews in their mess. It was especially enjoyable, according to Nelson, "because it was not marred by a lot of unnecessary speeches."[3]

The temperatures that night varied only between 102 and 106 degrees and although Indians waved *punkas* over them all evening and while they slept, they did not rest well. Concerned when they saw that the Americans were not tolerating the heat well and were still wearing the regulation flying clothing used in temperate climates, the British pilots told stories about airmen going mad from the heat. They gave each of the Americans an RAF pith helmet which the fliers wore on the ground until they left the desert countries. They also adopted British shorts and light shirts.

The Cruisers left for Multan on 3 July and climbed to six thousand feet to escape the heat. The route of flight was over the Sind desert and Smith was following a railroad line that would take them to their destination. They soon encountered a sandstorm that completely obscured both the earth and the railroad. The sand was so fine that it sifted through their clothes and stung their faces. In order to keep the railroad in sight, they descended to fifty feet but were severely blinded by the sand that tore at their planes. They flew right over Multan without seeing it. Colonel Butler, the British commander, had ordered hundreds of troops to line up around the airfield but they didn't see the planes cross overhead. When Smith realized that they had passed the airport, he returned to the area, finally saw the field, and made several passes before leading the other two planes in for a landing.

The planes were led into a parking area and the seven men with bloodshot eyes, lobster-red faces, and dry and parched lips had difficulty getting down from their cockpits. Butler, before he shook hands, handed each flier a tall glass of ice-cold lemonade. "I have had many delicious drinks in my life," Arnold wrote in his diary, "but none to compare with that one in Multan."[4]

Arnold thought the name Multan should be changed to "Molten" since the temperature that day was 120 degrees and only cooled off to 98 degrees at night with no breeze. Butler confirmed that it was the hottest place in all of India. Wells commented that "no sensible person would ever go there voluntarily. Like the Royal

Welsh Fusiliers and other British army men, they are always sentenced to Multan. And what a deadly monotonous life they lead; there are no white women because of the climate, and only the constant threat of revolt by fanatical, unfriendly Indians makes the place endurable."[5]

The crews fueled their planes, then went to the officers' guest quarters for a bath and a nap. Thoroughly fatigued from the flying and the heat, Nelson, Wade, and Smith, his rib still hurting from his injury, did not accept the invitation to attend a formal dinner as guests of the regiment that evening. Arnold, Harding, Ogden, and Wells did go and were entertained with a picturesque ceremony outdoors by a regimental band that had been held over for five days awaiting the Americans. None of the four got much sleep that night but were up at daybreak next morning, the fourth of July, and the three planes were off the ground at 6 A.M. heading for Karachi. Again they flew over more of the Sind Desert but there were no sandstorms this time, although they could see them swirling in the distance on both sides of their route of flight.

The flight was cruising at 4,000 feet to escape the heat and all went well except for Nelson. When about an hour out of Karachi, the engine of the *New Orleans* suddenly started to rattle and bang as if it were coming apart. Puffs of white smoke trailed behind and Nelson throttled back. Oil spewed down the sides of the engine and the fuselage and there were a number of holes in the fabric. Both men looked for a likely place for a landing on what appeared at first to be open desert. As they began a slow descent, though, they found it was really baked mud that had cracked into hard, open seams and would have spelled disaster for any plane trying to land there.

Nelson knew there was a railroad about thirty-five miles to the east that ran from Lahore to Karachi. He signaled his intentions to Smith and Wade and headed toward it so that if they had to go down they would at least be near a means of transportation to get to Karachi. When he was near the railroad, he turned toward Karachi seventy-five miles away. Pieces of a cylinder continued to be ejected through the engine cowling and thrown out the bottom of the engine. A chunk of metal ripped a hole in the wing; another blasted into a strut; a third grazed Harding's head as both men frantically continued to look for a place to land.

Nelson throttled back some more and the engine still responded enough for him to keep flying speed just above stalling. It coughed and died briefly several times and both men expected it to catch on fire but Nelson was able to keep the plane in the air and continued to fly along the railroad to Karachi, fully expecting at any moment to make a forced landing during the flight. Nelson later wryly reported that the engine continued "to run very nicely on eleven cylinders."[6]

Harding passed pieces of cheesecloth to Nelson in the front seat so he could wipe the oil off his goggles. While the *New Orleans* pressed on, Smith in the *Chicago* sped ahead to locate the landing field and circled so Nelson wouldn't have to search for it. Wade, Ogden, and Wells in the *Boston* looked for relatively safe landing spots in case Nelson had to land. Nelson continued to nurse the Cruiser carefully and landed safely at the large RAF flying field, home of one of the best repair depots in the world at the time. This was still the fourth of July, a day that the British do not celebrate.

A large crowd was waiting and the six fliers and Wells were welcomed by British RAF officers and administrative officials. William B. Douglass, the American consul, stepped out of the crowd and approached Smith with a cable in his hand. It was from General Patrick. Smith's request to allow Wells to accompany them was disapproved. Douglass also handed Wells a cable from the Associated Press office in Tokyo. It was the official notice from his boss that he was fired for disobeying orders to return to Tokyo after the fliers left Calcutta.

Wells was concerned that Wade and Smith might be court-martialed for taking him across India but nothing was ever said. Wells thought that since a reporter for Reuters News Agency in Allahabad had reported him as a stowaway who had been found in Wade's baggage compartment, it satisfied anyone who might be critical. The story apparently assured General Patrick and others as to how he had come to be with them, and Wells was content to have everyone believe that he was the world's first aerial stowaway until his memoirs were published in 1937. Smith and Wade were never chastised for the incident, probably because Smith accepted full responsibility for allowing Wells to accompany the flight and there had been no unfavorable publicity as a result.

Having gone that far, Wells tried to find ways to keep up with the flight and report its progress as a roving, freelance reporter. There was no airline service to Europe at that time but he found that he could book passage to Egypt and said he would try to rejoin them in Constantinople. He never did but instead got involved in reporting riots in Sudan and later appeared in London in time to accompany the Prince of Wales during his visit to America where he met the fliers again.

The fliers had dinner that evening with the RAF officers, the first time they had dinner with ladies present since leaving the States. They were reminded in a speech by the base commander that they had flown 12,577 miles after leaving Seattle, farther than any of the others, but still had nearly 14,000 miles to go. They had been in the air a few minutes over 178 hours.

The men worked in the daytime for the next two days changing engines on all three planes. The work went rapidly with the help of British mechanics. Returning tired and dirty in the evenings, they split up and accepted invitations for dinner at the homes of the British commissioner, the tax collector, and the commanding general of the Sind Rajputana District. They were up at 3 A.M. for breakfast on 7 July and were in the air by 6:30 headed west for Chahbar.

The route of flight took the trio of planes across Baluchistan, an uninteresting countryside totally without vegetation except for a few date trees and cactus. "Great stretches of sand, sand hills, ancient lava flow, some 5,000-foot mountains—the most lonesome, barren and desolate place imaginable," Arnold scratched in his diary.[7]

Shortly after noon, they crossed into Persia (now Iran) and descended at a small port city on the Gulf of Oman. They were met by George A. Tomlinson, a representative of the Indo-European Telegraph Company who had arranged for a supply of gas and oil and also a group of Indians to help with the tedious task of refueling. The fliers hurriedly ate sandwiches provided by the wife of the British consul and were airborne at 2:35 bound for Bandar Abbas, one of two chief Persian ports on the Strait of Ormuz that connects the Gulf of Oman with the Persian Gulf.

They were met there by a Mr. Richardson, the British consul, who had volunteered to act as an advance agent for the World Flight and had been instrumental in improving the air strip east of the city. Lieutenant Halverson, the advance officer, had made all the necessary arrangements and had left for Baghdad before their arrival. Richardson warned them to stay away from the Indians as much as possible because there was an epidemic of cholera raging at the time and hundreds had fled to the mountains to avoid it. The six men split up for the night to stay in two houses and were up at 3:30 A.M. They themselves had not refueled the planes after they landed when they saw that the gasoline was piled up in two-gallon cans. They hired a group of locals and had them form a line to pass the cans along from the cache to the planes where the crews put the fuel into the gas tanks. The process worked and they were off two hours later without eating breakfast.

They arrived at Bandar Abbas on 6 July. Between that date and 21 June when they'd left Bangkok, they had covered 3,710 miles and had made eleven stops. During this period they had overhauled their planes, fitting them with new engines and new wings, and had substituted the pontoons for wheels. The official report noted, "There is no question but that the change of landing gears will speed up their progress in no small measure."[8]

The next destination was Bushire, considered then as the most important seaport on the Persian Gulf. They landed at 9:30 A.M. beside the shore on an excellent airfield that had been built by the French. They were met by George Fuller, the American consul, who offered to send to the city for sandwiches while they loaded up with fuel, oil, and water. When this refueling was completed in about ninety minutes and the sandwiches had not arrived, they quashed their hunger and departed for Baghdad, Mesopotamia (now Iraq).

The route from Bushire took them over a vast desert to Basra; they followed the Euphrates River to Hilla and then took a compass course direct to Baghdad. It was 5:55 P.M. when they landed at a large British Royal Air Force airdrome and were surprised by the size of the crowd of British civilians and military personnel who greeted them. They were immediately offered sandwiches and cold drinks while they tended to their planes. RAF officers then took them to the officers' club for dinner. Afterwards, noting that they were greatly fatigued, their hosts showed them to the guest quarters. "I remember getting into bed," Arnold wrote, "but I don't remember lying down." He added that they all were suffering from sunburned knees since they had adopted the English shorts at Calcutta.[9]

The fliers, used to getting up long before daybreak, slept until 7 A.M. the next morning. They left at 11 A.M. for Aleppo in northwest Syria and were escorted for the next hour and a half by five British fighter planes. The weather was excellent. The flight followed the Euphrates River and took them over more monotonous desert. "Sometimes we could see as many as fifteen or twenty small-sized sandstorms traveling along the ground," Arnold noted. "About sixty miles from Aleppo we encountered some good-sized ones. The dust extended to 4,000 feet and the sun striking on the top of this white dust gives it the appearance of a real vapor cloud."[10]

Aleppo, located in a semidesert area, had been a French mandate since 1918. Grains, cotton, and fruit were grown there and it was a center for silk, wool, hides, and dried fruits. The fliers landed at the French airdrome north of the city and were immediately surrounded by laughing French pilots who insisted on toasts with champagne of a special vintage that they had saved for the occasion. The crews as always worked on their planes first before accepting transportation to the principal hotel in the city.

After a reception by the French, the Turks gave a dinner which lasted until 2 A.M. They were nonetheless up at 6 A.M. and en route to the airport were able to see a little of the local lifestyle as they traveled through the ancient city. Nelson commented, "Camels were burbling and complaining as their drivers loaded them. Merchants were on their way to the bazaars, and nearly every other person sat astride a diminutive donkey."[11]

Departure on 10 July was at 9 A.M. for Constantinople (now called Istanbul), which had been occupied by the Allies from 1918 to 1923. The trio of planes passed over miles of cultivated lands and then over a stretch of desert where camel caravans plodded relentlessly. Ahead were the 10,000-foot, snow-capped Taurus Mountains which the planes could not possibly top. Smith chose to lead them along the Berlin-Baghdad railroad that had been cut through the valley. They followed it single-file at 4,000 feet with the mountain walls uncomfortably close to their wing tips. It was their first experience with real cold air since they had left the Kurile Islands. The route took them over the rich homeland of the Turks and the Sea of Marmora to Constantinople with its picturesque cathedrals, minarets, mosques, red-roofed houses, ancient forts, and walls.

There had been some concern about this leg of the flight because the Turks had not readily accepted the idea of foreigners flying over their country and had delayed approving the request from the U.S. State Department for overflight and landing privileges. Smith landed first at 2:30 P.M. at the San Stefano airdrome, an excellent facility. In addition to a few Turkish officials, they were met by Admiral Bristol, American ambassador to Turkey, Lieutenant Halverson, the division advance man, and Maj. Carlyle Wash, U.S. air attaché at Paris who had been assigned as advance officer for the flight through Europe. There were a few other Americans on hand and there would have been more if the messages Smith had sent from Baghdad and Aleppo had reached Constantinople and the public had been informed. The telegraph system in that part of the world had not yet caught up with the technology of the day.

Excusing themselves after the introductions, the fliers worked until 4:30 P.M. and then were taken into the city. There were no dinners or receptions to attend since no one knew exactly when they were coming. They had dinner that evening at a hotel and went to a cabaret. They hoped to get off early the next morning, but the Turks had requested that members of their air force be permitted to inspect the American planes. Realizing that the Turkish government had been reluctant to let them land in the first place, Smith agreed they would stay another day.

The group went on a sightseeing tour the next morning and had lunch in the American embassy with the ambassador and his family. They spent the afternoon talking with the Turkish general and his staff and answering the questions of the flying officers. That evening was spent writing letters, packing, studying maps, and resting.

The crews were up before dawn on 12 July and were off the ground at 7:45 A.M. bound for Bucharest, largest city and capital of Romania. It is located in the southeastern part of the country on the Dimbovita River, a tributary of the Danube. The city had been occupied by the Central Powers from 1916 to 1918.

The three Cruisers made the flight in four hours and landed at the Franco-Romanian Aero Company airdrome shortly before noon. They had flown over some of the battlefields and ruined towns where trenches, pockmarked fields, wreckage of military equipment, and destroyed bridges were still in evidence from battles that had been fought a decade before. Dark clouds formed but threatening weather did not materialize and after crossing the Transylvanian Alps, the weather was clear.

When the crews landed and taxied to the Franco-Romanian hangars, strangely there was no official party to greet them. They were relieved that they could service their planes with the help of local airport personnel without a crowd of officials and curious spectators to slow them down. Smith located a telephone in a hangar and called the American embassy. Colonel Foy, the American consul, was embarrassed and thought they were still hundreds of miles away since he had received no word of their progress for days. They were treated to an impromptu dinner by members of the foreign colony in the city and while they dined, the chief of the Romanian Air Service rushed in from the country's summer capital. Breathless, he apologized on behalf of the government for not welcoming them with a formal reception. The crews made a quick sightseeing trip through the city and turned in early at a hotel. Arnold's diary reports: "Bucharest is a clean and snappy-looking place, has numerous cafes and cabarets, and many well-dressed and attractive-looking girls."[12]

The three planes departed Bucharest at dawn, 13 July, for Budapest via Belgrade. They flew due west in remarkably clear weather, crossed the Carpathian Mountains to the Danube River where it flows through the Transylvania Alps, and then to Belgrade, Yugoslavia. They flew directly over Panchevo Airport at Belgrade where diplomatic officials were waiting for their arrival. But despite having made arrangements to land there, with plenty of fuel on board and engines purring contentedly, Smith decided to continue to Budapest. (He later wired an apology.) They followed the Danube and crossed into Hungary. It was a six-hour, fifty-minute flight to Budapest's Matyasfold Airdrome and once again they landed with only a small crowd on hand. Earlier, hundreds had gathered to witness their arrival but when a rumor had passed through the crowd in midmorning that the Americans were not coming, many had gone home. Cornelius Poppe, the Hungarian air director, government official representatives, members of the Hungarian Aero Association, and Robert Brentano, the American minister, had remained. There were congratulatory speeches, followed by signing of autographs before the fliers were invited to a nearby hangar where a lunch was hastily provided.

They departed at 2:10 P.M. for Vienna, Austria's capital, and arrived there two hours later. This time there was a huge crowd waiting; to their surprise, they were mostly American tourists, all armed with cameras and shouting for them to pose.

"Kodaks to the left of us. Kodaks to the right, front, and rear," Arnold said. "It looked as though we were not going to be able to get our planes ready for the next day's flight to Paris. So Smith finally announced that if they would all line up with their picture machines, we also would line up and then they could get us all with one volley. But in spite of this, the Kodaks clicked until dusk, and indeed long after, for the amateur photographer is not particular about lighting."[13]

When they were finally able to get their work done, the crews were taken for a quick drive through the city, around the famous boulevard, the Ringstrasse, to the Imperial Palace and the shopping district, and then to the luxurious Imperial Hotel. They were told that the hotel was once the palace of the Prince of Wittenburg and that he had lost it in a game of cards.

They went to bed soon after dinner and were impressed with the tasty food, wonderful room service, and the size of their hotel rooms with twenty-foot ceilings and 500-light chandeliers. The room assigned to Smith and Arnold had twin beds on raised daises draped with silk canopies. According to Arnold, "The mattresses were so soft that we sank right down almost out of sight."[14]

The six airmen had breakfast next morning where they were served bowls of raspberries and cream, so delicious that to Arnold, "it was almost worth flying around the world to eat them." He was reminded of those long days and nights in the shacks in the Aleutians "where we made our beds on boxes to keep the rats from running over us, and where Smith had fed us on 'eggs Vienna.'"[15]

Anxious to continue, Smith had promised the others in India that if they could get to France twenty-four hours ahead of schedule, they would all take a holiday in Paris. They had already gained four days by spending minimum time in each city after leaving Calcutta. Although they would have liked to spend more time enjoying the deluxe accommodations of Vienna and seeing the sights, they all wanted to push on and left the ancient city before 7 A.M. on 14 July in good spirits, intent on reaching Paris on that very French national holiday known as Bastille Day.

It was raining heavily when they left Vienna. They flew in restricted visibility all the way across Austria and into France. "The rain and fog drove us down to the river," Wade said, "and often we shot around sharp bends and kicked rudder just in time to avoid crashing unannounced into a castle. For several hours we followed the winding Danube, flying against a stiff head wind that held us down to fifty miles an hour."[16]

As they crossed the dark pine trees of the Black Forest in southwest Germany, they suddenly emerged into bright sunshine, a welcome change from the gloom and danger of the first several hours. After flying for more than six hours, they landed at Strasbourg, capital of Alsace in northeast France, which had been regained by France from Germany in 1919. Although elaborate arrangements had been made to entertain them, they stayed only long enough to refuel and have a quick lunch before they were off on the four-hour flight to the famous City of Light.

The route took them north to Nancy, then swung northwest over the trenches and fortifications of the famous battlegrounds of World War I: Verdun, the Argonne Forest, Rheims, Saint-Mihiel, and the old Hindenburg Line. On this day, the trees and grass were green and the growing fields were cultivated, a much different scene from the days when the Allies had challenged the Germans in French skies six years before.

About a hundred miles from Paris, a flight of French Aviation Service planes met the American trio to escort them to the city. Fifty miles out, they could see the Eiffel Tower and the white dome of the Church of the Sacré Coeur on Montmartre. Nearing the famous capital city, they could see thousands of people in the streets celebrating Bastille Day. Accompanied by the French planes, Smith led the flight over the many famous landmarks and, as a mark of respect, circled over the Arc de Triomphe. Built originally to commemorate Napoleon's victories, in 1920 the Arc had become the national tomb of the French Unknown Soldier.

They approached Le Bourget Airport and were saluted by a parachute rocket that was lofted high over the field in welcome. There were more than five thousand Parisians on hand shouting, waving flags, and crowding onto the airport; many of them had been waiting since early in the morning. The three planes landed and taxied to the hangar line where they were mobbed by the throng that was intent on taking pictures up close and grabbing at the American fliers. Reporters shouted questions in French and English while French officials and diplomats tried to shake their hands while they posed for photographs.

"During that hour on the outskirts of Paris," Wade recalled, "we met more generals, ambassadors, cabinet ministers, and celebrities, than we had encountered in all the rest of our lives. There were so many of them that we couldn't remember their names, despite the fact that they were all men whose names are constantly in newspaper headlines."[17]

It took an hour before the fliers had a chance to get their planes into a hangar and conduct a postflight inspection and refueling. Smith, always cordial but a man of few words, answered reporters' questions in short bursts. He in turn asked reporters how the Americans were doing in the Olympic Games that were being held in Paris that summer. He learned that the Americans had won a number of track and field events and claimed two world records. Smith met with Maj. Carlyle Wash, American attaché to France and advance man for the European division of the World Flight, to discuss the schedule for their stay in Paris and on to England. A French reporter, commenting in the sensational style of the day, reported their arrival in the next day's newspaper:

> Flying in a perfect triangle above us, the great planes come, with the sunlight glinting on their wings. One by one they drop to earth with the light grace of a dragonfly. Slim khaki figures emerge from the cockpits—one cries, "Just in time for tea!" . . . Wade lifts his goggles with a placid air. Nelson pulls off his helmet, watches the cameramen, and then, with a full-throated laugh, takes a Kodak and shoots back in return. Congratulations, speeches, glasses of champagne. The heroes, with Generals Niessel and Dumesnil, pose for posterity before the newsreel men and press photographers.

There are cries of "Vive la France!" and "Vive l'Amérique!" But where are the heroes? They have vanished. "Feeding their horses," someone explains. And in fact, the fliers have left the throng, and with a gesture that is simple as it is symbolic, they are wiping down the engines to which they owe a part of their glory.[18]

The men were whisked into the city by staff cars from the French Aviation Service after finishing their chores. Dead tired from more than ten hours in their cramped cockpits, they bathed, changed their coveralls for clean uniforms, and had dinner in their rooms. An invitation from the Vacuum Oil Company had been extended to them to attend the famous Folies Bergère and they felt they couldn't turn it down. They were ushered into a special box along with other guests and settled into their soft seats. When the lights were lowered to signal the beginning of the show, the six fliers promptly fell asleep. Next day, one newspaper editorialized, "If the Folies Bergère won't keep these American airmen awake, we wonder what will?"[19]

Those who fly in open cockpit, single-engine airplanes will understand the fatigue the fliers must have felt. They had made the fastest time across Europe and Asia of the pilots of any nation before them and had clipped two days off a record over the distance that the French national hero Pelletier d'Oisy had set flying from Tokyo to Paris. They had not had any real time to relax and be on their own to act like tourists since arriving in Tokyo. They had hoped to have time to see the sights without the public crowding their every move but their bodies were not up to such pleasure. Returning to the hotel, they hand-lettered a sign and placed it on each room door:

PLEASE DO NOT WAKE US
UNTIL NINE O'CLOCK TOMORROW MORNING
UNLESS THIS HOTEL IS ON FIRE
AND NOT EVEN THEN
UNLESS THE FIREMEN HAVE GIVEN UP ALL HOPE

Any plans they had to "do" Paris by themselves the next morning were shattered when they learned the schedule for the day. Wash had arranged for them to place a wreath at the Tomb of the Unknown Soldier at the Arc de Triomphe and then make a number of official calls. The surprise of the day to them was a luncheon at Foyot's Restaurant with Gen. John J. Pershing, commander of the American Expeditionary Force during World War I. "As we were lieutenants in the army," Wade said, "he had seemed about as far from us as the Dalai Lama of Tibet. But there in Paris he put his arms around us, told us funny stories, and proved himself a genial host and a regular fellow!"[20]

They were officially welcomed to the city in the afternoon and signed the Golden Book of the City of Paris for the Vice President of the municipal council and at 6 P.M. met President Gaston Doumergue at the Palais de l'Elysées, where they expected to stay only a few minutes. But the French leader was effusive about meeting them and kept them for about an hour. Instead of letting them go, he invited them to accompany him to the Olympic Games and stood with him as he reviewed the four thousand participating athletes. Afterwards he said he wanted to bestow on each of them the French Legion of Honor. Smith thanked the president but said that the United States government would not allow military men to accept foreign decorations without the consent of Congress. In place of this award he gave them each autographed photographs of himself.

There was a banquet that evening at the Allied Club. It was attended mostly by French ministers and high-ranking military officers of several nations who were assigned to duty in France. Anxious to experience the city's night life, albeit briefly, several of the fliers who had served in France during the war made a quick trip to Maxim's and the Montmarte "for old times' sake."[21]

The next morning, 16 July, they were back at Le Bourget Airport and were impressed with the number of airliners taking on passengers and taxiing out for takeoffs to the other cities of Europe every few minutes. The European nations had truly pioneered commercial airline operations and proved that schedules could be set and met. What he saw caused Nelson to exclaim, "The era of transport by air is not coming some day in the future. It is here!"[22]

The airport had been decorated in their honor and the planes were rolled out of the hangar. Major Wash and a number of French airmen were on hand to see them off and the flight was in the air by 11 A.M. bound for London. As they climbed on a westerly heading, two airliners with passengers flew alongside the Cruisers. A motion picture cameraman could be seen filming from one of them. A squadron of French fighters joined in and soon the occupants of a dozen planes were waving them on. The Americans would soon be off on what promised to be the most dangerous leg of the entire flight plan.

# 10. Preparing for the North Atlantic

It was an overcast, hazy day when the three Cruisers took off from Le Bourget Airport. They circled the city and elected to fly in loose formation with the two commercial planes en route to London. A squadron of French fighter planes escorted them to the English Channel and at one time there were a dozen planes heading toward the French coast in formation. They all climbed above the clouds to 7,000 feet where it was uncomfortably cold for the World Fliers in their open cockpits, a foreshadow of what they would have to contend with over the North Atlantic. They could see briefly through breaks in the clouds that the English Channel below was being whipped by angry waves. The clouds became thinner over land as they neared London and it took three hours, ten minutes to fly the 215 miles between the two capitals because of stiff head winds. They flew over the city without trying to search for its famous landmarks and instead continued toward Croydon, a major airfield south of the city, for their first landing on English soil.

The three crews were mobbed by photographers and autograph collectors as they climbed down from their cockpits. The London bobbies were unable to contain the enthusiastic crowd that was so anxious to speak with the fliers and touch them. The press of the onrushing crowd alarmed the fliers who were afraid that they would push against the planes and cause damage to the fuselage and control surfaces. Many who had rushed from the two commercial passenger planes that had escorted from Paris were Americans, all shouting for them to pose for photographs and sign their names to bits of paper. Reporters shouted questions and tried to get answers. With great effort, the bobbies locked hands and were finally able to push the crowd back and allow the official greeters to approach. On hand were

Maj. Howard C. Davidson, the American assistant military attaché, RAF representatives, and British officials. Also there was Mrs. A. Stuart MacLaren, wife of the British World Flier, who thanked them and the U.S. Navy for the assistance they had provided her husband in the Far East. (At that time, he had left Etorofu for Paramushiru and, although no one knew it then, was soon to reach the end of his World Flight attempt.)

When the fliers were able to break away from the crowd, they were given a luncheon in an airport hangar and returned to the parking ramp to service their planes. They were then taken to the Royal Air Force Club on Piccadilly where excellent quarters were waiting for them. They were guests of the top officials of the British Air Ministry for dinner that evening. Leigh Wade put on a magnificent demonstration of snoring and Nelson delighted in telling about it:

> It was at the table and on one side of Leigh sat a dignified general and on the other sat Lord somebody. Well, with a knife in one hand and a fork in the other, Leigh fell sound asleep—and snored. Nor was this his first offense for he had done the same thing at a dinner after one of our long flights in the Kurile Islands. But folks insisted on entertaining us, so listening to Leigh's imitation trombone solo was the price we paid.[1]

They returned to the airport the next morning and took off in excellent weather for northwest Scotland. After cruising over the Tower of London, Saint Paul's Cathedral, Buckingham Palace, and the Houses of Parliament, they headed for Brough near Hull, a large seaport on the Humber River. The 165-mile flight took them over hundreds of mills, steel works, coal mines, and factories of all descriptions, then over green areas and farm lands that lent an idyllic atmosphere to the trip. Nelson remembered the flight as "something that pulls the heart strings [but] I hardly know why."[2]

They also saw many emergency and RAF flying fields, all plainly marked, which showed the extent to which the British were advancing aviation. A number of small planes came up to fly formation briefly; the pilots would wave and then quickly depart.

The landing at Brough was made on 17 July at the airdrome and seaplane base of the Blackburn Aeroplane and Motor Company, a manufacturer of land and seaplanes, that was exceptionally well-equipped with machine shops, ground support equipment, and comfortable quarters. This was a major depot for supplies for the Cruisers and the advance arrangements had been well executed. The boxes containing spare parts had all arrived in time and there had been no damage of any kind.

Looking back on the flight from Calcutta to Brough, the fliers had covered 6,025 miles in seventeen days with just under eighty-five hours of flying time. By then they were only two weeks behind the schedule they had set before leaving Seattle. Rear Adm. Thomas F. Magruder, commander of the Light Cruiser Division of the Scouting Fleet in the North Atlantic, was to patrol the route across the Atlantic. He had not expected the fliers to catch up on their schedule so soon and his ships were not yet in position for the crossing.

Lieutenant Crumrine, during his visit to Brough, had left instructions to spare no expense in expediting the overhaul of the planes when they arrived there. He was particularly concerned about the reports of ice at Angmagssalik, Greenland. In a letter to Lt. St. Claire Streett in Washington, he said he hoped they would arrive at Reykjavik by 15 August because the Angmagssalik harbor was landlocked. New ice would be created because of its far northerly position and the absence of the warm Gulf Stream, plus the runoff of a freshwater stream that empties into the harbor.

The fliers were greeted by a small, enthusiastic group of local townspeople, airport workers, and Norman Blackburn, one of the owners of the aerodrome, as they parked at the large hangars. Here the planes would be thoroughly inspected and have new engines installed. The wheels would be exchanged for pontoons for the Atlantic flight. Anxious to have the engines replaced as soon as possible, the three crews had them ready to be lifted out before dark. They were given quarters at the Blackburn Club on the field and that evening were treated to a dinner and a dance.

There was much to be accomplished in the days ahead. The great advantage to having their rooms on the field was that it saved time getting to work and there were few visitors and autograph hunters to disturb them as they labored to recondition their planes for the most dangerous leg of their flight. All cowling, propellers, radiators, engines, and tail-skid assemblies were removed and replaced. The planes were thoroughly cleaned; the gasoline and oil tanks were drained and flushed. All rigging wires were scraped, polished, and repainted; and all metal parts in the fuselages were heavily coated with rust-resistant oxide.

The ailerons were removed and all the fairing strips replaced that had been damaged by the damp and hot climates the planes had passed through. Smaller radiators were installed and all cowlings were painted with aluminum gilt paint. It had been planned to have a radio transmitter and receiver installed in the *Chicago* and Army Captain H. F. McClelland, a radio specialist then on leave in England, was ordered to proceed to Brough to install the equipment. This was not done, however, because of the increased weight. When the inspection and replacement work on all the planes was completed, the magnetic compasses were swung to assure their accuracy and test flights were made.

The English public meanwhile wanted to see and learn more about the Americans who seemed soon to claim the honor of being first to achieve the world-girdling honors. (This was while their own countrymen were having difficulty in the Far East.) The Americans were invited to a formal banquet in London the first night after their arrival but, as Arnold explained, "we were about as well-equipped with clothes as the head hunters of Borneo."[3]

Smith gave Arnold a shopping list and money and delegated him to go to London to buy what they all would need to look far better than they did in their rumpled flying clothes. Arnold left Brough early by train for London and dashed around to haberdashers and tailors to fill a long list of size and style requirements for everyone. He was joined later by Smith and Wade while Nelson, Harding, and Ogden elected to remain in Brough to work on the planes. They would visit later in the week and then all would return to continue their work.

The banquet held in their honor at the posh Savoy Hotel was certainly impressive. There were lords, earls, and dukes accompanied by their ladies resplendent in their best finery. The fliers in their new clothes were announced individually by a crimson-coated majordomo with a thundering voice and then each strode cautiously into the banquet room to tumultuous applause. There were many speeches that night all praising the fliers but also thanking them for the help given MacLaren in his quest for world-circling honors. Smith, always a man of few words, responded to his introduction by referring to MacLaren, saying that such flights were made not for personal glory but to further aviation progress. He added that he and his men were members of America's principal air arm and were just doing what they had been assigned to do.

The Prince of Wales did not attend the affair but was upstairs in the hotel dining with friends and sent word that he would like to meet the Americans after dinner. They were escorted to his suite and found him to be an affable man eager to hear about their trip. He said that he planned to sail to New York aboard the *Berengaria* in a few days and hoped he could greet them when they arrived at Mitchel Field, Long Island. He reportedly made a bet of five dollars with each of them that he would beat them there. A group of newspaper correspondents invited the airmen on a quick trip around the city after the banquet and then dropped them off at the train station for the return to Brough.

On 22 July Smith and several others narrowly escaped a fatal accident while working on the *Chicago.* He explained:

> We were taking off the landing gear and putting pontoons on the plane and in order to do this we used a crane and a heavy chain to lift her up on the dolly. As we had to get right in under the plane to do some work while it hung suspended in the air, we first tested the chain. It stood a strain of six and a half tons, and as the plane only weighed two and a half tons, we naturally thought it more than strong enough.
>
> We had to work in a cramped position, so several of us took turns. A moment after we had crawled out, the chain broke, and the plane crashed to the floor. Why it took a notion to break at that particular moment, we don't know. But we got a bit of a kick out of seeing those two and a half tons fall where we had been just a few seconds before. Of course, it was nobody's fault. It was just one of those things that occur without one's being able to prevent them. The pontoons were badly damaged, so we had to take them off and put on new ones. Fortunately, there was another set, the ones that had been sent from America for Major Martin's *Seattle.*[4]

During the short time the fliers had been in Constantinople, they had received the first information about the assistance they would be provided by the U.S. Navy for the Atlantic crossing. The scouting fleet in the Atlantic consisted of thirty-six ships that had modified their summer maneuvers and were prepared to take part in assisting the Army flight in North Atlantic waters. The details would be revealed after their arrival at Brough.

Rear Adm. Thomas P. Magruder, commander of the scouting fleet, arrived in the Firth of Forth aboard his flagship, the *Richmond,* and had a conference with

Maj. Howard Davidson, the assistant American military attaché. Using notes and drawings given him by Smith, Major Davidson made preliminary arrangements whereby the U.S. Navy would position a fleet of five to seven ships at regular intervals across the North Atlantic from Brough to Pictou, Nova Scotia, to provide weather information and be available for rescue if any of the three planes went down. A memorandum for the captain of the *Milwaukee* stated that "the success of the flight . . . is dependent primarily on the procurement and dissemination of weather data. This in turn is absolutely dependent upon the establishment and maintenance of an uninterrupted chain of communications. Shore facilities are so meager and unreliable that this problem in its entirety must be handled by the naval radio."[5]

The instructions to the captains of the ships assigned to assist the fliers reminded them that each destroyer on the line of flight was responsible for the safety of the planes until they were sighted by the next vessel in line. They would report the sighting of the planes and the time they landed to all other ships in the line. The instructions specified that each vessel would throw out heavy black smoke from its funnels fifty minutes before the planes were due to pass over them and keep the smoke going until the planes passed overhead. This would help the pilots navigate and also indicate the direction and approximate velocity of the wind.

Each vessel would also place boards twelve inches wide by twelve feet long on the forward deck to indicate the latest known weather conditions to the passing planes at the flight's destination. Placing the boards in a T formation indicated good weather ahead; an L would mean unfavorable weather at the destination, and H would signify that dangerous flying conditions were reported at the destination. All ships were to report weather information, including sea conditions, at specified times using call letters of the base vessel followed by the words WEATHER WORLD FLIGHT before the planes' arrival. The vessels at the bases would place mooring buoys for the planes in position, clear anchorages of small boats, and have two small boats ready at the anchorages to proceed to the planes when signaled by the crews. The ships would also provide guards to prevent the planes' being molested or set adrift during the night.

The memorandum noted that the fliers would arrive at each stop tired and hungry and "will desire rest and refreshments above all else. They will desire to retire early and will be very grateful if no arrangement of any kind is made for entertainment."[6] The cooperation of the commanders of the base vessels was requested to prevent newspapermen and photographers from interfering with work on the planes or bothering the fliers until an agreeable time for interviews could be arranged.

The designated ships steamed toward their assigned positions in the North Atlantic and began reporting the weather conditions. These were definitely not good. The ice conditions off Greenland were reportedly the worst experienced in twenty years. Every weather impediment for flyers in arctic conditions that could be imagined was being radioed to the *Richmond,* the admiral's flagship. It looked like a long wait before the planes could proceed.

Smith and the others worked on their planes daily but took some time to rest, tour the area, shop, and enjoy the superb food. They thoroughly enjoyed being at Brough and, outside of the short, single trip to London, had no desire to return to the capital city or take any lengthy side trips. They were invited by the King and Queen to a garden party at Buckingham Palace but respectfully turned it down, hoping to receive word any day from Admiral Magruder that his ships were in position and the weather was favorable for the next leg to Iceland.

On 24 July, they were invited to the luxurious home of Robert Blackburn, head of the company, on the outskirts of Leeds. The next day they drove through York to see the magnificent cathedral. They made a tour of Hull and the site of the tragic crash of the British dirigible *R.38* in August 1921 at the time on final trial flights with a joint Royal Navy/RAF/US Navy crew. It had been newly designated as the U.S. Navy's *ZR-2;* sixteen of the victims were Americans.

Anticipating the weather they would encounter on the next leg of the flight to Iceland, the fliers bought heavy flying clothing and returned to the airport to clean up odds and ends on their planes. Their concern about the weather grew daily. But the word did not come for another week. On the evening of 29 July, they finally received word from the U.S. Navy that they should be able to leave on the thirtieth.

They were up at 4 A.M. that day and supervised the launching of their planes down the ramp to the Humber River. After loading up with gas and oil, each plane was given a short test hop and then tied up at the moorings to top off the fuel tanks. A low fog hung over the area so they could not get away until after 10 A.M. Smith led the takeoffs and headed out over the North Sea toward the Orkney Islands, an archipelago of about seventy islands in the Atlantic Ocean and the North Sea off the northern tip of Scotland. As they proceeded north, the clouds forced them down to the wave tops so Smith climbed on top of the overcast with the others following.

They flew for an hour without seeing anything below. The mist gradually dissipated and they could see beach resorts, beautiful estates and crumbling ruins. They flew to Dunkensberry Point, then to Scapa Flow. This place represented a significant moment in history, for it was there that the German fleet had surrendered at the end of World War I—and then been scuttled. They landed near Kirkwall, a small fishing village on Pomona, one of the larger islands of the Orkneys on the north side of Scapa Flow, where the *Richmond* could be seen waiting in the bay.

The *Richmond*'s crew had prepared the plane moorings as had been agreed and the crews were given quarters aboard the ship. They discussed the details of what the Navy planned to do to monitor their passage for the 555-mile flight to Horna Fjord, Iceland. Then they visited the quaint town of Kirkwall with its small stone houses, heated by peat, and a church built in 1137. They bought Fair Island wool sweaters, a specialty of the area, and then retired to a local pub that sold "the biggest drinks anyone ever saw," according to Arnold.[7]

Although they expected to get off the next day, the fog was too dense and the ships stationed between Scapa Flow and Iceland reported bad weather along the route. The airmen could only wait. They spent some time going over maps and trying on the clothes that had been ordered from London. All were getting restless and several decided to visit some of the seventy-four half-submerged German ships that dotted the sea beyond the bay. They chose to climb the masts of the *Hindenburg,* a large battleship, which was half out of the water and found they could walk out on its two great long-range guns on the stern. Wade walked out on one while Arnold and Harding walked out on the other. The two dared Wade to try to leap from one to the other and bet he couldn't do it. Wade, always a risk-taker, tried but fell in the water fully dressed and had to be pulled out, fuming at his distress and thoroughly chilled.

Harding and Arnold lounged around their quarters and chatted at length with Damon Runyon, a journalist covering the World Flight. He would become known later for his humorous stories written in the slangy idiom of New York City's Broadway and underworld characters. Smith played a round of golf with Major Davidson and officers from the *Richmond.*

Lt. Clayton Bissell, who had been the advance officer for the flight down the Aleutians, was ordered meanwhile to board the USS *Milwaukee* and make arrangements for the three planes in Labrador and Nova Scotia, then assist Lieutenants Crumrine and Schulze on the Iceland-Greenland legs. On board were E. F. Porter representing the North American Newspaper Alliance and E. Pierson of United Press.

On 29 July, Bissell received a radiogram from General Patrick advising him that Antonio Locatelli, the Italian pilot, was attempting a round-the-world flight and would be following the same route across the North Atlantic. He had previously considered flying from Spitzbergen to the North Pole alone but abandoned that plan in favor of a westbound World Flight with three other crew members. Commander Cardenas, the Italian air attaché, had asked Patrick to allow use of the bases and left-over supplies from the American flight and this request was approved. Patrick warned, however, that he could not guarantee there would be sufficient supplies of gas and oil to satisfy his needs. Patrick could not guarantee either that there would be U.S. Navy vessels patrolling anywhere along the route for any period of time after the Cruisers had passed over them.

Bissell was directed to arrange to leave mooring buoys for Locatelli at all the bases the Americans were to use, except Pictou, Nova Scotia. Smith was informed that arrangements had been agreed upon between the American and Italian governments but was assigned no responsibility for assisting the Italian flier. No further information about Locatelli's estimated time of arrival at any of the North Atlantic bases was forthcoming at the time.[8]

It was 2 August before the weather cleared enough for the crews to attempt the flight to Iceland by way of the Faeroe Islands. The three planes began their takeoffs; the official report of the flight tells what happened next.

> The *Chicago* in attempting to take off, had considerable difficulty in getting up on the step of the pontoons and could not do so until the *Boston* came down, landing directly in front. This created sufficient roughness of water and currents of air to help the *Chicago* off. The flight started at 8:34 A.M.

Fog was encountered within five miles after departure and finding it impossible to go under, the Cruisers climbed above the fog, continuing on the course for about thirty minutes when all three planes were trapped in a heavy fog. It was impossible for the planes to see each other. The *Chicago* and *Boston,* using their instruments, climbed and turned back out of the fog, coming out at an altitude of 2,800 feet, where they circled for about thrity minutes looking for the *New Orleans.* Fearing some accident had befallen Nelson and Harding, the two returned to Kirkwall, dropping a note at the [Kirkwall Hotel] to immediately give out information regarding the separation."[9] The note read:

SEND A MESSAGE TO THE RICHMOND THAT WE ALL BECAME SEPARATED IN THE FOG AND THAT WADE AND I HAVE NOT SEEN NELSON SINCE WE BECAME SEPARATED ON THE COURSE TWENTY-FIVE MILES FROM BIRSAY.[10]

Smith and Wade landed at Kirkwall and returned to their moorings to see if any information had been received about the missing plane. About four hours later, a message arrived from one of the Navy ships stating that the *New Orleans* had been sighted passing over the Faeroe Islands. When more time passed and hope seemed to fade, the *Richmond* received some good news from Nelson himself:

GOT INTO PROPELLER WASH IN THE FOG WENT INTO A SPIN PARTIALLY OUT OF CONTROL CAME OUT JUST ABOVE WATER CONTINUED ON LANDING AT HORNA FJORD ALL OK NELSON[11]

It had been a near-tragedy and Nelson knew how close they had come to crashing. He tells his own story:

After losing sight of the *Chicago* and *Boston* in the fog, the weather became so thick that we could see nothing six inches from the cockpit. But we felt ourselves being jerked and thrown about and knew that we had got into the propeller wash of one of the other ships. This threw the plane out of control, and once one loses equilibrium in a fog, it is very difficult to regain it. With fog everywhere there was no basis of comparison and it was difficult to tell whether we were flying north, south, east, west, up or down. An instant later, my instruments indicated that we were descending in a spin at great speed.

Finally we managed to straighten her out. Not a minute too soon. As we pulled level, we shot into a clear spot, and from then on we were lucky enough to be able to fly under the fog until we were nearly out of it. Once clear, we flew back and forth for a time, hoping the other planes would show up. When they failed to appear, we climbed higher, and after flying for three hours over another fog bank we saw something black jutting up through the clouds. It was Sydero Island.

Twenty-five miles farther on, the fog ended abruptly, the sky became perfectly clear, and straight ahead we sighted the smoke of the first destroyer we had encountered. Gliding down, Jack wrote a note asking them if they could give us any news regarding the other planes and requested them to verify the direction of the course ahead of us. We flew right across the bow of the destroyer, but the first message bag fell into the sea. The second time we had better luck, and a moment later we had our signals, as well as the news that no other planes had passed that way.[12]

The ship was the *Billingsley* and the message read: IF PLANES 2 AND 3 HAVE PASSED BLOW TWO BLASTS ON WHISTLE IF NOT BLOW ONE.[13]

While Nelson circled with the engine throttled back, the ship gave one long blast so he continued on course toward Horna Fjord. The *New Orleans* soon passed over the cruiser *Raleigh,* another welcome sight, but were again enveloped by a fog bank that continued the rest of the way to Horna Fjord. The engine suddenly began to run rough as the oil pressure dropped ominously. Nelson thought that a landing to determine the cause of the pressure drop would have been exceedingly dangerous along the Icelandic coast, so he continued to fly a compass course directly toward the destination. Both men anxiously searched ahead for any signs of land, hoping they would not have to ditch in the frigid water among the floating ice cakes.

As they neared the Icelandic coast, the fog dissipated and their destination lay directly ahead—a tiny village with a population of eighty nestled against towering mountains with glaciers drifting down to the sea. They landed at 5:37 P.M., moored the plane, and hurried ashore where sailors from the *Raleigh* had established a radio station.

The news of Nelson's safe arrival at Horna Fjord spread fast among the news correspondents on shore and aboard the *Richmond* who quickly radioed their stories to the world's newspapers.

At Kirkwall, Smith was anxious for the *Chicago* and *Boston* to join Nelson and Harding as soon as possible. With excellent weather on hand on 3 August, they took off from the bay at Scapa Flow at 9:30 A.M. while motion picture photographers cranked their cameras, boats whistled, and local fishermen waved and cheered. Smith assumed the lead and headed west over the sea, with the *Boston* flying on his right. There was a stiff tail wind and Smith estimated they were doing better then 100 miles an hour.

About 11 A.M., Arnold, looking back, noticed that he could not see the *Boston.* He tapped Smith on the shoulder and both started looking for them as Smith circled. Down below they saw the *Boston* turn to head into the wind and land easily on a huge swell. Smith continued to circle lower to see if Wade and Ogden were signaling what their difficulty was but it was soon obvious: the engine oil pump had failed. They could see that the plane was smothered with oil and was leaving an oily trail in the water.

Wade was standing up in the cockpit waving frantically for Smith not to try to land because of the swelling sea and the mountainous waves that were developing. Although Wade had ditched seemingly without difficulty, he did not want Smith to risk a landing. Any attempt to taxi in the high wind to assist the *Boston* would be nearly impossible and could mean that there would be two planes down in the vast stretches of the Atlantic off the regular shipping lanes. A takeoff in the increasingly heavy swells would be extremely risky.

Smith circled several more times and then headed at full throttle for the destroyer *Billingsley* which was nearly 100 miles away. "Before we reached her," Arnold said, "Lowell had written two notes, each identical, describing Wade's mishap, the peril he and Ogden were in, their approximate location, time of landing, and the condition of both sea and wind, so that the naval officers could estimated how far the wind might blow them in the interval before a rescue could be effected.

"The first note we put in a message bag and dropped on the *Billingsley* but she was making twenty knots and I missed her deck by several yards. We had only one note left, and every moment was precious. It was imperative that this one should get to the destroyer, so I tied it to my one and only life preserver. When I dropped it this time, I again missed the deck, but a sailor dived overboard and fished it out of the sea.

"The note ended with a request that if they understood our message and were ready to start at once to the rescue, they were to give us three blasts from the whistle. We circled around, saw the captain seize the message, read it, and run across the deck. A moment later we saw three long streaks of steam coming from the whistle, and almost at the same moment clouds of smoke poured from the funnels, and the destroyer shot ahead like a greyhound whose leash has been slipped. Never have I seen a vessel jump into high speed so quickly. Later we learned that she had traveled so fast she burned all the paint off her stacks.

"As she raced through the sea at thirty-one knots, the captain wirelessed to the cruiser *Richmond* and the latter immediately started to the rescue also, at a speed of thirty-three knots."[14]

Once the ship acknowledged the message, there was nothing else Smith and Arnold could do but head the *Chicago* for Horna Fjord, Iceland, speeded along by a strong tail wind. They soon ran into light rain and fog and passed the destroyer *Reid* positioned halfway between the Faeroes and Iceland without seeing her. It later developed that she had drifted thirty-two miles south of her assigned position because of the navigator's inability to take sun shots with a sextant for several days. Smith continued to fly a compass course for the remaining 250 miles without any checkpoints to determine if he was nearing land until he saw the *Raleigh* offshore of Horna Fjord and knew they had found their destination.

Smith landed quickly and the two fueled the *Chicago* immediately before they went ashore. Nelson and Harding greeted them warmly and were shown their quarters in a large fisherman's hut which they shared with sailors from the *Raleigh* who had set up a temporary radio station. Soon there was good news. The *Boston* had been located and was in tow by a British fishing trawler. The *Richmond* would arrive soon and take over the tow. It was hoped that the *Boston* could be repaired and Wade and Ogden would soon join the others at Horna Fjord.

# 11. North America at Last!

The *Boston* was wallowing helplessly in the heavy ocean swells as Smith and Arnold in the *Chicago* disappeared in the mist toward Horna Fjord. Wade and Ogden wondered if they would ever see their fellow fliers again.

Wade had made a smooth landing but soon realized how extremely fortunate he was. The sea was running at cross-direction from the wind and the ocean had looked fairly smooth at five hundred feet. But after he touched down, he found it so rough that the left pontoon nearly wrapped itself around the lower wing and snapped two of the vertical wires attached to the upper wing. The oil pump failure meant that no repairs could be made at sea without a replacement and there was no spare on board. Even if it were replaced, the left wing would probably crumple if he attempted a takeoff. Wade describes what happened next:

> The first thing we did, after Smith and Arnold left, was to fasten the anchor to the bridle and heave it overboard. We hadn't been bobbing up and down on the waves for many minutes before we discovered what a nasty business it is to be in midocean on a fragile plane with the waves hitting her at right angles. Soon we both grew dizzy. But we realized that unless the vertical wires were repaired, the ship might not ride out the sea until help arrived. So we managed to crawl onto the wing and get them fixed. Then, climbing back into our cockpits, we settled down for a little rest.[1]

The two hapless airmen had landed just before 11 A.M., and knowing the approximate positions of the *Richmond* and *Billingsley*, thought it would be late afternoon before they could be located. The sea began to surge, twisting the plane around with the wind. Although both men were confident that they would be rescued soon, they gradually realized that they were mere specks in the middle of a vast ocean where few ships traveled. If the pontoons were damaged by the waves, the plane would sink and they would never be able to survive; they'd die within a few minutes from hypothermia. Never in their lives had either of them felt so lonesome, so helpless. A light rain developed and the wind increased making the sea become dangerously choppy. It looked as though the wings would buckle under as they dipped into the water from side to side.

> We settled ourselves in our cockpits and waited, rationing our water and food in case fog came and complicated our rescue [Wade recalled]. About 2 P.M., I sighted smoke on the horizon. I mounted the wing and began waving a sheet of canvas while Hank shot off the Very pistol. The ship didn't see us.
>
> A light but steady rain was falling and we were really feeling the cold. I'll never forget my feeling of isolation and helplessness. It seemed like hours went by and nothing improved. Instead a growing wind foamed the sea and it looked like we might drift to God knows where.
>
> Finally we sighted another ship. We were determined not to go unseen again. We rigged up a flag-type signaling device and Hank balanced on the wing waving furiously. We were in luck. The ship was crossing in front of us. I got our flares and the rifle, hoping the ping of a bullet hitting the bow would attract their attention. At last they spotted us and turned our way. It was a trawler and it reached us at 3:30 P.M. Our 4½ hour ordeal had seemed twice that long.[2]

The trawler was the *Rugby-Ramsey,* a British fishing boat whose captain had decided that day to look for a catch in that area. When it was within hailing distance, he shouted, "What can we do for you?"

"Just throw us a towline," Wade answered, hoping the boat could tow them to the Faeroe Islands. Wade tried to give the captain directions for getting a line to the plane but the wind howled so much that his words were lost. After one futile attempt, in which the ship and plane almost collided, a sailor attached the towline to a float that he had thrown overboard and the trawler went around in a circle so Ogden could fish it out of the water and fasten it to the plane.

Wade and Ogden sat in their cockpits while the trawler tried to keep the towline taught. Yet each time the trawler arose on a wave she would seem to stand still, and at these moments the *Boston* would swing around and head into the wind; then when the trawler would drop off from the crest of the wave, the *Boston* would quiver and groan and get a jerk that would almost shake her to pieces. More than once the pontoons were yanked down under the swells. Finding that she wasn't making any headway, the trawler stood by and awaited the arrival of one of the destroyers.

The *Billingsley* arrived alongside and a sailor tossed out a line. Ogden cast the trawler's towline adrift and picked up the destroyer's line. A few minutes later, the *Richmond* arrived and the line was passed to the larger ship. The *Boston* was drawn alongside and Wade and Ogden drained the water, gasoline, and oil out of the tanks to lighten the plane. They quickly removed everything that was loose in the plane, including baggage, tools, and spare parts while sailors tried to make emergency patches on the broken pontoons with fabric and glue. Wade thought they might disassemble the plane by taking off the wings and then hoist the fuselage onto the *Richmond*'s deck where they could make repairs. But the wind increased in violence and soon it became impossible to stay on the bobbing plane. Wade and Ogden hurriedly climbed from the plane to the ship. Struggling to follow them, one of the sailors fell overboard but two of his shipmates grabbed him before he was violently swept away.

A sling was then dropped down from the ship's crane; a sailor put it under the plane at its center of gravity and the plane was slowly lifted toward the ship's deck. Suddenly, as the plane was about three feet in the air, the ship rolled suddenly, dropping the five-ton boom on top of the plane with a thunderous crash. Three compartments of the left pontoon were punctured, the propeller was broken, and holes were punched in the center section and upper left wing.

"There seemed to be three possible solutions to the situation at this point," according to the official report of the incident: "First, to keep the plane afloat in the lee until after the storm subsided; second, to disassemble the plane and save the fuselage; and third, to attempt towing again. The first decision was to try the first solution and while the pontoon was being repaired, the plane was stripped and work was rushed to repair the boom. This was soon abandoned due to the continued increasing intensity of the storm. The third plan of towing was then resorted to and the plane rode through the night, suffering greatly, however, from the rough sea."[3]

As the *Richmond* turned toward the Faeroes with the crippled *Boston* in tow, the two fliers walked to the stern of the ship and watched it wallow helplessly in the waves. At midnight, Wade sent a radiogram to Smith via the *Raleigh* at Horna Fjord telling of the damage and that the *Boston* was being towed to the Faeroes for repairs and a new engine. He and Ogden then sat on the pitching stern of the ship, drinking hot coffee, to keep an eye on the machine that had taken them this far. They stayed until almost midnight, then thinking it would survive the towing, turned in. They took a last look at the plane wallowing in the destroyer's wake before going to sleep.

Shortly after 5 A.M. Wade was awakened for a talk with Capt. Lyman Cotton. The *Boston*'s front spreader bar had collapsed and allowed the pontoons to squeeze together. Cotton told Wade that his charts of the coast were not reliable enough to maintain a safe speed for quick maneuvering while towing the plane in that condition. He said there was a possibility that the ship could be wrecked on the rocks if the plane was not cut loose.

Fearing that this might happen, Wade and Ogden had left all the filler caps of the water, gas, and oil tanks open so they would fill with sea water and help the plane to sink instead of drifting, thus possibly becoming a menace to shipping. Yet it still might drift for hours so the decision to deliberately sink it was left up to Wade. "The hardest words I have ever had to speak to the ship's captain were: 'Abandon the airplane.' "[4]

The plane was pulled alongside and sailors went down the ropes with axes to hack holes in the wooden pontoons, then came back aboard, and cut the tow lines. As the *Boston* slowly began to capsize, the two fliers saluted and said goodby to the faithful machine that had carried them so far around the globe. They headed for Reykjavik aboard the *Richmond* with heavy hearts. Wade radioed the bad news to Smith and Nelson at Horna Fjord:

PLANE TOTAL LOSS RICHMOND SAILING REYKJAVIK TO ARRIVE EARLY AFTERNOON TUESDAY 0530 WADE

After Wade's message was received, there was little joy in Horna Fjord. Such an accident could have happened to any of them. The engine failure was probably due to a sheared off drive shaft to the oil pump. Unlike the fuel pump, there was no emergency hand pump to keep oil circulating to the engine. It was a new engine that Wade and Ogden had installed themselves at the Blackburn factory. The luck of the draw had been against them.

"We were all torn between two emotions," Arnold wrote in his diary, "one of relief that Wade and Ogden were safe, and the other of sorrow that after coming 20,000 miles they should so suddenly lose their plane through absolutely no fault of theirs."[5]

Realizing the disappointment that Wade and Ogden shared, General Patrick directed that the prototype Cruiser that was still at Langley Field, Virginia, be put in good condition on floats and sent to Pictou Harbor, Maine, one of the scheduled stops north of Boston, or to Hawkes Bay, Newfoundland, and await the other planes there. Wade and Ogden would then fly with the others to Boston and across the United States to Seattle.[6] Maj. John F. Pirie and Capt. Willis Hale and two mechanics were ordered to transport the Cruiser's set of wheels and fittings in two Martin bombers to Boston to replace the pontoons. Two other unnamed mechanics familiar with the Cruisers were also to proceed to Boston to assist the three crews in the final change from the pontoons to wheels.[7]

Smith, Arnold, Nelson, and Harding at Horna Fjord made plans immediately to continue the planned itinerary. Lieutenant Crumrine, the advance officer, had rented a fisherman's cottage for the fliers and stocked it with blankets and food. The *Raleigh,* anchored twenty-five miles offshore because of the shallow harbor, had sent sailors to stay with them, cook their meals, help refuel and guard the planes, and establish a radio station. On the night of 4 August, they were entertained with Danish songs by the six daughters of a Mr. Danielson, all dressed in native Icelandic costumes. Still, gloom hung over the evening as the Americans thought about the loss of the *Boston.*

At midmorning, 5 August, the two remaining planes departed for Reykjavik, a 290-mile trip, against a stiff head wind. The harbor at Horna Fjord was very shallow, and it was difficult to find an area long enough for the takeoff.

They followed the coast where very few safe landing harbors could be seen. They passed many glaciers running down toward the sea and saw the hulks of ships wrecked in years past. As they mused about that, the engine of the *New Orleans* suddenly began to run rough and the oil pressure dropped from sixty psi to twenty-seven. Nelson decided the better course of action was to continue rather than attempt a landing along the rocky Icelandic coast.

They passed the *Billingsley* at Portland Point and unexpectedly ran into several severe dust storms, a rare phenomenon in the Arctic, until they reached the narrowest point of the peninsula on the southwest end of Iceland. They crossed it and headed directly for Reykjavik. When they arrived at the Reykjavik harbor at 2:15, there were many boats inside a breakwater to escape the wind-whipped seas outside. Buoys had been placed in a sheltered area and Nelson and Smith were able to land close to them and tie up without difficulty.

The four fliers were surprised to see about 25,000 cheering people waiting to greet them onshore. Just as the launch was taking them in, the *Richmond* arrived and whistled a greeting. Wade and Ogden soon joined the others on the dock. Wade greeted Smith with a bear hug and there were tears in his eyes. The others knew how he and Ogden must have felt after surviving what they had all been through so far and then suddenly to end the flight so ingloriously. A mechanical failure of a vital part attached to the engine had finished the trip for them. Yet they knew that the same fate could have forced Nelson and Harding down had their engine failed.

Smith sent a radio message to General Patrick and reported that Wade and Ogden were there on the *Richmond* and requested that "the old Douglas" be sent to Boston with the World Flight insignia and the number 3 painted on it, and thus allow them to continue the rest of the trip.[8]

Lieutenant Crumrine met the fliers and confirmed previous reports that Lt. LeClaire Schulze was on board the *Gertrud Rask,* a Danish ship, which was taking supplies for them to Angmagssalik, Greenland, the next stop. He reported that ice was blocking the harbor there and the ship was unable to reach the town dock. Smith and the others were not discouraged because records maintained for the previous twenty years gave the average date for Angmagssalik harbor to be ice-free was 15 August, ten days later.

Contingency plans had to be made. Admiral Magruder and Smith decided to have the *Raleigh,* with two seaplanes aboard, make scouting forays to see if there were any other harbors so that Angmagssalik could be bypassed, or if it was possible to find a harbor where the planes would just refuel from a ship and continue. Wade went aboard, made two flights, and confirmed that the harbors were filled with icebergs; landings would be impossible. Schulze aboard the *Gertrud Rask* was also asked to scout nearby harbors as best he could on the ship. While they awaited word that the harbor at Angmagssalik was clear, the crews were entertained, along with Admiral Magruder and his staff, at a luncheon by Iceland's prime minister. They were embarrassed that they had only their flying clothes to wear, a distinct contrast to the naval officers in their full-dress uniforms.

The fliers enjoyed the hospitality of the Icelanders for the next two weeks. The prime minister offered them his residence but they elected to stay in a hotel near the beach where they could watch their planes and be ready to depart on short notice. Within a short time, there were five American battleships in the harbor with a total of 2,500 sailors and some newspaper reporters on board. According to the townspeople, it was the first time that any American warships had ever visited them.

The fliers were surprised to find that Reykjavik was a modern city with well-paved streets, electric lights, excellent hotels, banks, shops, cafés, taxis, and even motion pictures. And the Icelanders could speak English! They were especially pleased to see the beautiful blond-haired, blue-eyed girls. Since Nelson could speak Swedish and Danish, his hosts were delighted that a Scandinavian was represented among the fliers.

On 6 August, the fliers were invited to a buffet and dance aboard the *Richmond* with many of the townspeople attending. It was the *Billingsley*'s turn to entertain the next evening with a dinner. Then it was the *Reed*'s turn to meet them and serve dinner. The next several days were spent seeing the Great Geyser and the hot springs over which Reykjavik is situated.

But there was still work to be done. The planes had remained in the harbor and had not been brought ashore because of high winds until the eighth of August. The hauling operation up the launching ramp brought a great crowd out to see the planes and, as had happened many times before, the police had to be called out to protect them from souvenir hunters and allow the men to work. Engine repairs were made on the *New Orleans* and a new propeller was installed.

During the two weeks they were in Reykjavik, a forty-foot boat named the *Leif Ericsson* arrived with four men aboard. They were attempting to duplicate the route of Eric the Red, the famous Norseman, on his Atlantic crossing to the North American continent around the year 1000. The fliers enjoyed hearing about their experiences and went to the dock to see them off to continue their journey to America. They were reported later as having reached Greenland but were never heard from again.

The *Gertrud Rask* meantime waited ten miles off the harbor at Angmagssalik. The ice was so heavy that even a ship that was constructed for navigation in the ice fields could not force her way through the belt of floe ice. She was pinned fast for days and slowly drifted southward away from the destination. Suddenly when the ship was seventy miles south of Angmagsalik, the ice opened up. The amount of ice floes still in the harbor worried Schulze and he decided to place the plane moorings about fifteen miles north of the settlement where there was less floating ice.

While Schulze worried about whether there would be enough room for the Cruisers to take off safely if they landed at Angmagssalik, Clayton Bissell aboard the *Milwaukee* had succeeded in establishing a base at Frederiksdal on the southwest tip of Greenland. The Danish steamer *Danepy* had already transferred the necessary spares and fuel supplies to the *Milwaukee* at Ivigtut. The Danish warship *Island Falk* joined the *Milwaukee* to lend assistance. On 11 August, the light cruiser *Raleigh* sent two observation planes on several reconnaissance flights to locate suitable emergency landing areas. Wade transferred from the *Richmond* to the *Raleigh* and volunteered to lend another pair of eyes to the search for open water.

He flew with Cmdr. Bruce G. Leighton. They didn't see anything except "horrible weather and lots of ice." When they did find a suitable harbor "it was filled with icebergs, some over a hundred feet high."[9]

Smith received some information that disturbed him during this frustrating period of waiting for decent weather and better ice conditions. He heard that a rumor was circulating among the newsmen that the Americans were going to abandon the flight. Fearing that this speculation would get to Washington, he sent a radiogram to General Patrick reassuring him that if Angmagssalik did not open soon, they were going to fly directly to Frederiksdal where an emergency base was being established. He noted that there were two other options but he did not say which he preferred: a refueling at sea or putting wheels on the planes and flying directly to Labrador.[10] This rumor which implied that the Americans were afraid to tackle the next leg--the longest and most dangerous of all—made Smith and the others even more anxious to continue. They visited the radio station frequently to read the hourly weather reports from the *Gertrud Rask.* Smith increasingly favored the long flight 830-mile flight to Frederiksdal if Angmagssalik continued to be closed for safe landing. They inspected their planes thoroughly and knew the risk they were taking. More fuel would have to be carried so the total weight was reduced considerably by discarding many tools and even their spare clothes. The items removed were placed aboard the *Richmond* which would meet them eventually in Labrador.

On 11 August, an Italian naval officer named Marescalchi, an advance agent for Lt. Antonio Locatelli, arrived in Horna Fjord. As had been expected from General Patrick's radiogram, he announced proudly that Locatelli, Lt. Tullio Crozio, and two mechanics, Bruno Fulcinelli and Giovonni Braccine, were proceeding westbound in their German-designed, Italian-made Dornier Wal (Whale) twin-engine seaplane. They had left Pisa on 25 July, landed in Swiss lakes as they traversed the Alps, followed the Rhine River to Rotterdam, then flew to Brough. They stopped at Stromness and the Faeroe Islands and planned to join the Americans at Reykjavik. Maresalchi said that when Locatelli arrived at Reykjavik, he would request cooperation from the Americans and accompany them to North America. This was denied.

Locatelli arrived on 16 August. He was not pleased about the agreement between the two governments that prohibited him from flying with the Americans if he chose to do so. He asked Smith if he could accompany the Cruisers across the rest of the North Atlantic. Smith and Nelson conferred and realized that it would probably be mutually helpful by providing an added rescue capability if Locatelli were with them, in view of what had happened to Wade and Ogden. Smith wired Washington requesting authority for this from General Patrick and it was granted on 18 August 1924.

The Americans were impressed with the Dornier's streamlined construction, 74-foot wing span, and especially its tough metal hull made of duralumin. It was a Type J Dornier which was large enough to carry nine passengers but as many as fourteen could be crowded in for short distances. It was much heavier than the

Cruisers and faster. Its two Rolls Royce engines, mounted in tandem, gave it added safety in case of failure of one. Arnold commented that "It appeared to be the most efficient plane for long-distance flying that we had ever seen, and Lieutenants Locatelli and Crozio and their two assistants were dashing fellows."[11]

Everyone involved in the American World Flight was getting anxious for the two Cruisers to depart, especially the bored news correspondents traveling on the Navy ships. The weather experts studying the route reported that fogs were prevalent along the coast of Iceland and rolled into the area without warning. The Danish government advised that the ice conditions were worse in 1924 than they had been in many years. Many icebergs had been sighted between Iceland and Greenland that were larger than normal and drift ice was found more than a hundred miles south of the course between the two land masses.

The weather remained stormy with gale winds and the news from Schulze in the *Gertrud Rask* continued to be discouraging. On 12 August, Wade was flying as an observer with Commander Leighton again from the *Raleigh* when they spotted the Danish cutter in an ice-free cove near Angmagssalik and Leighton prepared to land nearby. Unknown to them, the crew of the *Gertrud Rask* had attached steel cables from her bow to abutments on shore. Wade tells what happened:

> We were making an approach across the cutter's bow to an area of clear water. A few feet above the water I spotted the cables. I shouted to Leighton while pounding on the fuselage with one hand and pointing with the other. Leighton gunned the engine . . . there were only inches between life and a dunking in freezing water.[12]

Leighton hopped over the cables, landed, and taxied back to the *Rask.* A message was waiting for them from the *Raleigh:* RETURN IMMEDIATELY FOG. Leighton made a quick takeoff and climbed to 12,000 feet to begin looking for the ship. He landed, the plane was hoisted aboard, and by the time it was stowed on deck, the fog was so thick they could not see either the bow or the stern from the center of the ship.

After thirteen days of waiting, all hope was abandoned that the iced harbor at Angmagssalik, the most inaccessible point on the entire crossing, would clear in a reasonable time before the first freeze. Smith conferred with Admiral Magruder and decided they would instead make the nonstop flight from Reykjavik directly to Frederiksdal where Bissell had now readied the emergency base. The new routing would add an additional 335 miles over ocean and ice fields but seemed to be the only feasible course to avoid the closed harbors. It was the most dangerous leg of all because it was far north of the steamship routes across the Atlantic and on the edge of the Arctic fogs. Extremely high winds swept down from the Greenland ice cap.

On 18 August, the four fliers were up before dawn and in their planes waiting for favorable weather reports. Good news arrived at 10 A.M. and the two Cruisers, more heavily loaded with fuel than ever before, taxied to the outer harbor for takeoff, followed by Locatelli and his crew of three in the Dornier. There were heavy swells and very little wind. As they lined up for takeoff, a large wave suddenly swept over the *New Orleans* and shattered its propeller. At the same time, another large roller smashed into the *Chicago* and sheared off the front pontoon spreader bar at the nose fittings. Both planes had to be towed back to the dock for repairs. Seeing what had happened, Locatelli turned the Dornier around, tied up at a buoy, and the crew came ashore. Ironically, Schulze reported at that time that the harbor at Angmagssalik was now cleared of ice. If they had been headed there, they could have carried a much smaller load of gas and, being much lighter, could have probably been able to take off without damage.

All the excess supplies and spare parts for the Cruisers had been put aboard the *Richmond* to be returned to the States and it had steamed off to take up a position near Greenland. Admiral Magruder immediately ordered the ship's skipper, Capt. Lyman A. Cotton, to return to Reykjavik where it docked on 20 August. Since there were seventeen hours of daylight at this latitude, the crews were able to work most of the night and both planes were ready by early morning. They took off for Frederiksdal at 6:55 A.M. on 21 August, followed by the Italian plane.

The planes leveled off and Locatelli tried to fly formation but the Dornier was so much faster that Locatelli had to circle a few times to allow the Cruisers to catch up. The impetuous Italian soon grew impatient. He wagged his wings in farewell and forged ahead. He was out of sight in the mist in a few minutes.

There were five naval vessels patrolling the line of flight that Smith and Nelson intended to follow. Captain Cotton on the *Richmond* described this 835-mile leg from Iceland to Greenland as "the longest and most difficult leg of the transatlantic flight . . . and [it] was truly a flight to test the skill and courage of the hardiest aviator."[13]

They passed the *Richmond* ninety miles from Reykjavik; then flew over the *Reid* 115 miles farther. At about the 140-mile mark beyond that ship, the planes were checked out by the *Billingsley*. According to the plan approved by Magruder, this was the last time they would see the *Billingsley* so they flew low overhead and waved to the sailors in thanks for their help. They were cheered to find that the ship's crew had painted in huge letters the words GOOD LUCK in white paint on the open deck. It was an encouraging sight. They would remember this moment forever.

After the next 140 miles or so, they came upon the destroyer *Barry*. Wade and Ogden were aboard and would be taken to Pictou, Nova Scotia, once the Cruisers had passed and assuming no search was required. The ship was displaying two flags from its mast, the signal that dangerous weather lay ahead. In a few minutes after passing the *Barry,* they ran into heavy fog but continued on course. As so many times before, the planes were forced to fly close to the wave tops in the limited visibility.

The *Raleigh* was 160 miles farther on from the *Barry* and they never saw it. Estimating the distance from the Greenland coast at about 150 miles, Smith swung to a course toward the shore barely on top of huge waves, hoping that the fog would be lighter close to the land. Seventy-five miles before the coast was reached, the flight began to encounter large icebergs and winds estimated at about sixty mph. The combination of fog, the many icebergs of all sizes, and the rocky coast made the flying extremely dangerous. Just before rounding Cape Farewell, the two planes lost sight of each other and separated.

Smith admitted he was terrified as they played tag and leap-frog with the towering icebergs because they could not see them until they were upon them:

The presence of all these bergs and so much ice made the fog even more dense than before. We were traveling along at a speed of ninety miles an hour, and could see only between a hundred and a hundred and fifty feet ahead, so use your own imagination as to how soon a plane traveling at that speed could use up the distance that we could see, and then try and figure out how little time was left us to sight a berg ahead, decide which way to turn, and then execute the maneuver. Three times we came so suddenly upon huge icebergs that there was no time left to do any deciding. We simply jerked the wheel back for a quick climb, and were lucky enough to zoom over the top of it into the still denser fog above. Here we were completely lost and unable to see beyond the prop and wing tips. Blindly, we would grope and feel our way downward, hoping against hope that the little space we should eventually descend into just above the surface of the water would be clear of ice for a great enough distance to enable us to glance around, size up the situation, and get set for dodging the next one.[14]

After the flight, Smith and Nelson were often asked why they didn't climb above the fog. They both did try but the fog apparently had no limit and with the extra load of fuel and oil they were carrying, they could climb no higher than 8,000 feet. The mountains along the Greenland coast were known to be eight to ten thousand feet high and they could easily have flown into them as Martin had done in Alaska. Smith decided the better part of valor was to stay low, inches above the water, and take their chances: He describes their near-miss with death:

Diving through a small patch of extra heavy fog that was clinging close to the water, we emerged on the other side to find ourselves plunging straight toward a wall of white. The *New Orleans* was close behind us with that huge berg looming in front. I banked steeply to the right while Erik and Jack swung sharp to the left. Les shouted, "Hold on, God!" and I'm sure I did some rapid praying myself. Both left wings seemed to graze the edge of the berg as we shot past it. And in far less time than it takes to tell it the two planes were lost from each other.[15]

Smith headed the *Chicago* in toward shore while Nelson turned out to sea for about thirty miles before swinging back on course. Neither saw the other and neither knew whether or not the other had crashed into that iceberg. Each had to continue dodging bergs, ghostlike shadows and then, suddenly, dark patches that were the sides of mountains; this meant they had reached the mainland of Greenland and could follow the coastline. They each flew a compass course toward Frederiksdal while keeping as close to shore as they dared. They broke out of the fog briefly into bright sunlight, only to plunge back into a layer of fog that topped out at 1,500 feet. Unable to get under it, they flew on top and had only distant mountain peaks to reassure them they were still on course toward their destination.

> Finally, we arrived over where, according to our charts, we thought Frederiksdal ought to be, and watched anxiously for an opening in the clouds [Smith continued]. We circled around several times, and then the All-Wise Providence, who had already spared our lives a dozen times on this day's journey, parted the clouds for us to see there was a shaft of light extending down to the sea. Far below we spied a boat emitting clouds of black smoke. We knew this must be the Danish coastguard cutter, the *Island Falk,* sending up smoke signals for us, because there was no other ship in these waters. Her guns were firing and her whistle was blowing, but, of course, we could hear nothing above the roar of our Liberty.[16]

Smith landed the *Chicago* in very rough water beside the ship at 5:30 in the afternoon. The *Island Falk* was anchored far out at the mouth of a large fjord and Smith had to taxi several miles to calmer waters upstream between the towering mountains to the tie-up buoys. He and Arnold were exhausted after ten hours and forty minutes in the cold, cramped cockpits. A launch came alongside and a Danish officer asked if they knew where the *New Orleans* and Locatelli were since no one had heard from either of them. Smith nodded negatively and replied that they had been lost in the fog and had no idea where they might be.

Fearing the worst for Nelson and Harding, Smith and Arnold said little to each other as they refueled and inspected their plane but each reflected mentally on how fortunate they were to escape what could have been a quick death from plunging into a berg or a rock outcropping. "We simply couldn't see how anyone could be as lucky as we had been," Smith said.[17]

Then suddenly, as they were finishing their servicing chores, the beautiful, familiar sound of a Liberty engine echoed across the harbor. Nelson and Harding in the *New Orleans* were circling above the fog layer looking for a break in the clouds just as the *Chicago* had done an hour before. They, too, found a hole in the low clouds, saw the Danish vessel, and glided down for a landing. As the plane was leveling off, however, it caught a pontoon on a large wave, slightly damaging it. Considering what they had also been through during their 11 hours, 17 minutes in the air, it was insignificant damage that could be easily repaired. The four men and two planes had survived this, the longest and most dangerous leg of the entire flight.

Nelson and Harding, after turning left and barely escaping the berg when Smith turned right, had flown south to escape the thickening icebergs near the coast. They looked for their leader when they rounded the tip of Greenland and feared he had crashed into a berg or a rock outcropping on the coast when they could not see the *Chicago*. It was a most welcome and joyful sight to see it sitting calmly at rest in the harbor.

The two exhausted crews went aboard the *Island Falk* and sent a radio message to the *Richmond* of their arrival. They willingly went to bed after a welcome dinner. They had been without sleep for about forty-two hours.

Now that the Americans were safe, the attention of all was focused on the whereabouts of Locatelli and his crew. The Dornier had not been sighted and it was quite possible that he and his three crew members could have crashed into one of the icebergs that the others had escaped. Admiral Magruder, with permission from Washington, ordered his ships to concentrate on searching for the Italian flying boat. All the vessels were ordered to patrol in a 12,000-square-mile area of an angry sea covered with floating cakes of ice. They spent the days and nights of 21 to 24 August conducting search patterns. The two cruisers each catapulted their two Vought UO-1 observation planes several times but the fog seriously hampered visibility and made it difficult for the planes to be launched and retrieved safely. By midnight of the twenty-third, some of the vessels were running short of fuel and the destroyers *Billingsley* and *Reid* were sent back to European ports for restocking. The *Richmond, Raleigh,* and *Barry* also would soon need refueling but for the moment continued the search.

From the time the first message was received that Locatelli was probably lost, the Danish administrator at Julianhåb immediately ordered two search parties of Greenlanders sent out on foot and with dog teams. They concentrated on likely spots along the coast and inland.

Captain Cotton, skipper of the *Richmond,* cruising about 125 miles east of Cape Farewell, Greenland, was about to recommend to the admiral that they abandon the search when a lookout saw a flicker of light on the horizon. Cotton colorfully describes what happened next:

> The *Richmond* turns and speeds toward the spot, throbbing with her hundred-thousand horsepower. A red star, fired into the air, lights up our decks with lurid light, as officers, men, correspondents, and cameramen rush up on deck, half-clad, hair disheveled, with heavy overcoats and trailing blankets hastily thrown around them. An answering star from the darkness ahead. Can it be that the lost are found? Can it be? Our searchlight feels along the horizon, groping over the hostile sea that is loathe to surrender its prey. The light touches a small object, bobbing like a cork on the water. All eyes are strained toward the plane, through moments of tense silence. How slowly it seems to draw near! The beams of our searchlights catch it again as it rises to the crest of a breaker, and this time we see the red, white, and green rudder of the Italian monoplane. One, two, three, four—-the crew are all visible now. All are alive and safe![18]

It was 11:35 P.M. when the *Richmond* sidled carefully up to the plane and one of the *Richmond*'s crewmen threw it a line. The line was, Locatelli told the press later, "like the first thread connecting us with life again." They had almost given up hope as heavy waves and icebergs had battered and rammed the Dornier to near destruction. The ailerons, vertical stabilizer, and elevators were shattered and the engine mounts were bent. It probably would not have stayed afloat through the night; certainly it would never fly again.

Traumatized by their ordeal, Locatelli and his three crew-mates were so seasick and exhausted that they had to be lifted aboard the cruiser in cargo nets. Sailors punctured the plane's gas tanks and hull and set it on fire so it wouldn't become a hazard to shipping. The four Italian airmen watched soulfully as it sank out of sight. Locatelli turned toward Admiral Magruder and gratefully handed him an Italian flag as thanks for their rescue. When he looked at the ship's navigation charts later he was told that the Dornier had drifted into an area that had already been searched. Had the *Richmond*'s lookout not seen their flares, no one would have ever known what had happened to them.

The airmen were fed and afterward Locatelli told their story to the assembled newspaper correspondents on board. When they ran into dense fog, he said he decided to land on the sea rather than fly at wave-top level and risk ramming into the towering icebergs or a mountain. He intended to take off when the fog cleared. But the heavy seas and floating ice damaged the plane so severely that takeoff would have been impossible. Locatelli was criticized in the press for leaving the Americans behind but Smith disagreed. "I think Locatelli did right in going ahead," he said. "To have gone slower he would have had to use up more gas."[19]

While this episode was unfolding, messages had been flowing back and forth between Washington and the *Richmond.* General Patrick decided that Wade and Ogden should be given the opportunity to resume the flight. He had ordered the prototype DWC to be flown on pontoons to Nova Scotia, where Wade and Ogden would meet the other fliers and continue with them to Seattle. The plane would be named the *Boston II.*

Smith and Nelson still had much dangerous flying ahead of them. They were preparing on 21 August for the next leg to Ivigtut, a small village and mining camp that the advance officers had made into a regular supply base one hundred and fifty miles farther up the west coast of Greenland. They were planning to depart when they found that the *Chicago*'s pontoons had been punctured. The men who had been posted to watch the planes during the night had allowed some cakes of ice to drift into them. While Nelson, Harding, and Arnold pumped the pontoons out, Smith took off his flying suit and dove into the icy water to apply temporary patches of canvas and sheet aluminum on the undersides. It was hard work and the others took turns to relieve Smith since only a few patches could be attached at a time. They rubbed their hands and arms vigorously with oil to overcome the numbness of the cold water.

It wasn't until the twenty-fourth that good weather was reported at Ivigtut; Smith decided to take advantage of it even though it was raining and foggy at Frederiksdal. The two planes taxied out and dodged large cakes of ice to get airborne. During the first attempt to take off in rough water, the engine on the *New Orleans* cut out several times and Nelson made a quick landing in heavy swells. This damaged both vertical wing wires and caused the pontoon brace wires to loosen up. He and Harding tightened them while Smith waited to take off in the *Chicago.*

The two planes finally got off and flew for two hours along the frigid, dismal coast. The wind gradually increased to gale force and the airmen were reminded of the Aleutian williwaws as they were jolted and thrown about in their cockpits. Contrary to what they had been led to expect by the weather reports, they had to fly through freezing rain, snow, fog, and sleet before they sighted the Ivigtut harbor. They found it to be mercifully well-protected from the high winds and waves.

The village was at the head of a fjord surrounded by high, rugged mountains. Glaciers flowed down the mountainsides to the sea and huge ice chunks would "calve" or break off and come crashing down to separate and float out to the Davis Strait. Nelson noted that the area was the scene of the "last and barrenmost" of the emergency repair depots that were established.

Waiting in the harbor at Ivigtut was the *Milwaukee* and on board was Clayton Bissell who had been their advance officer for the Aleutian segments. They were as surprised and pleased as he was. Bissell was the last person they had seen in the Aleutians and the first person they met who had been with them previously on the flight. With his experience at Dutch Harbor in the Aleutians to guide him, Bissell had supervised the construction of excellent ramps on the beach so the planes could be pulled up out of the water and floating ice for easier maintenance. After their planes were towed up and tied down, the four fliers got in a launch and went aboard the *Milwaukee* to find that the entire crew had been called to the deck to give them a rousing welcome.

The village of Ivigtut consisted of a few men and women and about 150 Danish miners who extract cryolite from the hills during the summer months. Cryolite is a rare mineral consisting of sodium and aluminum fluoride used principally in the smelting of aluminum. Discovered in Greenland in 1794, it occurs almost nowhere else. The fliers found that the work was hard but the miners were provided with quarters, food, clothing, tobacco, and alcoholic beverages. Unable to spend their earnings in Greenland, they returned to Denmark in the fall with tidy earnings that allowed them to resume the good life until the next spring. The arrival of the *Milwaukee* and the World Fliers provided unequaled excitement in the form of a dinner for all the miners as guests of the ship's crew, followed by a motion picture shown on deck in the rain.

The fliers went trout fishing one day and Smith was able to try a rod and line that had been given to him by a well-wisher before he left Seattle. He was delighted to catch forty trout in less than two hours and prepare them for his teammates.

A 560-mile risky flight over water now faced the two planes to get to Icy Tickle, Labrador, the last over-ocean leg of the flight. If they succeeded, they would be the first airmen to have flown westbound across the Pacific and the North Atlantic. The planes were carefully inspected. One of the *Chicago*'s pontoons that had been punctured during takeoff at Frederiksdal was repaired. Smith decided that since new engines were available at Ivigtut, they should replace the used ones as a safety precaution. The pontoons on the planes were revarnished and despite the fact that all work had to be done in the open, both planes were actually ready in three days because Smith wanted to delay no further if the weather cleared. Short test flights were made to check them out and both crews were ready to go on 28 August. This day happened to be Les Arnold's birthday. Although the weather was reported better for flying all the way to Labrador, the U.S. Navy ships were just not in position along the route. The weather meantime deteriorated and did not break for the next four days.

In addition to the foul weather, the fliers met a new surprise enemy: billions of tiny, biting gnats that caused Nelson to describe as "the most troublesome brutes you ever saw—worse even than tropical insects. They flew into our eyes, and we had to talk with our lips shut, to keep them from swarming into our mouths. In fact, they were so bad that we finally couldn't work at all until we got some netting draped over our heads and tied around our necks."[20]

Smith had time to think during the many hours of waiting about what might be in store for them after they reached the North American continent. He felt they had already had their full share of welcomes, and it was the consensus that they all wanted to get to Seattle without any more delays for ceremonies, speeches, and parties. He asked Bissell to send a message to General Patrick requesting "that no entertainments, receptions, or escorts be arranged for them previous to the completion of the round world flight by arrival of planes on Pacific coast."[21]

It was to be a fruitless appeal. They would be welcomed en route by literally thousands of people, all anxious to see and talk with the World Fliers, to hear about their adventures, and to touch their planes. The seemingly endless period of waiting at Ivigtut ended on 31 August when en route weather reports were favorable from Labrador, the *Richmond,* and the four destroyers—*Coghlan, McFarland, Ausburne,* and *Lawrence*—all standing by in their assigned positions along the route to Labrador. The *Brazos,* an oiler, was ordered to stand by at the Bay of Islands with fuel while the *Milwaukee* was to remain and report the flight's departure from Ivigtut, then proceed to Icy Tickle, Labrador, and replace the *Richmond* that would be there to meet the planes. The fleet's operations orders stipulated that searchlights for signals were to be used in thick weather, and flags and whistles otherwise when the planes passed.

Smith had difficulty getting off and it took two hours of taxiing to finally become airborne. Nelson, however, was able to use his wake and took off easily. When only about ten minutes from Ivigtut, they encountered heavy fog. Knowing there were many icebergs ahead, they carefully hugged the water until they broke out into the clear after about thirty minutes of flying.

The *Chicago* and *New Orleans* chugged along peacefully in bright sunshine. They were about two hundred miles from Labrador when they ran into head winds. Then "the cold hand of Failure suddenly tried to claw us down," according to Smith. The *Chicago*'s motor-driven fuel pump suddenly failed; a few minutes later, the wind-driven pump clattered to a stop. Oil began leaking out of the engine nacelle and ran down the sides of the plane. Smith switched to the 58-gallon reserve fuel tank that had only enough fuel for about two hours of flying. Smith immediately throttled back and yelled to Arnold to start using the hand-operated wobble pump in his cockpit that boosted the fuel from the lower tanks into the gravity-feed reserve, allowing the engine to continue operating.

Arnold pumped furiously with his right arm, then when his arm grew numb after an hour or so, he made a sling with his belt, attached it to the hand pump, placed a handkerchief around his neck to relieve the chafing, and pumped with his other hand to keep up the steady beat. He was sweating profusely and every time he thought he would quit for a minute or so to rest and the engine would sputter. He looked down at the icy water below and continued to pump with renewed determination. He pumped for nearly three hours, knowing that remaining airborne was his sole responsibility.

But there were two more worrisome developments. The *Chicago*'s engine was losing oil and Nelson signaled from the *New Orleans* that they could see it streaming down the fuselage. There was no way to determine how much oil was left in the tank and how long the engine could run without it. Smith also found that the earth-inductor compass had ceased to operate. The sun's position, however, enabled them to continue heading westward where land was certain to appear in time.

After what seemed a lifetime to both men, the faithful *Richmond* was sighted ahead sitting confidently in the calm bay at Indian Harbor. They knew they had reached North American soil. Smith and Nelson landed their ships in the bay off the tiny settlement of Icy Tickle at 3:20 P.M. while the ship blew its whistle in greeting. They had achieved a historic aviation "first" and soon were to be honored far beyond their wildest dreams.

# 12. Mission Accomplished

It had been a grueling 6-hour, 55-minute flight from Greenland to Icy Tickle, especially for Arnold, who could not raise his painful right arm. After tying up at the buoys placed by the sailors of the *Richmond,* the fliers were taken to the beach by a motor launch where Smith, as the expedition's leader, had the honor of being first to step ashore, just as he imagined the English Pilgrims had done at Plymouth in 1620. They were officially welcomed by Admiral Magruder and his staff before a group of news reporters and photographers. The admiral then invited the fliers to the *Richmond* for a rousing welcome from its crew.

On deck, Magruder read several messages from Washington, all sent ahead of time in anticipation that the *Chicago* and *New Orleans* would reach Labrador safely. The one from President Coolidge read: "Your history-making flight has been followed with absorbing interest by your countrymen and your return to North American soil is an inspiration to the whole Nation. You will be welcomed back to the United States with an eagerness and enthusiasm that I am sure will compensate for the hardship you have undergone. Your countrymen are proud of you. My congratulations and heartiest good wishes go to you at this hour of your landing."[1]

Acting Secretary of War Dwight F. Davis sent radiograms to each of the fliers, including Wade and Ogden, to be delivered to the latter when they arrived at Pictou, Nova Scotia by ship. The message to Smith congratulated him for his "bravery, hardihood, and modesty" and added that as leader of the flight, "I desire to say that your courage, skill, and determination have shown you to be a fit successor to the great navigators of the Age of Discovery. The whole country, the War Department, and the Air Service are very proud of you."[2]

General Patrick added his greeting, saying, "We have never had any doubts regarding the successful accomplishment of your task. You have done well. We are rightfully proud of you now that your task is nearly completed as you near Boston."[3] Although Smith was pleased to receive these messages, he was concerned that there would be an excessive demand on their time at each stop en route to the West Coast. He was to find that his prior request to General Patrick had been ignored as the cities on the itinerary continued to plan their individual rousing welcomes.[4]

The fliers were assigned cabins on the *Richmond,* and each hoped that they could get something to eat since they hadn't had any food since early that morning. They then wanted to get some rest. This was not to be. Arnold's diary for 31 August records that "in the evening we had a dinner at five, at six we dined in the wardroom mess, and at 7:00 were unexpectedly called to the admiral's cabin and had dinner there. We ate all three of them and enjoyed them all. Afterward we lost little time in climbing into a bunk for a good sleep."[5]

The fliers spent the next day preparing their planes for the next leg to Hawkes Bay, Newfoundland. This is a 350-mile flight, where the destroyer *Ausburn* would be waiting with fuel. Smith and Arnold washed the oil from the *Chicago* and replaced the engine pump. The *Richmond* moved out of the harbor in the afternoon, and was replaced by the *Milwaukee* on which they spent the night.

A little after 11 A.M. on 2 September, even though the weather reports were far from favorable, the two planes took off from Icy Tickle and cut across a narrow peninsula covered with scrubby pines, the first trees they had seen since they left the British Isles. Nearly three hours out as they followed offshore of the Newfoundland coast, they ran into heavy fog, their old, unwelcome adversary. As nearly always before, they lowered to wave-top level above heavy swells and plunged along, eyes glued ahead to sight any obstacle that had to be avoided. At one point, they zoomed over a coastal steamer and missed hitting its bridge by what Nelson estimated was only thirty-five feet. The weather cleared slightly and the shoreline revealed several ships wrecked against the unforgiving rocks in years past. They passed many small fishing villages and were surprised to see the inhabitants waving as they passed by.

The wind had strengthened and it took nearly six hours to reach Hawkes Bay. The planes were towed to the moorings placed by the *Ausburn,* and the fliers were taken aboard for the night. The weather was discouraging at dawn the next day but cleared up quickly and they were off by 11 A.M. They passed the *Milwaukee, Brazos, McFarland, Cogland,* and *Richmond,* all plying their way along the route to Pictou. As they neared the small Nova Scotian town, they were met by a plane from the Royal Canadian Air Force and escorted to the harbor where they saw Wade's plane, the *Boston II,* floating peacefully. There were several American and Canadian destroyers there, all whistling a welcome, along with crowds of people waving along the waterfront.

They tied up at the buoys, refueled, and were met by Wade, Ogden, and Lts. Victor E. Bertrandias and George C. McDonald, who had flown the replacement

Cruiser from Virginia to Pictou. They were taken ashore, where despite Smith's message requesting that there be no such welcomes, the six men were placed in automobiles and joined a parade that included a Scotch band, bagpipers, American and Canadian sailors, and school children. The streets were decorated with flags, bunting, and signs at every corner welcoming the World Travelers. They soon discovered that they were en route to a park where the fliers were ushered to a decorated platform. Short speeches of welcome were made by local townsmen and each of the fliers said a few words of thanks for the reception. They were then taken to a hotel and were hosted later at a lobster party and dance.

The next day was too windy and rainy to attempt a flight. The Pictou Chamber of Commerce treated the fliers to a noon concert by the bagpipers and that evening they all boarded the *Patriot,* a Canadian destroyer, for another lobster banquet. They turned in early, anxious to leave the morning of 5 September for Boston.

In mid-August, assuming that the flight would successfully cross the Atlantic and arrive in Labrador, it was planned the planes could land at Eastport, Maine, in case of an emergency, whereas St. Johns, Newfoundland, was an original choice. In a memorandum to General Patrick, Major H. C. Pratt, now chief of the Air Service Training and War Plans Division, reported that Boston had been given to understand that the first landing in the United States would be made there and that any change would be sure to bring confusion and result in embarrassment to the Air Service. He sent a telegram telling Smith not to arrive in Boston earlier than 2 September.[6]

Permission had already been given to land at St. Johns, Newfoundland, two hundred miles from Boston and supplies and facilities were made available there. Smith disagreed with this plan and intended to lead the flight all the way to Boston.

The three planes left the harbor at Hawkes Bay at 11:15 A.M. on 6 September and headed west along the coast of Nova Scotia through a rain squall but then soon came out into good weather. After passing St. Johns, they ran into fog that got thicker as they progressed over large rocks and tiny islands. They tried to climb over it and under it, to no avail. Just before reaching Portland, Maine, visibility was down to a mere few feet. When they had a few narrow scrapes with trees on the islands, Smith decided it wasn't worth the risk just to get to Boston because the city fathers expected them to arrive that day. He turned back and headed inland for a few miles and landed in a sheltered cove on Casco Bay near Mere Point, Maine, a summer colony. They stayed that night in cabins offered by the local residents where photographers and reporters found them. They accommodated their requests and were kept busy running to the local store where the town's only telephone was located. Boy Scouts volunteered to stand watch over the Cruisers during the night.

The fliers were anxious to leave early on 7 September but a stiff head wind was blowing. Smith decided they should take on more gasoline to ensure getting to Boston without another landing. The fuel had to be bought from a commercial gas station in Brunswick, the nearest town. As they waited for it to be brought to them, ten de Havilland DH-4s arrived overhead and waggled their wings in greeting. The old DHs had been flown north to escort them to Boston and were led by General Patrick. Among the other pilots were Streett and Brown, two of the flight committee members. Seeing their old friends who had supported them so magnificently was a great thrill. As the planes flew low, Smith held up a funnel and a gas can to signal what was holding up their departure. After circling for awhile, the DH-4s flew to Old Orchard, Maine, to wait until the Cruisers came into view.[7]

The three Cruisers were off about noontime and after an uneventful flight arrived over Boston about 2 P.M. None of the men were prepared for what was in store for them when they circled the airport. Nelson explains:

> We all remembered the mere passing interest which the American public had taken in the remarkable flights from New York to Nome, to Puerto Rico and return, and the nonstop flight from New York to San Diego. After all, the receptions given to us in foreign countries were accorded to us mainly because we were representatives of the air force of the United States of America who had been entrusted with an important and somewhat spectacular mission. So as we winged our way down from Greenland we simply took it for granted that our countrymen would look upon our flight much as they had looked upon the others, and little did we dream that what in some respects was to be the most thrilling part of our journey still lay before us.[8]

There was a great crowd milling around the airport as they circled for an approach to the harbor. Every boat there was blowing its whistle in salute; fire boats spouted spears of water; U.S. Navy ships fired their guns; factories spewed smoke in salute. The three planes landed in the harbor with Smith leading while the escorts landed at the airport. While they watched from a Navy motor launch, their planes were towed to a Navy crane lighter and lifted onto the dock where the pontoons would be exchanged for wheels for the last time.

The six fliers were taken ashore where a huge cheering crowd waited. Someone shoved a microphone in Smith's face as he alighted and he looked at it in surprise. "What am I supposed to do with this?" he asked. These were his first words to a waiting American public that was listening in from coast to coast, including his parents in California. All he could think of to say was, "Hello, folks. I'm glad to be home."

A pretty young lady pushed her way through the crowd that surrounded the fliers and kissed Nelson on his bald head, then on each cheek. Neither he nor the others knew who she was but one thing was certain: it wasn't the woman whose picture Nelson had carried around the world. Nelson's brother Gunnar surged through the throng and surprised him with an enthusiastic Scandinavian hug. Out of the crowd came Squad. Ldr. Stuart MacLaren, the British flier, who thanked them for having his spare plane sent from the Kurile Islands to Burma by the American destroyer so he could complete his flight. He said that after losing his plane in Japan he was en route home to Britain now to plan another expedition around the world.

The six men signed the airport entry book and then were hustled into Rickenbacker automobiles, escorted by a cavalry guard, and driven to the state capitol building where they were officially greeted by the governor of Massachusetts, the mayor of Boston, the assistant secretary of war, General Patrick, and other military and political officials, all of whom made short speeches of welcome and congratulations. The fliers were given valuable presents and mementos and then boarded limousines for a fast ride through the city to the Boston Common with a police escort on motorcycles. Cheering crowds jammed the sidewalks on every street. Not having seen any newspapers in Iceland, Greenland, or Labrador, they had no idea that there would be this much public enthusiasm about what they had done when they reached America. They were off-loaded at the foot of a speakers' platform where reporters and photographers pushed forward shouting questions and requests for posing. They were presented with the keys to the city by Mayor James M. Curley; various individuals and groups gave them sabers, silver Paul Revere bowls, silver wings, American flags, and silver mesh bags for their mothers or girlfriends. When the mayor presented them with watches, he noted they were all inscribed, "In the future you will have no alibi for not arriving on time."

When the presentations were over, they were taken by motorcade to the Copley-Plaza Hotel where an entire floor had been reserved for them. Brown told them they were to have dinner that evening with General Patrick but as they went to their rooms, each wondered if their chief would appreciate being with them while they were still wearing their sweaty flying clothes. They were surprised to find that Brown and Streett had thoughtfully placed neatly pressed uniforms, clean shirts, and other clothing items in their respective closets. It was just one more example of the thoroughness and efficiency of their brother officers who had planned and carried out so many details to make the flight a success.

The next few hours were a blur of ringing telephones and people running in and out of the six rooms. It seemed the whole world was trying to get in touch with them for statements and invitations. Many telegrams were delivered, including one from Edward, Prince of Wales, asking the British consul in Boston to convey his warmest congratulations "on their wonderful achievement and safe return home."[9] Another arrived for General Patrick from England's King George V who asked Patrick to convey his congratulations and added, "I have followed with interest and admiration the progress of their heroic undertaking."[10]

With the bedlam of the afternoon in mind, guards were posted so the dinner that evening with General Patrick could be a quiet affair where they had the opportunity to tell him of their grand adventure. At one point, a radio microphone was brought in and each of the fliers was asked to comment on the flight. Smith wasn't pleased; he was not comfortable making speeches or speaking into a microphone. "Whenever I get in front of one of those instruments," he said, "my gas pump refuses to feed, lung compression drops to zero, my heart starts to knock, and the old think-box freezes."[11]

Smith admitted later that he was "uneasy and fidgety" about the reception they received from the Bostonians. Although grateful, he thought everyone seemed to think the flight was completed once they landed there. They still had to cross the continent via New York and Washington, D.C., to complete the flight officially at

Seattle and anything could happen to spoil the effort they had made so far. He very fortunately did not realize then how many more parades, receptions, speeches, banquets, and handshakes they would have to endure that would be more strenuous and fatiguing than the flight itself. Smith, ever anxious to complete his mission, was handed a cautionary letter from Major W. G. Kilner of the army adjutant general's office, indicating that Capt. Burdette S. Wright had been assigned as the flight's advance officer for the rest of the flight to Seattle and that Lt. George Goddard would accompany Burdette in another aircraft carrying a motion picture photographer.

"Our countrymen are very proud of you and your comrades," Kilner added, "and they will be eager to show you their appreciation for what you have done. Fortunately, it has been possible to prevail upon those waiting to welcome you in most of the cities through which you will pass en route to Seattle, to defer their plans for an elaborate welcome until after you have completed your mission.

"Nevertheless, some demands will be made upon you which cannot be avoided. In these cases, remember that the Air Service is just as anxious as you to bring your wonderful undertaking to a quick and successful conclusion but the eyes of the entire country will be critically focused upon you and your comrades and any show of resentment to what you may justly consider as unnecessary interference with the purpose of the flight will be noticed and commented upon."[12]

Smith was also instructed that on the route from Boston he was to fly over New London, Connecticut, the home town of Arnold, where a festival welcome would be going on as they passed overhead. Between Mitchel Field and Washington, he was also instructed to fly over Philadelphia because "the Air Service has promised that this will be done."[13]

It was 7 September, a Sunday, and the fliers were up at 4 A.M. to spend the day at the airport supervising the exchange of pontoons for wheels, refueling, and checking the planes thoroughly for the next leg to Mitchel Field, Long Island. A large crowd had gathered but were held at a distance by soldiers and police to allow the men to work. That night they packed their gear, arranged to have souvenirs and personal items shipped, and answered more phone calls. They conferred with Wright, the advance officer, about the arrangements and the schedule to be followed for the stops across the country. It was well after midnight before they could get to bed.

It was an exceptionally clear day on 8 September and the three planes were off at noon for Mitchel Field. They passed over Providence, Rhode Island, and New London, Connecticut, Arnold's home town. After passing Bridgeport, ten planes arrived to escort them to Mitchel Field; there was a passenger in each, including General Patrick, New York Senator James W. Wadsworth, and Erik's brother Gunnar. The formation flew over the center of Manhattan where traffic had stopped and thousands of people could be seen waving from the streets. In the harbor, boats of every description were blowing their whistles; fire boats gave the traditional water salutes. They flew over the Statue of Liberty in tribute, then turned east to Mitchel Field where automobiles jammed the roadways and the airport was absolutely covered with a large mass of people.

General Patrick and two planes accompanying him landed first and the crowd thought it was the World Fliers. The mob surged forward and covered the landing area so that the three Cruisers had to circle until the field was cleared by soldiers. As soon as they landed and tried to taxi, the crowd broke through the restraining lines and surrounded them. As the pilots quickly shut off the engines and dismounted from their planes, they had to shout at the aggressive spectators sternly and push souvenir hunters away who were trying to cut the planes' fabric and take away any equipment that could be easily dismantled. The fliers were eventually rescued by police and escorted to a speakers' stand where they met Charles Nungesser, famous French ace. The Prince of Wales was escorted through the crowd and congratulated each flier with a handshake and said, "Shall we settle our bets, gentlemen?" Senator Wadsworth and others made speeches but Wadsworth's was the most memorable.

> If our hospitality seems ferocious, forgive us because it comes from the heart. You will find as you proceed along the home stretch that these receptions are the first evidence what all Americans long to show you. The world never forgets its pathfinders. Those who trod the wilderness and cross the seas filled with dangers are never forgotten by posterity.[14]

The senator then presented them with the handsomest engraved green-gold cigarette cases the fliers had ever seen. On one side was a platinum replica of a World Cruiser; the other side depicted the route they had flown and the places they had stopped. That night they were given a reception and buffet dinner in the quarters of Col. William Hensley, the base commander, and attended a dance at the officers' club where they were treated to a surprise showing of movies made at the different stops since their arrival in North America. Afterward, even though tired from the day's activities, several of them made a quick trip into New York City "to see the bright lights once more."[15]

The three Cruisers and their ten escorts left Mitchel Field next morning at 9:30 A.M. headed for Washington, D.C., and plunged into a strong head wind, so strong that they made a ground speed of only 35 mph. They flew over Philadelphia and stopped at Aberdeen, Maryland, so the escorts in their short-range de Havillands could gas up and were met there by Gen. Billy Mitchell, Assistant Chief of the Air Service. Resuming the flight, the planes took off and ran into rain over Baltimore. Eight miles south of the city, the engine of the *New Orleans* suddenly quit without warning and Nelson made a smooth forced landing in a large pasture. General Patrick and several other escort planes landed beside him while the other two Cruisers circled.

Knowing that President Coolidge and his cabinet were waiting for them at Bolling Field in Washington, General Patrick decided that Nelson should take the escort plane. This was piloted by Lt. Louis Meister, who had carried Gunnar Nelson, Erik's brother, in the passenger seat. The Nelson brothers then continued the

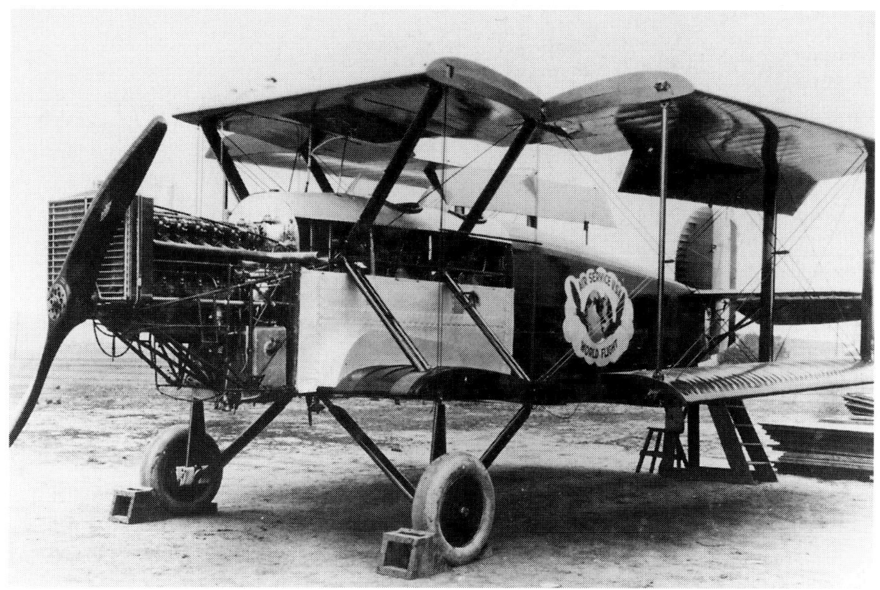


*Above:* The Douglas World Cruisers were modified versions of DT-2 Navy torpedo planes and were powered by 12-cylinder Liberty engines reconditioned from Army Air Service stocks. They had dual controls and could be fitted with wheels and pontoons. (Photo: U.S. Air Force)

*Below:* Three-quarter front view shows wings folded and engine without the cowling. The engine had two types of coolers: one for hot climates and a smaller one for arctic flying. (Photo: McDonnell Douglas Company)

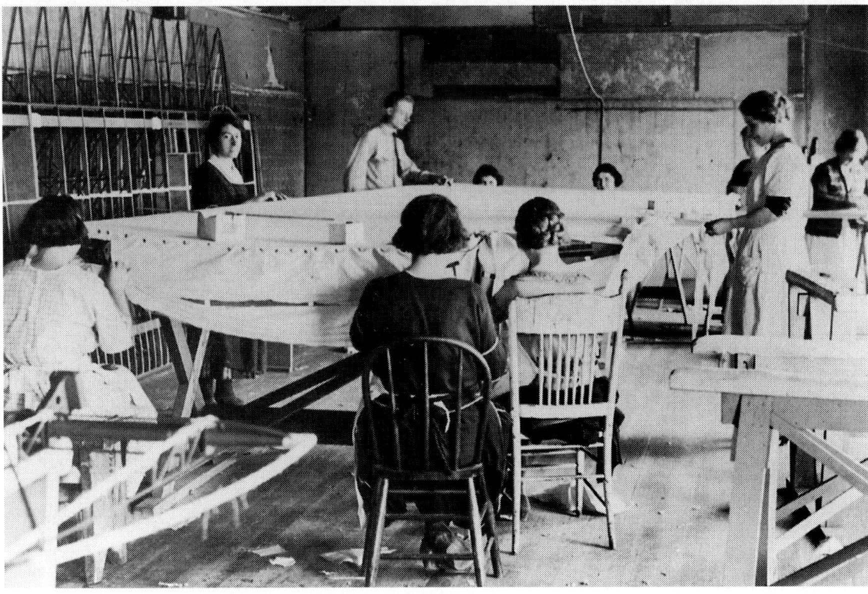

*Above:* Seven of the original World Flight crew members pose in their winter flying suits. *Left to right:* Sgt. Arthur Turner, Sgt. Henry H. Ogden, Lt. Leslie P. Arnold (who replaced Turner), Lt. Leigh Wade, Lt. Lowell H. Smith, Maj. Frederick L. Martin, Sgt. Alva L. Harvey. *Not shown:* Lt. Erik H. Nelson and Lt. John Harding Jr. (Photo: U.S. Air Force)

*Below:* Women sew cloth on wings of a World Cruiser. The work was pushed ahead rapidly so the planes could depart from Santa Monica on 15 March 1924. (Photo: McDonnell Douglas Company)

*Above:* The *Seattle (right)* has had the pontoon installation completed before the official departure from Lake Washington, while the *Chicago* waits its turn. Wheels would not replace the pontoons until the planes reached Calcutta, India. (Photo: U.S. Air Force)

*Below:* Major Martin and Sergeant Harvey at Kanatak, Alaska, after the *Seattle* had an engine failure. The U.S. Coast Guard rushed a new engine to them which they installed and resumed the flight. (Photo: U.S. Air Force)

Fuel and oil for the World Cruisers while in Alaskan waters was transported by U.S. Navy, U.S. Coast Guard, and a Bureau of Fisheries ship. Cooperation of these organizations was essential for the transit of the planes through the Aleutians to Japan. (Photo: U.S. Coast Guard)

Two views of the *Seattle* after it crashed into a mountain on the Alaskan Peninsula during the flight from Chignik to Dutch Harbor. Martin and Harvey suffered only minor injuries but the plane was totally destroyed. Years later, the engine and parts of the plane were brought to Anchorage and are on display at the Alaska Aviation Heritage Museum at Lake Hood, Anchorage. (Photo: U.S. Air Force)

Major Martin and Sergeant Harvey traveled for ten days after the *Seattle* crashed. They eventually found their way to a cannery at Port Moller on the Bering Sea side of the Alaska Peninsula. (Photo: U.S. Air Force)

The *Chicago, Boston*, and *New Orleans* are pulled up on the beach at Dutch Harbor to protect them from the frequently violent williwaws. (Photo: U.S. Air Force Museum)

*Above:* Two ships that helped the World Fliers were *(left)* the USS *Brookdale* and the *Eider,* The *Eider* was provided by the U.S. Bureau of Fisheries. (Photo: Wade/Morrow Collection, U.S. Air Force Academy)

*Below:* The World Fliers relax at the large Japanese naval air station at Kasumigaura while waiting for transportation to extensive welcoming activities in Tokyo. Nelson *(holding map)* confers with a Japanese naval officer about the route to Kushimoto, the next stop. (Photo: Wade/Morrow Collection, U.S. Air Force Academy)

Three of the four Cruisers *(top photo)* are pulled up on the Resurrection Bay beach at Seward, Alaska, for protection from wind and high waves. En route to the next stop, the *Seattle* had engine failure and landed at Cape Igvak near Kanatak. (Photo: Wade/Morrow Collection, U.S. Air Force Academy)

Thousands *(right photo)* of Chinese junks and sampans crowd the harbor at Shanghai, China. They posed a great danger when they deliberately crossed the takeoff paths of the planes. (Photo: Peter M. Bowers Collection)

The engine of the *Chicago* (*bottom photo*) is changed at Hue, French Indochina (now Vietnam), with the help of American sailors under the supervision of Smith and Arnold. The bridge allows for the engine to be dropped into place. (Photo: U.S. Air Force)

*Above:* Lts. Lowell Smith and Leslie Arnold wait for a boat to take them ashore at Saigon, then known as the “Paris of the Orient.” The crews were invited to several social events by the French and had to borrow white shirts and trousers from U.S. Navy officers. (Photo: Mobil Oil Company)

*Left:* Erik Nelson and John Harding in the *New Orleans* nearly had a forced landing when an engine connecting rod broke, splattering oil over the plane during the flight from Multan to Karachi, India. Nelson was able to nurse the plane for nearly an hour to a safe landing. (Photos: U.S. Air Force)

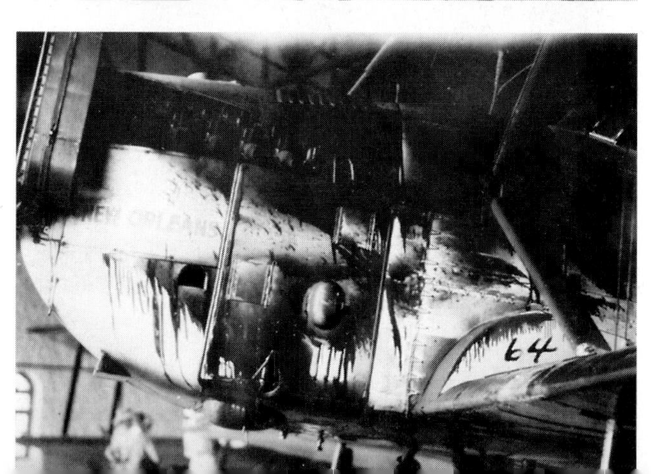

*Above:* American sailors from the destroyer *Hart* assist the fliers at the Maidan, a large park in Calcutta, India (now Pakistan). Wheels replaced the pontoons here and the planes were overhauled. (Photo: U.S. Air Force)

*Below:* The fliers were greeted by the largest crowd at Vienna, Austria, since leaving Japan but were able to stay only one night. Viennese of all ages pose happily for the camera. (Photo: U.S. Air Force)

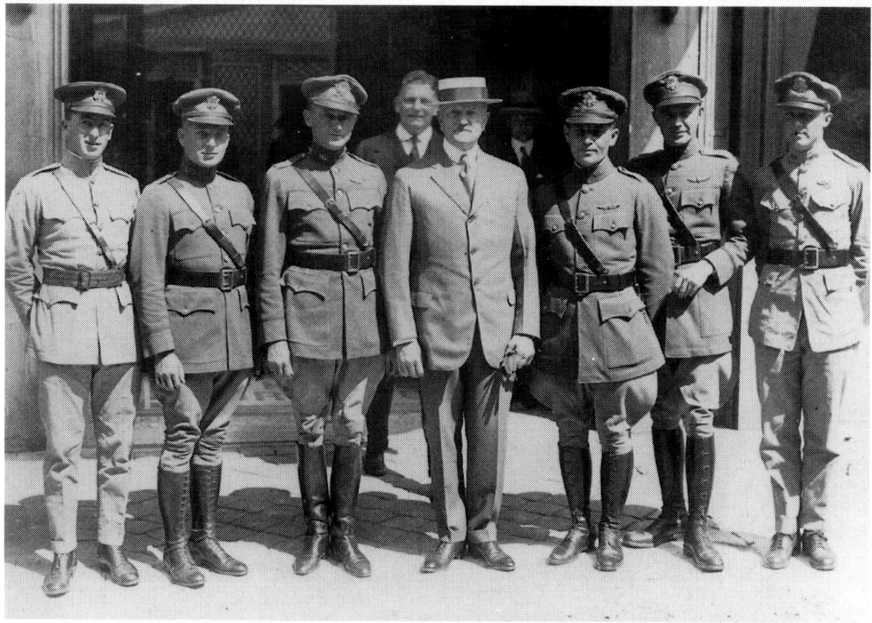

*Above:* Henry Ogden, promoted from sergeant to second lieutenant during the flight, completes filling the oil tank of the *Boston* at Le Bourget Airport in Paris. (Photo: U.S. Air Force)

*Below:* The World Fliers met in Paris with Gen. John J. Pershing, leader of the Allied Expeditionary Forces during World War One. *Left to right:* Lts. Henry Ogden, Leslie Arnold, Lowell Smith, General Pershing, Lts. Leigh Wade, Erik Nelson, and John Harding Jr. (Photo: U.S. Air Force)

*Above:* One of the World Cruisers flies formation with a British passenger plane en route from Paris to London. French planes escorted the Cruisers to the English Channel. (Photo: U.S. Air Force)

*Below:* A crowd surrounds the fliers and planes when they arrived at Croydon Airport near London. Many were American tourists who had departed at the same time from Paris and were allowed to greet the fliers. Others were restrained behind a fence at left. (Photo: U.S. Air Force)

*Above:* The *New Orleans* is readied for towing through the streets of Reykjavik, Iceland, for maintenance with the help of sailors from the *Richmond.* (Photo: U.S. Air Force)

*Middle:* The *New Orleans* is towed through the streets of Reykjavik, Iceland, before an admiring crowd. The crews were surprised to find that the city was very modern and that most of the inhabitants could speak English. (Photo: U.S. Air Force)

*Below:* The damaged *Boston* was towed to land until it became too dangerous. Wade made the decision to cut the tow lines from the *Richmond* loose and allow the plane to sink. Wade and Ogden would be given the prototype aircraft, named the *Boston II,* and permitted to join the other two planes at Nova Scotia. (Photo: U.S. Air Force)

*Above:* A World Cruiser lands near an iceberg in the harbor at Frederiksdal, Greenland. The 830-mile flight from Reykjavik, Iceland, to Frederiksdal was the longest nonstop flight of the whole journey. (Photo: U.S. Air Force)

*Below: Seattle, New Orleans,* and *Boston II* fly down the Hudson River to Manhattan and the New York harbor on 8 September 1924. They landed at Mitchel Field, Long Island, before a large crowd that included the Prince of Wales. (Photo: U.S. Air Force)

*Above left:* President Calvin Coolidge greets Lt. Leslie Arnold as Secretary of War John W. Weeks looks on. To the left is Herbert Hoover, who was then Secretary of Commerce. (Photo: U.S. Air Force)

*Above right:* Lowell Smith speaks at welcoming ceremonies at San Diego. The city claimed that the World Flight started there, rather than at Santa Monica or Seattle. (Photo: Wade/Morrow Collection, U.S. Air Force Academy)

*Below:* The single-engine *New Orleans* is parked beside a Pan American four-engine Boeing 707-321 after the intercontinental jet transport completed a world flight in 2½ days in 1959. The World Cruiser was borrowed from the Air Force Museum for a special event before being returned to Dayton in an Air Force transport. (Photo: Pan American World Airways System)

*Above:* The small country of Monaco issued a stamp honoring the World Flight on the fortieth anniversary in 1964. A U.S. Postal Service committee turned down a commemorative stamp on the flight's fiftieth anniversary as not being of sufficient public interest. (Photo: C. V. Glines)

*Below:* President Calvin Coolidge *(in raincoat)* and Secretary of War John W. Weeks pose with five of the world fliers at Bolling Field, Washington, D.C., on 9 September 1924. (Photo: U.S. Air Force)

*Above:* A rare photograph of the four World Cruisers on wheels after their christening at Seattle in April 1924. Shortly thereafter pontoons were attached and the *Seattle* crashed on a mountainside in Alaska. (Photo: U.S. Air Force Museum)

*Below:* The *Chicago* passes a cargo ship along the east coast of North America before landing at Boston, where the pontoons were exchanged for wheels for the last time. (Photo: Wade/Morrow Collection, U.S. Air Force Academy)

flight together. Harding would remain with the *New Orleans* and see that the engine was repaired or replaced. The nonscheduled stop at Aberdeen and Nelson's forced landing meant that their arrival in Washington would be about three hours late.

It was still raining when the two Cruisers circled Bolling Field and landed at 3:55 P.M., followed by the escorts. Smith and the others parked hurriedly and were greeted by the president and Mrs. Coolidge and most of his cabinet members. They had been waiting in the rain so patiently since 11 A.M. Although the president had many appointments scheduled, he sent aides to the White House to apologize and change his schedule. When one of them suggested that he might like to leave, he said, "Not on your life. I'll wait all day if necessary."[16] This was a compliment that all the fliers appreciated. It was the first time in history that a president had ever left the White House to greet American citizens to Washington.

The president shook hands with the five fliers and asked many questions. Smith then showed the president and Secretary of War Weeks around and inside the *Chicago* and explained how things worked. Gen. Billy Mitchell arrived from Aberdeen resplendent in uniform, including spurs and a riding crop. He talked briefly with the crews and was surrounded by newspapermen who wanted to take note of any remarks he might make about the flight. The *New Orleans* meantime had been repaired by Harding overnight in the pasture and was flown to Bolling Field. Harding then joined the others in the welcoming activities.

The fliers were guests that evening of General Patrick at the Army-Navy Country Club where Secretary Weeks, generals, admirals, and other notables were present. The next day they made an official call at the White House, then assembled in General Patrick's office in the War Department. They visited General Pershing in his office where they received his compliments on their achievement and were introduced to the army adjutant general and other top Army staff members. That afternoon the three pilots went to Walter Reed Hospital to visit injured Army personnel while the mechanics returned to Bolling to prepare their planes for Defense Day activities.

The fliers remained in Washington for the next three days to grant interview requests from press and radio reporters and participate in Defense Day ceremonies on 12 September. During the activities in Washington, Gen. Billy Mitchell introduced the airmen to the young journalist named Lowell Thomas and recommended that they cooperate with him as the World Flight historian. Thomas was permitted to follow the fliers as a passenger in Army Air Service aircraft for the rest of their trip to Seattle and their return to McCook Field.

The resulting book, *The First World Flight* with the crews' personal accounts, was published the following year and became a best seller. It marked the continuation of recognition for the then-32-year-old journalist who became world famous as a radio/television commentator, lecturer, and writer. He had been a war correspondent during World War I and President Woodrow Wilson had appointed him to head a civilian mission to Europe to prepare a historical record of the war. His book on the World Flight is extremely valuable today as its major record not only because it is well written but because it contains extensive quotations provided by the fliers from interviews Thomas had conducted soon after they returned to American soil when their memories were fresh.

All other air traffic around Washington was halted on 12 September as the three Cruisers took off at 1:15 P.M. and flew in formation over the city, then across the Potomac River to Arlington National Cemetery where they dropped flowers on the amphitheater containing the tomb of the Unknown Soldier. They took another route around the city to return to Bolling Field so more people on the ground could see them. They landed and were immediately ushered into limousines and joined the parade on Pennsylvania Ave. They dropped from the parade at the Ellipse and joined President Coolidge, General Pershing, and other dignitaries reviewing the parading troops from the stands in front of the White House.

"The reception and applause given to us all along the line of march was wonderful," Arnold wrote. "And to be so received by our own people thrilled us all. It was probably the greatest moment in our lives and never again will we reach as high a pinnacle."[17]

The departure for Dayton next day was made in marginal weather, but all were fatigued by all the attention that had been directed to them and were very willing to press on. Five escorting planes joined them as Smith led the flight heading west. Between Cumberland, Maryland and Uniontown, Pennsylvania, they ran into heavy fog near Harpers Ferry and the escorts left hurriedly. Smith deviated to the north and flew through the valleys hugging the treetops and telephone poles and following the railroad. About eighty miles east of Dayton the first escort planes from McCook Field joined the Cruisers. The number of planes increased until there were about twenty flying formation with them, including the Barling XNBL-1, a giant, one-of-a-kind, six-engine bomber, flown by Lt. Harold Harris.[18]

They saw that they were in for another big welcome when they flew over McCook Field, then the Air Service's major aircraft evaluation center where three of the six men (Nelson, Wade, and Harding) were stationed before the flight. "WELCOME WORLD FLIERS" had been laid out in huge white letters on the ramp and a crowd estimated at nearly 10,000 was milling around waiting for their arrival. They were swamped with shouted greetings from old friends when they dismounted from their cockpits; Major Martin and Harvey quickly emerged from the crowd to extend their congratulations. Handsome "Smiling Jack" Harding was set upon immediately by fellow mechanics he had worked with for several years. They all yelled for him to share souvenirs they claimed he must have stashed away during the trip. When he said he had only himself to offer, they flipped him upside down and shook all the tools out of his flight suit pockets to keep as mementos of his trip. A comely young lady broke through the crowd, threw her arms around him, and kissed him firmly. It was a scene his fellow fliers had seen before and would witness many times later. He always claimed they were "cousins." The hours that followed were filled with presentations of flowers, Liberty bonds, traveling bags, and other welcoming gifts. Nelson was happy to see Nome, his Siberian sled dog, that he had carried with him in the cockpit of his de Havilland on the return from the highly successful New York–Nome round trip flight in 1920.

Mechanics meanwhile rolled the planes into a hangar and inspected every nut, bolt, wire, and piece of fabric to see how the planes had held up. They worked in shifts round the clock for two days and replaced anything that showed any wear and tear. The planes were then pronounced ready to continue. It was the first time the fliers had allowed anyone to work on their planes without their presence since they had started.

Nor were the men themselves immune from having themselves inspected. They were subjected to a rigorous physical examination at the base hospital, similar to the one given to aviation cadets before acceptance for flying training. They all passed but admitted they were very tired.

A citation was presented to "the conquerors of the World's uncharted aerial sea" by the City of Dayton, the Dayton Chamber of Commerce, and the Dayton Chapter of the National Aeronautic Association, welcoming them "to the Birth Place of the Airplane." It stated:

> All Dayton pours forth the warmest greetings of her heart, born of an understanding of the trials of flying. What you have endured, we shall probably never know, but posterity will never cease to recall what you have accomplished. Even while we have watched distance annihilated under the wings of the airplane upon this continent, by spanning it from dawn to dusk you have linked by air the nations of the world bringing all mankind within the scope of aerial navigation. As you near the end of your voyage, our emotions are only restrained by your wishes. We await your return to the International Air Races to express fittingly our full appreciation of what you have done.

Smith had decided earlier, after discussions with General Patrick, that they would not follow the originally planned route to Seattle by following the airmail route over the Rocky Mountains via Cheyenne, Wyoming, and Salt Lake City. The lowest point of the Continental Divide was 6,500 feet and the mail planes had to fly sometimes at eight or nine thousand feet to clear the mountains. Smith wanted to avoid the risks that were associated with the higher altitudes and the summer thunderstorms. They would fly to Chicago as originally intended but then head southwest to Dallas, west to San Diego, then north to Seattle. Lts. George A. Goddard and John A. Brockhurst, flying a specially modified de Havilland DH-9 would continue to photograph their flight across the country to Seattle. In another plane was Capt. Burdette S. "Birdie" Wright, the advance officer, who preceded the Cruisers to every stop to make arrangements for their arrival.

It had been obvious since their return to the States that the fliers would be asked to make many talks about their adventure to civilian audiences. General Patrick furnished each with a three-page "talking paper" that provided points they could use in preparation. Included were the purpose of the flight and the intended benefits. More important, there was information about the current condition of the Air

Service, why aircraft were needed in times of peace, and the need for a separate promotion system for Air Service officers. "Most of the flying officers in the Army Air Service are men who came into the Army upon entry of the United States in the great war," the paper stated. "A deplorable condition now exists because these Air Service officers are so far down on the promotion list of the Army that they are outranked by officers in other branches who are younger than they and who have not had their length of service. This is directly due to the fact that, because of the technical requirements for officers in the Air Service, it became necessary for these men to undergo a longer period of training than was necessary to qualify for a commission in any other branch. This makes promotion in our branch very slow, and so discouraging that a great many valuable officers have resigned because they see no possible future advancement in their chosen profession."[19]

The three Cruisers left McCook Field for Chicago on 15 September and followed the railroad lines that all seemed to point toward their destination. Huge crowds had seen them off and even larger crowds were waiting in Chicago. They landed in midafternoon at the Maywood airmail field outside the city. Crowds converged on the planes but policemen formed a cordon around the fliers and they were hurried into limousines and taken at high speeds with a motorcycle escort, sirens screaming, to the Drake Hotel. That evening at a large banquet at the Chicago Beach Hotel, they were presented with engraved cigarette boxes filled with five dollar gold coins. Inside were cards saying, "May this box never be empty. Enclosed is the wherewithal to keep it filled."

They hoped to get off next morning but a heavy fog hung in all day long. They remained at the hotel that night but were off the next morning for Omaha, 460 miles away. They landed at Jarvis Offutt Field, the Army airport at Fort Crook, and again crowds converged on the planes and their crews while soldiers tried to hold them off. There was the usual dinner, speeches by local dignitaries, and presentation of souvenir medals and cigarette cases. Special entertainment was planned by Gould Dietz, their designated host, that pleased them more than the food and speeches. The citizens of Omaha chose a queen and five ladies-in-waiting who were to be hostesses for the six fliers.

"Instead of shaking hands for hours," Nelson explained, "we held one hand the whole evening. Instead of returning thanks to a civic welcome in stuttering sentences, we spoke in the more eloquent language of the eyes. The idea met with our unanimous and enthusiastic approval."[20]

The planes were off next morning for the short 125-mile hop down the Missouri River to St. Joseph, Missouri, after a crowd-pleasing aerobatic show by Lt. Reuben Moffatt. They stayed there long enough for a luncheon sponsored by a civic club and then departed for Muskogee, Oklahoma, where they received what they agreed was one of the warmest welcomes from a small community. En route to a landing at Hat Box Field, they were met by a large number of planes and, although Muskogee was a small town, there was a large group of fully-loaded chartered passenger buses that had converged there in greeting. That evening the fliers were given a banquet and presented with gold medallions for their "intrepid flying skill."

The next stop was Love Field at Dallas, Texas, which had been a World War I pilot training field and was growing into a large commercial airport. They had awakened to a heavy wind and rainstorm that blew in the windows of their hotel. They somehow managed to get off late in the morning despite the airfield being like a huge lake, and bucked heavy winds that slowed their planes to a paltry 45 mph. A passenger train passed below them at one point, seeming to mock the speed that airmen bragged about for their machines versus all ground transportation. They were met at Dallas by a large crowd, all straining to shake hands, touch their planes, and talk with the airmen. There was another banquet that night and more unexpected gifts from Dallas citizens.

The plan was to take off with plenty of gasoline and fly to El Paso, a 645-mile trip against strong head winds. But oil pump trouble on the *Boston II*'s engine caused them to land at Sweetwater to make repairs and take on more fuel, oil, and water. Although their stop was unexpected, airport personnel rustled up a picnic lunch and the fliers continued westward after only an hour on the ground.

El Paso was nearly in view when the photographic plane with Goddard and Brockhurst made a forced landing that badly damaged their plane. They were rescued by "Birdie" Wright flying a DH-9 and were dropped off at Pecos, Texas. They rented an ancient automobile, drove all night, and hurried to an airport along the Rio Grande where they borrowed another plane and caught up with the Cruisers in El Paso.

The landing at El Paso was made at dusk and once more waiting crowds surged through the police lines and surrounded the men so they couldn't service their planes promptly as they always insisted on doing soon after landing. It was state-fair time and they were given a banquet that night and more presents such as serapes that symbolized the culture and arts of the local area. The admiration and respect the public there felt for the fliers were clear.

They were off on 22 September at 7:15 A.M. for Tucson, Arizona, and it was the same pattern there when they landed: surging crowds, a fast ride to a hotel, a banquet, and presents of local significance. They left Tucson next day and crossed over the Crater and Growler mountains. Each man was lost in his own thoughts as they got closer to the coast. Smith, in a rare pensive mood, described what he felt to Lowell Thomas, the official historian for the flight:

> Every minute was bringing us a mile and a half nearer my California home, just over the desert's rim. We had been gone a long time. We had crossed vast continents and distant seas. We had passed through experiences when we lived a lifetime in a day. And now, on this radiant morning, San Diego lay ahead! When our wheels touched the soil of Coronado Island we had been around the world. How can I describe it? Ten years hence, perhaps. But now it seems like a dream.[21]

The citizens of San Diego considered their city the starting point of the World Flight and were prepared to show the fliers that they deserved that honor. They had been preparing for their arrival for several weeks and touted it as the biggest celebration in the city's history. At 9:20 A.M., announcements were made that the planes would arrive an hour and a half earlier than planned so only a few people were on the field when they landed. Boats, buses, cars, and airplanes quickly converged on Rockwell Field and the roads leading to it were jammed with traffic. Air Service planes were hurriedly launched. The first ones intercepted the Cruisers about a hundred miles out; eventually twenty-five planes were airborne to meet the homecoming heroes.

Smith wanted all three planes to land together so they got into a three-ship line-abreast formation and touched down at the same instant on Rockwell Field. As Smith shut his engine down, Major Fitzgerald, the base commander, mounted the *Chicago*'s wing and extended his hand in greeting. "Let me get down, Major, I want to get to my parents," Smith said. Fitzgerald beckoned and Jasper and Roberta Smith, who had driven down from Los Angeles the night before, pushed through the crowd and gave him great welcome hugs. Harding was also happily greeted by his mother and everyone posed for photographers.

The fliers were taken that afternoon to the stadium at Balboa Park where they received their largest reception so far with 35,000 people filling the seats. As the fliers ascended the stadium steps, a group of high school girls placed flowers around their necks and a band struck up a tune of welcome. There were speeches by military officers and local politicians, including San Diego's Mayor Bacon, who declared, "I would rather stand in your shoes today than be president of the United States."[22] Adm. Ashley R. Robertson spoke the most succinctly of all. "Probably in the near future others will fly around the world," he said, "but there will never again be a first time."[23]

San Diegoans honestly believed that the fliers had completed their circle of the world when they landed there. The rationalization was stated by Louis J. Arland, president of the junior chamber of commerce. "Whatever the official records may show as to the starting and ending of the World Flight," he said, "the close student of aviation history will realize that the prelude which made possible this magnificent achievement occurred on August 28, 1923, and the real termination of the World Flight was made this morning at Rockwell Field. For, after that memorable day in August when Lowell Smith and John Paul Richter electrified the world by the successful consummation of their midair refueling experiment, recognition of Lowell's superb flying ability could no longer be denied and inevitably led to his ultimate selection for the World Flight squadron."[24]

Smith responded in what was probably the longest speech he ever delivered during the flight. "All six of us are glad to be back in San Diego," he said. "None of us is gifted with words to express his feelings fully. We all got a big thrill this morning when we flew over the mountains and, side by side, came down and crossed for the first time a line that we had crossed before on this flight. It is a pleasure to have our planes again in a hangar in which they have been before. We cannot express our great satisfaction in the flight. Other officers of the Air Service could have done as well. We simply did it for the service."[25]

The fliers were presented with a large silver service set inscribed individually. Erik Nelson received a special gift from a group of fellow Swedes: a valuable antique copper coin that weighed four pounds. They were given rooms at the famous Hotel del Coronado where a party was held for Smith by old friends. The others went to a dance. During the night, new engines were installed on all three planes; it was only the second time they had allowed anyone else to perform maintenance on them without their presence.

The three planes left in the early afternoon of 23 September for the 115-mile flight to Santa Monica's Clover Field, home of the Douglas Company and the second city that claimed to have the honor as the starting place for the flight. A large number of planes from the San Diego Naval Air Station, Rockwell Field, and San Francisco's Crissy Field escorted them for the entire distance.

The scene at Clover Field in Santa Monica was the same as at San Diego, only there were an estimated 200,000 people crowded onto the field and the surrounding area, all trying to get a glimpse of the famous planes and their crews. A Los Angeles newspaper editorial stated, "Moses's flight into Egypt with the Children of Israel was an orderly procession compared to the army of enthusiasts that stampeded on Clover Field today."[26]

A grandstand had been erected on one side of the field fronted by an enclosure; truckloads of roses had been carefully laid out. The planes taxied to the area marked out for parking where a large line of guards was waiting. Smith described their arrival:

> As we crawled out of our cockpits, the crowd went wild. With a roar, they knocked down the fence. They knocked down the police. They knocked down the soldiers. They knocked us down. They tried to pull our ships apart for souvenirs, but somehow we fought them off. Los Angeles had a pot of gold waiting for us in the grandstand, we were told, symbolizing our arrival at the end of the rainbow. But we had as hard a time reaching it as the Forty-Niners had in winning gold from the soil of California. Burly policemen helped us on our way. People were tearing bits off our clothes and snipping off buttons for souvenirs. One lady cut a chunk of my collar with a penknife. And another got hold of my ear—I suppose by mistake. Somebody else took a keepsake out of the seat of my trousers. Luckily I had my old friend "Dutch" Henry for my bodyguard or I might have fared far worse.[27]

Smith wasn't the only one being besieged by the aggressive crowd. Harding and Arnold were being pawed by a dozen giggling young women; kisses were planted on Nelson's bald head. Burdette Wright, the advance officer, tried vainly to fight off the ladies who thought he was one of the World Fliers.

Leigh Wade struggled to get out of the grasp of a particularly husky, overenthusiastic man. In the skirmish he felt sudden pain in his sides and pushed away in distress. He later found that three ribs had been cracked. He said the enthusiasm of the welcome was a good feeling but it was countered by the three very sore ribs he received as a result. When Nelson wrestled himself away, he tried to locate Donald Douglas in the crowd. "I want to congratulate that boy." he shouted. "He sure does know how to build airplanes!"

No work could be done on the planes that night because of the harassing souvenir hunters and photographers so the fliers were motored into Hollywood to stay at the Christie Hotel. When they had been at the Douglas plant before the flight, they had tried to get rooms at several hotels nearby. An Air Service officer stationed there had asked for special rates for the fliers but he was refused. Yet one hotel owner in a Los Angeles suburb named Christie said he considered it an honor to give a special rate to those who had been chosen for the World Flight. When they had reached Boston and it seemed certain they would be able to complete the flight, several hotels in the Los Angeles area wired them offering free suites, hoping to gain publicity from their visit. They refused to consider the offers and stayed at the Christie Hotel where they occupied the same rooms they had used before the flight. When they checked in, they found a silver engraved plate on each door already noting which flier had stayed in that room upon completion of the flight.

There was an eight-column editorial of welcome in a Los Angeles paper that day hailing the achievement: "World Fliers, greetings! In the great battle with mechanics and the elements you may have overlooked the fact that your great achievement will go down in history along with those monumental feats which had recorded human progress. Today your names are household words and in the public schools of our country there is a splendid and youthful glamour attendant upon the mention of your flight. You are young now. The glory and the satisfaction of achievement is yours. But in other days and years to come, when you are old men and memories take the place of achievement and world flying has become an everyday instance, a great contentment shall be yours. You were first!"[28]

Next stop was San Francisco where the fliers headed for Crissy Field. En route the *Boston II* had generator failure and had to make a forced landing at a fairground a few miles south of the city. The *Chicago* and *New Orleans* circled and continued to Crissy Field when Wade and Ogden signaled that they were solving the problem, and landed at 3:10 P.M.

A young truck driver saw the *Boston II* land and offered help. When Wade explained that he needed a new battery, they found that his truck battery was similar and could be used on the Cruiser. They exchanged batteries but the man refused payment and said he was glad he could help. *Boston II* continued to Crissy Field to join the others. The engine ran very roughly and lacked sufficient power so Wade made arrangements for an engine change with Maj. Delos C. Emmons, the base commander.

Wade was grateful for the lad's assistance and had invited him to his hotel in the city that evening. When they met, Wade asked if there was anything he could do to repay him for his help. He replied that he would like to learn to fly. Wade told him that if he would go to March Field at Riverside, California, there would be a letter waiting for him recommending he be given a flight test to see if he was really suited for flying. He was. His name was Paul Mantz, who later became world-famous as a racing and movie stunt pilot.

The arrival at San Francisco was far different from their arrival at Santa Monica. Several hundred soldiers guarded the parking ramp from the large, well-behaved crowd and only a few local dignitaries were permitted near the fliers as they serviced their planes. They motored into the city without a parade to the St. Francis Hotel. Mayor James Rolph and the city fathers had planned a large series of dinners and entertainment for them, but Smith urgently requested that the entertainment be postponed until they returned from Seattle. They did meet with the mayor who presented them each with checks for $1,250.

Before their arrival, an unsigned editorial in a San Francisco newspaper criticized the Air Service for making the flight and stated that it was costing the taxpayers five million dollars.[29] The actual cost was reported to be $67,000 for expenses other than the purchase of the planes, engines, supplies, and spare parts.

The engine change on the *Boston II* required that the fliers remain an extra day so everyone slept late and went to the theater that evening. They departed Crissy Field at 9 A.M. in excellent weather on 27 September for Eugene, Oregon, a 420-mile trip. Smith called it his "second home" and was greeted by many friends who paid no attention to his request for a quiet welcome. Oregon's Governor Pierce and Mayor Parks were the instigators of a large reception and citizens had journeyed from all over the state to see them.

The fliers were getting nervous about making the last 240 miles of the trip safely. They left Eugene in midmorning of 28 September and while approaching Vancouver, Washington, the *Boston II* had trouble with the oil pump and landed at the Vancouver Barracks Field. The trouble was remedied quickly and the three planes took off in a V-formation for the final leg of their great adventure. Mount Rainier was shining in all its glory like a homing beacon. As they neared the Seattle area, Smith formed the planes in a line-abreast formation so that each plane would land at the same time as they had done at San Diego.

Although the fliers were assured that there would be a crowd waiting when they landed at the Sand Point Field, they were surprised by the huge numbers of welcomers that jammed onto the small airport. A welcome sign twenty feet high and one hundred fifty feet long was laid out on the ground. The planes taxied to the reviewing stand where a reception committee waited.

An estimated fifty thousand spectators witnessed the landings and swarmed around the fliers as they tried to climb down from their cockpits. A twenty-one-gun salute of French seventy-five artillery pieces was fired by soldiers from the 148th Field Artillery, a tribute that was normally reserved for presidents and sovereigns of foreign nations and members of royalty. Each was handed a bouquet of dahlias as reporters began shouting questions and photographers vied for position.

Shortly after alighting from their planes the six aviators were each handed the following telegram from President Coolidge: "On final completion of your flight, I desire to again offer my congratulations and express to you the thanks of the country. Under the law I do not understand that I have authority suitable to reward you by promotion and other appropriate action. I wish, however, to announce to you that on the convening of Congress I shall recommend that such authority by granted in order that your distinguished services may have a practical recognition from your country."

The next hour was a blur of speeches and presentation of mementos; among the latter were rings for each of them made of platinum and gold set with bloodstones that had been made in Alaska. They were then escorted to a yacht for a reception and more speeches. One of the most memorable was that delivered by Major Martin who was gracious in his praise of the men he had wanted so much to lead all the way around. He was in tears as he spoke of the contribution his men had made to aviation progress and was cheered as he concluded. When the informal ceremonies were over, the fliers were taken to Madison Park where they were greeted by about 5,000 persons, then were motored to Volunteer Park for a formal reception by 50,000 cheering spectators.

The successful completion of the flight made headlines around the world. Perhaps *The Times* of London summarized the accomplishment best: "It can hardly be supposed that there will not be fresh attempts, but the glory of being first will remain with the Americans. Nor should their achievement be judged too narrowly by utilitarian standards. The challenge thrown down by the sphericity of the earth was bound to be answered by airmen as it was generations ago by seamen. As a provocation it is like that of the North Pole or of Everest. It is a world to conquer."[30]

Congratulatory telegrams, cables, and letters poured in relentlessly from famous personalities as well as citizens who had followed the flight's progress since the previous April. Invitations to tour with vaudeville companies and appear in motion pictures were received. The fliers were surprised to learn that many babies born during the trip were named after some of the crew members and couples had arranged their marriages to coincide with the termination of the flight; for a time it was fashionable for women to wear beauty patches and pins in the shape of a World Cruiser. A song entitled "Out of the Skies" was composed by Louis De Jean and a poem, "An 'If' for the American World Fliers," was written by Abie E. Brown, wife of Lt. R. J. Brown Jr., chairman of the World Flight Committee. A parlor game was produced similar to the later Monopoly; aviation magazines published drawings of the Cruiser for model builders. Later the fliers posed for a sculptor and had their heads modeled for a large sculpture that was placed on display in the Air Service Museum at Dayton.

The following several days were filled with lunches, receptions, dinners, interviews, and talks before large audiences all intent upon the details of their experiences. One of the memorable side trips was made back to Sand Point Field on 29 September where Arnold's sister, Mrs. Francis L. Cole, unveiled a polished fifteen-foot granite monument commemorating the flight. This impressive memorial stands today at the entrance to the Sand Point Naval Air Station. It was designed by Victor Alonzo Lewis, a Seattle sculptor. The cost was reportedly borne by Alaska businessmen the previous August while the fliers were en route from Scotland to Iceland; their announced motivation was to symbolize the psychological, business, and physical connection between Alaska and Seattle. On top was a half globe about three feet in diameter surmounted with a pair of large, eagle wings; on one side was a bronze plate bearing the fliers' names. Senator Wesley L. Jones gave a dedication address and said he hoped that "the journey which began and ended here where this monument stands will intensify the interest of the American people in air navigation, making it a blessing to civilization and put an end to war and waste."[31] Smith wryly commented later that he had never expected to see their names on a monument until they were under it.

The fliers were given a luncheon by the Seattle Chamber of Commerce where each made remarks about their recollections of the flight. None wanted to speak but realized they were obliged to say something as a courtesy for all the attention they were getting. Smith, first to be introduced, said, "The hardest part of the trip was leaving Seattle, April 6, for Seattle, knowing that we would have to go all around the world to get here." Wade said it was harder to talk to this audience than it was to fly around the world. Nelson said he was the worst speaker of the bunch and had never made a talk in his life before until he was called upon at a dinner in Shanghai, China, and couldn't get out of it.

Reporters looked for quotes from the fliers about the trip and Smith seemed to summarize it for all. He was asked, "Would you do it again?" His reply was typical of the leader who had viewed the whole experience as a military mission. "Not for a million dollars," he replied. "Unless I was ordered to."

Les Arnold did not air his feelings in public but he wrote the following in his diary: "The best part of the trip—the finish—to have it all over with, to be through with the worry and strain of it all."[32]

Official timers representing the National Aeronautic Association (NAA) focused on the *Chicago* as the record-setting aircraft and recorded that Smith touched down at 1:28 P.M. Pacific time on 28 September 1924. Statisticians quickly went to work and the official record of the flight notes that the distance flown from Seattle to Seattle was 26,345 miles and the flight was officially timed as having been completed in 363 hours, 7 minutes—or 15 days, 3 hours, and 7 minutes of flying time. The average speed had been 72.5 mph. The flight was thus officially verified and the six fliers received medals from the NAA "in recognition of the first circumnavigation of the world by airplane."

The planes had used a total of 15 engines, 14 sets of pontoons, 42 sets of wheels, and an unspecified number of propellers during the flight. Nearly 27,000 gallons of gas and 2,900 gallons of oil had been consumed. There had been about 480 separate items such as spare parts, tools, tubing, and other materials placed at the supply points and 91,800 gallons of gasoline and 11,650 gallons of oil were scattered along the route and on board the navy ships. Most of the unused items were returned to government stocks.

Although the World Flight was over, there was much more in store for the six airmen. As the welcoming festivities came to a close, each wondered what they would be asked to do next. General Patrick supplied the answer with a telegram ordering them to leave the planes at Seattle and go by rail to Dayton to attend the International Air Races. "We were delighted," Smith recalled, "because we thought, oh, well, the flight's over and tomorrow the country will have forgotten about it and us, so on our way to Dayton we'll just catch up on lost sleep. But we were wrong."[33]

They did not realize it at the time but their lives were forever changed as a result of their experience. Each one of them would remain in activities related to aviation and would be involved in another world war two decades hence.

# Epilogue

The World Fliers welcomed the opportunity to be relieved of flying the Cruisers for a while. Would someone else fly them back to Dayton or would they fly them to the various cities that had requested a visit? Would the planes then be donated by the government to museums or would they be put into service as trainers?

Three alternative plans were presented to General Patrick for decision. Plan A was for the planes to make a complete tour of the United States to forty-two cities that had extended invitations. Plan B proposed a shorter itinerary that would bring the planes for display to only five cities, including New Orleans and Chicago. There was a Plan C that would end the flying activity of the World Flight as an organization at Rockwell Field and the *Chicago* and *New Orleans* would be crated and shipped to those cities for permanent retention provided (1) the cities would consent to pay transportation charges, and (2) the War Department would consent to having the planes disposed of in that manner. The *Boston II* would be flown to McCook Field by a Rockwell pilot. The final decision was to be made after the fliers returned to Seattle.[1]

In accordance with their orders, the six airmen boarded the Olympian of the Chicago, Milwaukee & St. Paul Railroad bound for Chicago, accompanied by Capt. Burdette Wright, the advance officer, and Joe Bahl, a railroad executive who was assigned to assure their comfort en route. They loaded their baggage aboard and then went forward to the engine cab where they were surprised to learn that they were being pulled not by a steam locomotive but by an electric engine. Just as they left the Seattle station, Bahl showed them a telegram from the Spokane

Chamber of Commerce saying the train would stop there for a short time to allow the city to give them a reception. They would be met by a Committee of Six which they assumed would be local officials.

The six airmen said they were fed up with receptions and under no circumstances did they want to stop more than the customary fifteen minutes the through trains usually stayed at each station for passenger and baggage transfers. But they were not to get their way. They were told that the "Committee of Six" had been carefully selected and it would be rude to ignore them. The Six turned out to be "the snappiest Spokanese that ever wore short skirts," according to Smith.[2] The fliers, all bachelors, said the train could wait until Doomsday for all they cared when they saw the six pretty girls who welcomed them. They delayed the train for an hour, which immediately put the famous Olympian behind schedule. Bahl had to order the train to leave.

It was on to Miles City, Montana, where a fleet of small planes dove on the train in greeting. When the train stopped, the airmen were presented with silk bandannas, loaded into an ancient stagecoach, and pulled up and down the platform to the delight of the citizenry. They were met from then on at the rest of the stops with more gifts representing each local area, including a case of canned corn at Aberdeen, North Dakota. Ducks, grouse, squabs, and prairie chickens were included at other stations; they graciously accepted but wondered what to do with them. When they arrived at Minneapolis, Smith was grabbed off the train by well-wishers, hustled into an automobile, and taken to a local radio studio to make a short speech. Cheering bystanders on the train platform shouted for Nelson, "We want to see the Big Swede!" Nelson accommodated them by waving his cap and showing them his bald head.

Bahl received stacks of mail for the fliers at each station. Most were letters of congratulation but a few also sought answers to strange questions, such as information about a brother who had been last heard of as a prisoner in a Siberian labor camp, and queries about tree-climbing fish that were said to be found only in Southeast Asia, and Alaskan ice worms they might have seen there. The greatest number of letters were from women, who no doubt had learned that the World Fliers were all bachelors. One classic letter gave a telephone number and said, simply, "My name is Carmen. I'm Spanish."

The group finally arrived in Dayton and felt truly honored when they were met at the station by Orville Wright. They stayed for the International Air Races and were introduced to the applauding crowd. Luncheons and receptions followed. When the races were concluded, Smith received a telegram from General Patrick ordering them all back to Seattle to pick up the Cruisers and fly them across the country to McCook Field in accordance with a combination of Plans B and C of the proposed alternatives. A decision would be made later as to the eventual disposition of the planes.

There had been concern in Washington about giving the men a rest and some feared that their appearance at different cities throughout the country would be an anticlimax. "We had better stop while this is at its height rather than to continue while it gradually dies out," General Patrick noted in a memorandum. "This people of ours does not think about the same thing for any great length of time. Like the Athenians of old, they are continually seeking for something new."[3]

The Training and War Plans staff recommended, and General Patrick agreed, that the crews should proceed to Rockwell Field, San Diego, via Vancouver, Eugene, San Francisco, and Santa Monica. Upon arrival there, no more flying activity would be planned for them as an organization. With "Birdie" Wright preceding them to make arrangements, the Cruisers were flown from San Diego to El Paso. From there the *Boston II* and *New Orleans* proceeded to San Antonio, Houston, and New Orleans. Wade had a minor mishap at the latter as a tail skid broke when he taxied over a filled ditch. It was quickly repaired.

For honoring New Orleans by their plane's name, Nelson and Harding were made honorary citizens and presented with huge loving cups four feet high. The *Boston II* and *New Orleans* then flew to Scott Field, Illinois, via Dallas and Muskogee, Oklahoma. Smith was directed to fly the *Chicago* directly from El Paso to Scott Field, Illinois, to await the other two planes. Despite pleas from prominent Chicagoans, its namesake would not be flown to Chicago.

W. A. Curley, editor of the *Chicago Evening American,* was unhappy with that decision and made a plaintive request that the *Chicago* return because "the plane was named for this city and because Chicago has been a leader in aviation affairs of the nation, the people of Chicago would appreciate this favor."[4] Chicago's Mayor William E. Dever requested the plane be awarded to the city permanently "as the appropriate depository for the machine that bears its name."[5]

Two months later, the *Chicago* was again the subject of a request from Frank Carson, managing editor of the *Chicago Herald and Tribune,* who said Chicagoans wanted it to land at a field in Lincoln Park on the lake front so it could be viewed "by the great majority of citizens who can't afford autos and can't spare time to go to Maywood" where it had landed previously. He said the field could be put in the proper condition "regardless of political assertions to the contrary. With election over and no chance to make political capital, won't it be possible to bring ship to Chicago November 9 and land it on field within reach of all the people?"[6]

Patrick could not be dissuaded. Smith and Arnold entrained for Chicago from St. Louis and were immediately inundated with invitations to luncheons and dinners by civic clubs, the Army and Navy Club, and the American Legion over the next three days. They were completely surprised at a huge rally on 9 November in the Chicago Auditorium when Mayor Dever presented them each with a new Packard eight-cylinder limousine. Too overwhelmed to find the proper words, they stumbled through thank-you remarks saying they were extremely lucky that they had been privileged to fly the plane named for the city that offered such extraordinary hospitality. All Smith could think of to say was, "of all the cities in America that our plane could have been named after, we were indeed thankful that Lady Luck had been kind enough to award us the name 'Chicago.'"[7]

When Smith and Arnold returned to Scott Field, Illinois, the six fliers were immediately engaged in an official welcome thirty miles away in St. Louis but the reception was not without a near tragedy. Lt. C. C. Moseley, the pilot of the plane that carried Lowell Thomas around the country trailing the World Fliers, invited Joseph O'Neill, vice chairman of the St. Louis reception committee, to make a local flight around Lambert Field with him. O'Neill, who had never been in a plane before, was to drop a bouquet of roses on the speakers' stand as the fliers were being officially welcomed by the city. He had been kidded beforehand that Moseley's plane was painted black and looked like a coffin so that all he had to do if there were an accident was to fold his arms. O'Neill was undaunted and threw the flowers at Moseley's signal but the bouquet caught in the plane's elevator wires and Moseley fought desperately for control. The plane pitched upward into a near-stall and threatened to crash onto the crowd but Moseley managed to shake the flowers free by skidding the plane and was able to recover from what could have been a tragic ending to a series of unprecedented American welcomes.

One of the lasting memories of the stay in St. Louis was a speech by Eugene H. Angert, a leading criminal lawyer and outstanding after-dinner speaker, who humorously summarized their flight:

"Colonel Perkins called me up late this afternoon and told me he had discovered why the visit of our distinguished guests was delayed for a whole week under such mysterious circumstances. They had been in a sanitarium. They had broken down under the strain of the dinners, luncheons, and banquets that were forced upon them in almost every city of the country since their return. It was not the food; and, strange to say, it was not even the drink, that did it. It was the speeches that had prostrated them. After-dinner speakers, or, in the vernacular, postprandial orators, had fed them on flattery until they became afflicted with acute mental indigestion. Extravagant praise, garnished with a sauce of superlatives, was served to them in celebration. They were gorged with hero worship and glutted with glorification. They were asphyxiated by adulation."

Angert reviewed the round-the-world trips by Nellie Bly, André Jaeger-Schmidt, and others by land and sea, then continued his mocking of the World Fliers:

"More in sorrow than anger, let us compare these trips around the world with the one we are celebrating tonight. Our guests were aided and abetted from the beginning to the end of their journey by an army of mechanics, radio experts, weather forecasters, cheerupidists, mah-jongg players, and ouija board mediuma—an army greater in numbers than Cornwallis surrendered at Yorktown. They were supported by a fleet of government ships scattered throughout the navigable and unnavigable waters of both hemispheres as large as the combined fleets which the Five Great Naval Powers have agreed to scrap and did not. And I tell you in strict confidence . . . that during the entire flight it was impossible for these aviators to have dropped into the Atlantic or Pacific, the Arctic or Antarctic oceans, the Dead Sea, Salt Lake, or Cripple Creek, or into any bay, islet, lagoon, or pond, within the jurisdiction of the League of Nations, without alighting upon the deck of a United

States warship." Angert continued kidding them about the length of time it took the World Fliers to make their trip and compared them with the others who did it in less time and did not use airplanes to set their records. He added:

"Then let your manly bosoms contract with humility when you think of these three strong, sturdy Americans comfortably seated behind a Liberty engine capable of doing a hundred miles an hour, each with a mechanician by his side to put cracked ice on his head when he was hot and a hot water bottle on his back when he was cold, and supported by enough accessories before the fact and accessories after the fact to make a lawyer green with envy, not able to finish the trip in less than one hundred and seventy-five days!

". . . But, after all, absence makes the heart grow fonder; and so, may I say to the guests of the evening, in all seriousness, that, despite your long absence, we are glad that you are back. . . . You have written an imperishable chapter in the record of American achievement—a record full of great accomplishments. You have met almost insurmountable difficulties and overcome them by your skill, your bravery, your endurance. It was an uncharted sea you sailed. It was a land of nothingness and space you conquered. The whole world acclaimed your flight, and we, your fellow citizens, are proud of the glory you have brought to the Nation."[8]

When the festivities were over, the three planes were flown to McCook Field to await a final decision on their disposition. Smith, Nelson, Wade, and Arnold were then ordered to Washington to meet with General Patrick and make out their official reports while the flight was still fresh in their minds. Harding and Ogden were ordered to Seattle to await further assignment.[9]

As soon as the flight was successfully completed, a bill was introduced in Congress to give each of the fliers $10,000, promotion in rank, and award of the Medal of Honor. The War Department did not favor this kind of recognition. It was argued that the World Flight was made in the regular line of duty and that it would tend to sow disruption and resentment if the fliers were singled out and placed ahead of others in the services who would have done the same thing if they had the opportunity. Secretary of War Weeks declared that it was the intention of the War Department to compensate the fliers—for any nonreimbursable expenses they suffered—either by departmental or by special authorization of Congress. If this was not possible, he said, he would dig down into his own pockets to repay them.

Many members of Congress were determined to reward the fliers and a bill was introduced in the House and Senate "to recognize and reward the accomplishment of the World Flyers." The bill authorized the promotion of Smith to captain and a gain of one thousand files on the Regular Army promotion list; Wade, Arnold, and Nelson were advanced five hundred files. Ogden and Harding, both second lieutenants in the Officers' Reserve Corps, were commissioned in the Regular Army and "placed on the promotion list next after the second lieutenant who immediately precedes them on the date of the approval of this Act." All the fliers, including Martin and Harvey, were authorized to receive the Distinguished Service Medal and "accept any medals or decorations tendered or bestowed upon them by foreign governments."[10] The bill was approved on 25 February 1925 and signed by the president.

The disposition of the planes was discussed at length in Washington and political pressure was brought to bear from several quarters. In addition to Mayor Dever's request the *Chicago* be awarded to the city and placed on permanent exhibition, other cities continued to ask that the crews and planes visit them for special occasions in the coming months. But to avoid and further adverse comment, the Secretary of War decided that the planes should not be flown again or loaned for expositions or air shows. The *Chicago* would be placed in the Smithsonian Institution in Washington and the *New Orleans* would remain at McCook Field for display in the Army Air Service Museum. Neither ever flew again; the *Chicago* was disassembled and sent by train to Washington.

The world soon forgot that other nations also had brave fliers who had wanted to have the honor of being first to blaze an aerial trail around the world. The world press had reported the various attempts as a race but none of the other contenders achieved their ultimate goal. They had limited financial and logistical support from their respective governments and each attempt had ended in the loss of the aircraft; few mementos of their flights survive today.

Squad. Ldr. Stuart MacLaren, navigator, Flying Officer W. N. Plenderleith, pilot, and Sgt. Richard Andrews, mechanic, had left Calshot, England, in a Vickers amphibian on 15 March 1924. With Lt. Col. L. E. Broome later substituting for Andrews, MacLaren's dream had ended with a crash landing in rough seas near Nikolski in the Soviet Komandorski Islands.

Two Portuguese fliers, Capt. Brito Pais and Lt. Sarmiento Beires, had left Lisbon on 2 April 1924 and were forced to abandon their attempt near Macao, a Portuguese settlement in southeastern China. Maj. Pedro Zanni, the Argentine pilot, with Lt. Nelson T. Page as navigator and Felipe Beltrame as mechanic, had left Amsterdam on 26 July 1924 and had crashed near Hanoi. They transferred to another plane to resume the attempt and on a takeoff from Osaka, Japan, overturned in heavy seas; Zanni decided not to continue even if repairs were made.

France's noted pilot Capt. Pelletier d'Oisy and Sgt. Bernard Vesin, mechanic, had crashed near Shanghai, which ended their effort to capture the honor for their country. And the Americans had known first-hand how Antonio Locatelli's attempt had ended. He had started in July from Pisa, Italy, and had to abandon his plane after landing at sea in foggy weather near Greenland on 21 August 1924. As the Americans neared their goal in September, no other nations indicated an interest in making a World Flight. There was no glory in being second.

The American success was destined to be remembered as a historic aviation way-point. It had been planned and executed as a military mission and had the support of several branches of the government. It had been a test of men, machines, and superior logistical planning. America would preserve the planes to remind all who see them in the future that the flight was made successfully when many thought it was an impossible task to ask in peacetime of men in uniform. Especially noteworthy was the exceptional cooperation recorded by the U.S. Navy during the Pacific and Atlantic oceans and Southeast Asia phases of the flight. This was during a period of much rancor between the services when Gen. William "Billy" Mitchell was fighting for a separate air force and the Navy was adamant that it was not needed. Unprecedented assistance to the flight was also rendered by the U.S. Coast Guard with great willingness during the Aleutian portion of the flight, even to the extent of putting their ships and crews into perilous situations.

Formal recognition for the 1924 achievement occurred in the spring of 1925 when the Army Air Service was awarded the prestigious Collier Trophy named for Robert J. Collier, a prominent publisher, patriot, sportsman, and aviator. Collier proclaimed the ideal that the flying machine should be unselfishly and rapidly developed to its ultimate possibilities for America's economic advancement and preservation. His trophy is awarded annually "for the greatest achievement in aeronautics or astronautics in America, with respect to improving the performance, efficiency, and safety of air or space vehicles, the value of which has been thoroughly demonstrated during the preceding year."

The three pilots, Smith, Nelson, and Wade, received honorary Master of Science degrees from Tufts University, Medford, Massachusetts, at the June 1925 commencement. After the three planes were flown to McCook Field to await their fate. Lowell Thomas, the flight's historian, was granted permission to fly from McCook Field to Washington with Lieutenant C. C. Moseley in a DH-4 and finish collecting their reminiscences of the flight for his book.

Smith made an extensive report of the flight and praised the outstanding work of the flight committee and the untiring and efficient manner in which the advance officers contributed to the flight's success under the most trying handicaps. He also commended the U.S. Navy, U.S. Coast Guard, and the Bureau of Fisheries, and especially the *Eider*'s skipper, who "was very resourceful and deserves the highest commendation on his efficient cooperation" during the Aleutian phase of the flight. He also noted that the inhabitants of every nation wherever a landing was made "were anxious to do everything within their power to assist the flight." Also praised was the Danish Coast Guard and the crew of the *Island Falk* who rendered every assistance, "both by the use of their radio and the actual servicing and guarding of the planes, and also in caring for the flight's personnel in Fredricksdal where no lodging facilities were available."[11]

Nelson submitted a forty-five-page report as the flight's engineering officer and pointed out failures or substandard aircraft parts and equipment and his recommended changes for future operations of this type. He commented on the mechanical difficulties experienced with the engines, ignition, cooling, and oil and fuel systems on each leg of the flight and the lessons and innovations the fliers and crews originated about servicing, docking, and caring for the planes. Of special concern to all the crews throughout the flight were the fragile pontoons; Nelson recommended metal ones for future use. His comments about the planes included the landing gear, tail skids, wings, fuselage, propellers, hand fuel pumps, instruments, and controls.[12]

Arnold submitted a finance report and stated his difficulties in paying the bills in foreign countries. Major Martin had been given about $17,000 to be used to pay local charges throughout the flight but after his crash in Alaska, Arnold had been given the responsibility to pay all bills after they reached Tokyo. He was given $17,000 of which $14,000 was converted into a letter of credit with the International Banking Corporation of New York. He noted that it was not always possible to keep money on hand of the country they happened to be in or to obtain it from the local banks. "Through China, the Mexican peso was used; in Indohina, it was the Indochinese franc and also the Mexican peso," he wrote. "From Burma through India and on to Baghdad, the Indian rupee is accepted, and from Constantinople on to England, either English, French, or American currency is accepted in all countries. Iceland has a currency of its own, but Danish currency is acceptable, while Greenland uses Danish currency only."[13]

Arnold revealed that the pilot of each plane had been given $1,000 in banker's checks at the start of the flight to be used as emergency funds. "The wisdom of this was proven when Major Martin was lost with the main funds. The combined amount from the remaining three planes was more than ample for things until the additional funds were secured in Tokyo."[14]

Smith wrote a separate confidential report for General Patrick. He commented on the severe weather they encountered and concluded, "An airway through the Aleutian Islands for the operation of planes during the entire year is believed to be quite impracticable with present aeronautical equipment." He commented that they were courteously received by the Japanese people, especially by the Japanese school children. "It is believed that they were sincere in their enthusiasm but that their friendship was to the personnel of the World Flight. That there was an underlying feeling against the American government which, to a certain extent, was shown in what may or may not have been false pride and a desire to show their importance. Many small incidents would bring out this feature of their character, some of them being the difficulty of obtaining permission to pass through Japan, unreasonable schedules for radio activities of the U.S. Navy patrol ships, the prevention of a landing party going ashore at Hitakoppu, although there was absolutely nothing on the island of military or naval construction, and the prohibition against taking photographs, or in several instances requiring the flight to take a round-about course to keep them away from some very minor forts, even though we assured them that our cameras were all sealed and that our mission was flying around the world and not to obtain military information.

"In one case, at a small dinner given by some Japanese officers to myself and Lieutenant Commander Frost of the U.S. Navy, a major in the Japanese infantry while slightly under the influence of liquor and in a very talkative mood, expressed his friendship for us and for all American Army and Navy officers, adding that Americans had frequently insulted Japan and slapped her face but that sometime Japan was going to slap back; further stating that when this was done, the Japanese Army and Navy officers would be fighting the American Army and Navy officers, not because they personally were enemies, but because it was their occupation to protect their countries. His views seemed to be the views of the other six or eight Japanese Army and Navy officers present.

"The American fliers were not given a decoration by the Japanese government as was given to the French flier, Captain d'Oisy. This may have been due to the unrest among the Japanese people caused by the Japanese Exclusion Act which had been passed about two weeks previously."[15]

Smith reported briefly on the aircraft activities he observed in the various other foreign countries with special mention of the established airway being flown by commercial aircraft between Constantinople and Paris by the Franco-Romanian Aviation Company. He was especially surprised to find that Romania was building an air force nearly as great as that of the United States. He also added that "we were all astonished to learn of the size and efficiency of the French Air Force."[16]

In a final paragraph, Smith commented, "It was very disappointing to us and humiliating to Americans to find that most of our country's representatives are not in as good standing with native-born and European inhabitants throughout the countries we visited as those from the European countries. This is due in a great measure to the small amount of pay they receive, to their inability to obtain funds for officers to compare with those of other governments, and to the fact that they are given very little if anything to carry on the necessary entertainment required of them. It is believed by the undersigned that frequent visits of American naval ships or distinguished American citizens would greatly help the situation, and also add to our trade relations with any of the countries throughout the world. It is believed that more can be done to establish permanent peace, or at least a postponement of wars, in this manner than in any other way."[17]

The question about the disposition of the *Chicago* and the *New Orleans* continued to be contentious as urgent requests were persistently received from politicians and civic leaders. Cities that had not been visited requested that the pilots and planes favor them with their presence for brief periods. General Patrick held fast and continued to feel that to accede to these requests would result in a storm of protest from those not so favored. In addition, because of their construction, the planes could be easily damaged if handled by inexperienced personnel. The decision was finalized after a careful study that was reflected in an answer to one of the requests: "If they were to be lent as exhibits to be used as celebrations and ceremonials throughout the country, they would soon be in such a state of repair that a great deal of the sentimental value which is now attached to them would be lost."[18]

Secretary of War Dwight F. Davis agreed and the issue was settled. He decided that the *Chicago* would remain in the Smithsonian Institution in Washington and the *New Orleans* would stay at the Air Service Museum at McCook Field. Neither plane was to be flown again or loaned for display at expositions and air shows. After negotiations with Donald W. Douglas Sr. in 1927, the *New Orleans* was subsequently sent from the Air Service Museum to the Los Angeles County Museum for display where it eventually fell into disrepair. When this became known to Douglas, he volunteered the services of his company to prepare it for shipment to the Air Force Museum at Wright-Patterson Air Force Base in Dayton and it was transported there in a Douglas C-124 in March 1957. In still another turnabout, it was returned to its birthplace in September 1988 and is now on display in the Museum of Flying, which stands on the site of the old Douglas plant, adjacent to the Santa Monica Airport. In its place at the Air Force Museum is an exhibit of items related to the flight, such as flying clothing, aircraft parts, gifts and medals awarded the fliers, and a diorama depicting the *Seattle* and the *Boston,* which appear to be tied up at a dock at Sand Point, Washington. Most of the personal items were donated by Leigh Wade, John Harding, and Erik Nelson.

The *Chicago* also suffered the ravages of time during its years in the metal shed at the Smithsonian Institution. The fabric started to split and crack and curators suspected that rot and corrosion were eating away at the wood and metal. Careful restoration began in 1971 and was completed in 1974. It has remained on display in the Milestones of Flight Gallery on the second floor of the Smithsonian National Air and Space Museum since its opening in 1976.

Some of the remains of the ill-fated *Seattle* that had crashed in Alaska have also been preserved. Employees of the U.S. Bureau of Fisheries found the crash site in late 1924, and $500 had been allotted to Lt. Robert Koenig, the base commander at Sand Point Airfield, to salvage parts of the plane that could be brought out by dog sled.[19] The main fuselage and engine remained at the site for many years until the engine and other parts were flown out by helicopter in the 1960s with the encouragement and assistance of Reeve Aleutian Airways president Robert C. Reeve and Lowell Thomas Jr. The engine and the rest of the displayable items were on exhibit at the Alaska Transportation Museum in Palmer, Alaska, until 1993, and were moved to the Alaska Aviation Heritage Museum near Anchorage International Airport where they can be seen today.

There were some missing items carried on the *Seattle* that had not been known about until a year after the crash. Clarence J. Bertler, a stamp collector, had persuaded Martin and Harvey secretly to carry a number of postcards in the plane. They could carry only a few with them when they left the crash site. The following spring, when the snow had melted and a search party reached the plane, the elements and wild animals had destroyed so much of what remained of the plane, the equipment, and the postcards that nothing of value was found except the plane's metal parts.[20] It is not known if any of the postcards carried by Martin and Harvey survive today.

The *Boston II* had a different story. It had a checkered career after the other four planes had departed the country. It had been transferred from McCook Field in the spring of 1924 to Langley Field, Virginia, when it was first thought it might be shipped to England so Major Martin could rejoin the flight. After it was uncrated and the decision was made not to have Martin rejoin the others, Lt. George McDonald was authorized to proceed with arrangements for making endurance tests at Langley and attempt to set a world seaplane distance and endurance record. Neither of these flights was carried out. The plane was returned to McCook Field in June 1924 to complete long-distance navigation and engineering tests because "a considerable misimpression of the performance of this aircraft is believed to exist."[21] It was used for further testing at McCook Field and was returned to Langley to be fitted with pontoons and tested for the flight to Nova Scotia for Wade and Ogden. After it was returned to McCook from Seattle, it was flown to Kelly Field, in San Antonio, Texas, home of the Air Service mechanics' school, and was eventually scrapped there on 14 May 1932.

The Air Service, impressed with the World Cruiser design, ordered five to be used as observation aircraft. Initially designated the DOS (Douglas Observation Seaplane), it retained its pontoon/wheels interchange capability but had its fuel capacity reduced to 110 gallons. Twin .30-caliber machine guns were mounted in the rear cockpit. Later designated O-5, the five planes were assigned to the Second Observation Squadron at McKinley Field in the Philippines.

The fliers all continued to lead interesting lives related to aviation after the World Flight. Frederick L. Martin, the original commander of the flight, returned to his assignment at Chanute Field, Illinois. He subsequently was commanding officer of Bolling, Kelly, Randolph, and Wright fields, before being assigned as commander of Barksdale Field, Louisiana, in 1937. In 1940, as a major general, he was named commander of the Hawaiian Air Force at Hickam Field and was in that assignment when the Japanese bombed Pearl Harbor on 7 December 1941. A staunch advocate of a stronger air force and additional air strength in Hawaii, he had warned eight months before in a report he coauthored with Rear Adm. Patrick N. L. Bellinger that there was the possibility that Japan could attack the islands by air and would probably do so on a Saturday, Sunday, or American national holiday. In the aftermath of the investigation of the surprise raid, he was relieved of command and transferred to head the Second Air Force with headquarters at Fort George Wright, Spokane, Washington. He retired in 1944 for physical disability and died in Los Angeles in 1954.

Lowell H. Smith remained in the service and held sixteen national and world flying records for speed, duration, and distance. He charted some of the earliest airway routes and in the mid-1930s flew tests on the original Northrop Flying Wing. He also contributed to the development of airborne assaults and participated in the first mass parachute troop drops before World War II. During World War II, he was a colonel and commanded Davis-Monthan Field near Tucson, Arizona. He was killed while riding his favorite horse during a vacation in the Catalina Mountains in 1945. He was inducted into the Arizona Aviation Hall of Fame in May 1994.

The year after the World Flight, Leigh Wade and Linton Wells teamed up to drive a Packard sedan from Los Angeles to New York City in 165 hours, 50 minutes without stopping, thus completing the first transcontinental nonstop automobile trip. Wade left active duty in 1926 and planned to make an oil survey in the Antarctic with Lowell Thomas, but the venture did not take place because of the lack of financial backing. He also planned a world flight in a seaplane in the summer of 1928 with Floyd K. Smith, president of New York & Western Airways, as copilot. The flight was to begin and end at Chicago. Capt. Bradley Jones, chief of air navigation of the U.S. Army was slated to go as navigator; a mechanic was to be named later. Although a syndicate of New York stock brokers was formed to back the flight, the $110,000 needed was not raised.

Wade next became a test pilot for Consolidated Aircraft Company and later was the company's representative in Latin America. He was recalled to active duty shortly before World War II, served in Cuba, and was air attaché to Greece, Brazil, and Argentina between 1941 and 1955 when he retired as a major general. He served as an assistant to the chairman of the board of an insurance company for the next ten years. He was enshrined in the National Aviation Hall of Fame in 1974 and died on 31 August 1991 at the age of 93.

Erik H. Nelson left active duty in 1928 and became a sales manager and later a vice president and director of the Boeing Aircraft Company. He was involved in the formation of the Boeing Air Transport Company that later became United Air Lines. After retiring from Boeing in 1936, he worked as an aviation consultant. During World War II, he worked on aircraft development which included the B-29 Super Fortress. He was appointed a brigadier general in 1945 and died in Hawaii on 9 May 1970 at age 81.

Henry H. Ogden left active duty in 1926 and helped organize the Michigan National Guard. He was a commercial test pilot and manager of the Mazatlan and La Paz Air Mail and Passenger Line for the Mexican government in the 1930s. He also helped organize construction of smelting and mining operations in that country. He designed and manufactured a small trimotor aircraft named the *Ogden Osprey.* He moved to England in 1939 with the Lockheed Aircraft Company and remained there until 1946. He became a vice president of Lockheed and retired in 1955.

After the World Flight, John T. "Jack" Harding Jr. teamed up with Lowell Thomas for a national lecture tour in 1925 that was widely acclaimed. Using motion and still pictures, the two entertained audiences with stories about the flight that Thomas accompanied with colorful descriptions and history of the countries the Cruisers had visited and flown over. Harding then worked for Boeing Aircraft Company and Menasco Manufacturing Company as a sales representative before starting his own company in Dallas, Texas. In 1940 he patented and manufactured electric fuel valves that were used on fighters and bombers during World War II. After the war, his interests turned to real estate holdings in Texas and California. He died at La Jolla, California, in 1968.

Leslie P. Arnold resigned from the Army Air Corps in 1928 and joined Maddux Air Lines that later was bought by TAT and became Trans World Airlines. He became a vice president of Eastern Air Lines in 1940 and was called to active duty as a colonel with the Eighth Air Force in Europe during World War II. He retired as a major general and died in 1962.

Alva L. Harvey completed flight training and was commissioned in 1926. In September 1941, while stationed in Puerto Rico, he piloted a B-24 over 3,150 miles to Moscow with members of a Lend-Lease delegation. He continued around the world via India, Australia, Wake Island, and Hawaii, completing 27,238 miles. During World War II, he commanded a group of the Twentieth Bomber Command in China and the Marianas, and retired as a colonel in 1956. Afterward, he was a sales manager for a real estate firm in northern Virginia and died in 1992.

In retrospect, these men had defied the odds by surviving at a time when planes were extremely fragile and parts of the world were not ready for aviation. They had flown over twenty-eight different nations and colonial mandates and made seventy-two stops for fuel and maintenance. Besides being the first airmen to circumnavigate the globe, they were the first to cross the Pacific, the first to cross the East China Sea, and the first to cross both of the world's largest oceans. The World Flight had resulted in a daring success and proved that aviation could significantly diminish the bonds of time and distance.

Despite the many successful world flights made since those trial-and-error days of aviation, it is significant that for seventy-five years none have been made in an open cockpit, single-engine plane. That was true until Robert Ragozzino of Norman, Oklahoma, completed a World Flight of more than 23,000 miles in a biplane between 1 June 2000 and 17 November 2000 in five days less time than the old World Cruisers. The differences were that he few alone and chose to go west-to-east instead of east-to-west as the World Cruisers had done. He began his flight from Oklahoma City, Oklahoma, in a World War II Stearman single-engine open-cockpit trainer modified to carry extra fuel. His purpose was to beat the 175 days it had taken for the 1924 flight. If he were successful but didn't make it within that time period, he would still have set a record by doing it solo.

Ragozzino's attempt was stalled on 29 September 2000 when he encountered stronger-than-forecast head winds on the 1,700-mile over-water leg from Kushiro, Japan, to Shemya, Alaska, and had to divert for fuel at Petropavlovsk on the Kamchatka Peninsula in Russian territory. He was detained for more than three weeks and was threatened with deportation and confiscation of his airplane, although he was in compliance with international aviation regulations. When he was finally permitted to depart, he flew to Attu and then to several more stops along the Aleutian chain to Anchorage, Alaska. He made eight more landings before reaching Will Rogers Airport in Oklahoma City.

The Stearman was equipped with modern navigation instruments, including three global position systems, advanced radio and radar systems, and a search and rescue organization. He was also able to take advantage of accurate weather reports and forecasts. His success nonetheless is a tribute to aviation progress and serves to memorialize the first World Flight made seventy-six years before.

# Appendix. The Route of the Flight

| Date | | Landing Point | Miles | Approximate Flight Time |
|---|---|---|---|---|
| Apr | 6 | Seattle to Prince Rupert, B.C. | 650 | 8:10 |
| | 10 | Sitka, Alaska | 282 | 4:26 |
| | 13 | Seward, Alaska | 625 | 7:44 |
| | 15 | Chignik, Alaska | 425 | 6:38 |
| | 19 | Dutch Harbor, Alaska | 390 | 7:26 |
| May | 3 | Nazan, Atka Island | 365 | 4:19 |
| | 9 | Chichagof, Attu Island | 555 | 7:52 |
| | 15 | Komandorski Islands | 350 | 5:25 |
| | 16 | Date change at 180th Meridian | | |
| | 17 | Paramushiru, Japan | 585 | 6:55 |
| | 19 | Hitokappu, Yetorofu, Japan | 595 | 7:20 |
| | 22 | Minato, Japan | 485 | 5:05 |
| | | Kasumigaura, Japan | 350 | 4:55 |
| Jun | 1 | Kushimoto, Japan | 305 | 4:35 |
| | 2 | Kagoshima, Japan | 360 | 6:11 |
| | 4 | Shanghai, China | 550 | 9:10 |
| | 7 | Tchinkoen Bay, China | 350 | 4:30 |
| | | Amoy, China | 250 | 2:47 |
| | 8 | Hong Kong | 310 | 3:24 |
| | 10 | Haiphong, French Indochina | 495 | 7:26 |
| | 11 | Tourane, French Indochina | 410 | 6:05 |
| | 16 | Saigon, French Indochina | 540 | 7:58 |

*Continued on next page*

| Date | | Landing Point | Miles | Approximate Flight Time |
|---|---|---|---|---|
| Jun | 18 | Kampongson Bay, French Indochina | 295 | 4:20 |
| | | Bangkok, Siam | 290 | 4:02 |
| | 20 | Tavoy, Burma | 200 | 3:55 |
| | | Rangoon, Burma | 295 | 3:08 |
| | 25 | Akyab, Burma | 480 | 5:38 |
| | 26 | Chittagong, Burma | 180 | 2:10 |
| | | Calcutta, India | 265 | 3:17 |
| Jul | 1 | Allahabad, India | 450 | 6:30 |
| | 2 | Ambala, India | 480 | 6:25 |
| | 3 | Multan, India | 360 | 5:45 |
| | 4 | Karachi, India | 455 | 7:08 |
| | 7 | Chahbar, Persia | 410 | 4:50 |
| | | Bandar Abbas, Persia | 365 | 4:05 |
| | 8 | Bushire, Persia | 390 | 4:05 |
| | | Baghdad, Mesopotamia | 530 | 6:30 |
| | 9 | Aleppo, Syria | 450 | 6:10 |
| | 10 | Constantinople, Turkey | 560 | 7:38 |
| | 12 | Bucharest, Rumania | 350 | 4:40 |
| | 13 | Budapest, Hungary | 465 | 6:50 |
| | | Vienna, Austria | 113 | 2:00 |
| | 14 | Strasbourg, France | 500 | 6:30 |
| | | Paris, France | 250 | 3:55 |
| | 16 | London, England | 215 | 3:07 |
| | 17 | Brough, England | 165 | 1:55 |
| | 30 | Kirkwall, Orkney Islands | 450 | 5:30 |
| Aug | 2 | Horna Fjord, Iceland | 555 | |
| | | *Chicago* | | 6:13 |
| | | *New Orleans* | | 9:03 |
| | 5 | Reykjavik, Iceland | 290 | 5:03 |
| | 21 | Fredricksdal, Greenland | 830 | |
| | | *Chicago* | | 10:40 |
| | | *New Orleans* | | 11:17 |
| | 24 | Ivigtut, Greenland | 165 | 2:12 |
| | 31 | Icy Tickle, Labrador | 560 | 6:55 |
| Sep | 2 | Hawkes Bay, Newfoundland | 315 | 4:56 |
| | 3 | Pictou Harbor, Nova Scotia | 430 | 6:34 |
| | 5 | Mere Point, Maine | 450 | 6:05 |
| | 6 | Boston, Massachusetts | 100 | 2:08 |
| | 8 | Mitchel Field, New York | 220 | 3:40 |
| | 9 | Aberdeen, Maryland | 160 | 3:38 |
| | | Bolling Field, Washington, D.C. | 70 | 1:05 |
| | 13 | McCook Field, Dayton, Ohio | 400 | 6:43 |
| | 15 | Chicago, Illinois | 245 | 2:58 |
| | 16 | Omaha, Nebraska | 430 | 4:48 |
| | 18 | St. Joseph, Missouri | 110 | 1:48 |
| | | Muskogee, Oklahoma | 270 | 3:53 |
| | 19 | Dallas, Texas | 245 | 3:45 |

| Date | Landing Point | Miles | Approximate Flight Time |
|---|---|---|---|
| 20 | Sweetwater, Texas | 210 | 3:06 |
| | El Paso, Texas | 390 | 6:18 |
| 21 | Tucson, Arizona | 280 | 3:23 |
| 22 | San Diego, California | 390 | 4:03 |
| 23 | Los Angeles, California | 115 | 1:25 |
| 25 | San Francisco, California | 365 | 5:05 |
| 27 | Eugene, Oregon | 420 | 5:20 |
| 28 | Vancouver Barracks, Washington | 90 | 1:08 |
| | Seattle, Washington | 150 | 1:43 |

| | |
|---|---|
| Approximate Distance | 26,345 statute miles |
| Flying Time: *Chicago* | 363 hours, 7 minutes |
| *New Orleans* | 366 hours, 34 minutes |

# Notes

NOTE: For authors or titles not given in full, please search in the list of further reading following these notes.

## Introduction

1. "World Race Rules Submitted," *Aero and Hydro,* 7 February 1914, 237.
2. Letter to the Editor, *Aero and Hydro,* 21 February 1914, 267.
3. Untitled editorial, by E. Percy Noel, *Aero and Hydro,* 21 February 1914, 266.
4. "First Aerial Derby Around the World," *Flying,* May 1920, 261.

## 1. The Challenge

1. *Aircraft Year Book 1923* (New York: Aeronautical Chamber of Commerce), 6.
2. *Aircraft Year Book 1924* (New York: Aeronautical Chamber of Commerce), 1.
3. Isaac Don Levine, *Mitchell, Pioneer of Air Power* (New York: Duell, Sloan, and Pierce, 1943), 301.
4. Henry H. Arnold, *Global Mission* (New York: Harper and Brothers, 1949), 80.
5. Levine, *Mitchell, Pioneer of Air Power,* 192.

6. Memorandum from H. A. Dargue, Chief, War Plans Section, Office of Chief of Air Service, for Lt. Robert J. Brown Jr., 13 April 1922. U.S. National Archives, File Entry No. E.140, RWF File, Box 5 (hereinafter referred to as National Archives, RWF File).
7. Associated Press, "Army Getting Data for World Flight," 23 October 1922.
8. Memorandum for Chief of Air Service from Major General J. G. Harbord, Deputy Chief of Staff, 24 October 1922. National Archives, RWF File, Box 5.
9. First indorsement by Major General Mason M. Patrick to Memorandum from Deputy Chief of Staff, 27 October 1922. National Archives, RWF File, Box 5.
10. "U.S. Not Planning Round-the-World Flight," by Myron H. Best, *New York Times,* 9 January 1923.
11. Letter, subject: "Airplanes for Round-the-World Flight" from Major W. H. Frank to Chief, Engineering Division, McCook Field, Dayton, Ohio, 7 November 1922. National Archives, RWF File, Box 5.
12. First indorsement by H. A. Mobrey, Assistant Chief, Engineering Division, to letter from Major W. H. Frank, 22 November 1922. National Archives, RWF File, Box 5.
13. Memorandum from C. E. Crumrine, Subject: Round-the-World Flight for Major H. A. Dargue, 10 January 1923. National Archives, RWF File, Box 6.
14. Report, Lt. Clarence E. Crumrine to Chief of Air Service, 28 March 1923. National Archives, RWF File, Box 6.
15. Document U-672-A.S. "The Round-the-World Flight," undated, unsigned, 1. Series Eleven, Leigh Wade/Cole Morrow Collection, Air Force Academy, Colorado Springs, Colorado (hereinafter referred to as Wade/Morrow Collection).
16. Memorandum from Lt. Col. J. E. Fechet, Chief, Training and War Plans Division, for Chief of Air Service, Subject: "Airplane Flight Around the World," 26 May 1923, 4. National Archives, RWF File, Box 7.
17. "Airplane Flight Around the World," Folder 8.
18. "Airplane Flight Around the World."
19. Letter, Lt. James H. Doolittle to Chief of Air Service, Subject: "Cross Country Flight," 4 June 1923. National Archives, RWF File, Box 7.
20. After the World Flight, the Air Service ordered five near-duplicates under the initial designation of DOS for Douglas Observation Seaplane. This title was changed to O-5 when a new designation system was adopted in May 1924. The five O-5s were delivered as twin-float seaplanes. The Army Air Service (later the Army Air Corps) began ordering O-2 observation aircraft, descendants of the Cloudster, in 1924. During the next twelve years, Douglas manufactured nearly 900 of this type in more than fifty versions for United States and foreign air forces.
21. Letter, Mason M. Patrick, Chief of Air Service, to Adjutant General of the Army, Subject: "Airplane Flight Around-the-World," 1 June 1923. National Archives, RWF File, Box 7.
22. First indorsement to letter from Chief of Air Service to Commanding Officer, McCook Field, 4 June 1923. National Archives, RWF File, Box 7.
23. General Specifications, Type D-WC, Douglas Company, 5 July 1923. Wade/Morrow Collection, Series 1, Folder 7.
24. Letter, Douglas Aircraft Company to Engineering Division, McCook Field, 10 August 1923. National Archives, RWF File, Box 7.
25. Letter, S. Whipple, Adjutant General, War Department, Subject: "Airplane Flight Around the World" to Chief of Air Service, 23 June 1923. National Archives, RWF File, Box 7.

26. Duplicate letters from General Patrick to Lts. Clarence E. Crumrine and Clifford C. Nutt, 15 August 1923. National Archives, RWF File, Box 7.
27. Duplicate letters, Box 7.
28. Telegram, Acting Secretary of State to Chargé in Japan, 30 August 1923. (All references to communications concerning the World Flight between the U.S. State Department and foreign governments are found in *Papers Relating to the Foreign Relations of the United States—1924, vol. 1.* Washington, D.C.: Government Printing Office, 1939.)
29. Telegram, Secretary of State to Chargé in Japan, 27 November 1923.
30. Telegram, American Ambassador in Japan to Secretary of State, 22 September 1923.
31. Telegram, American Chargé in Japan to Secretary of State, 30 November 1923.
32. Letter, American Chargé in Japan to Secretary of State, 14 December 1923.
33. Telegram, Secretary of State to Chargé in Japan (Caffrey), 10 January 1924.
34. Telegram, American Minister to China (Schurman) to Secretary of State, 26 January 1924.
35. Telegram, Secretary of State to Minister in China (Schurman), 28 January 1924.
36. Telegram, Ambassador to Germany (Houghton) to Secretary of State, 28 January 1924.
37. Telegram, High Commissioner in Turkey (Bristol) to Secretary of State, 30 January 1924.
38. Memorandum from Lieutenant C. E. Crumrine for Lieutenant R. J. Brown, 25 February 1924. National Archives, RWF File, Box 7.
39. Telegram, Ambassador to Japan (Woods) to Secretary of State, 6 March 1924.
40. Confidential message from CINC Asiatic to OPNAV, 2 April 1924. National Archives, RWF File, Box 7.
41. Letter, Japanese Ambassador Hanihara Masanao to Secretary of State Charles Evans Hughes, 10 April 1924. Also, Yugi Ichioka, *The Issei: The World of the First Generation Japanese Immigrants, 1885—1924* (New York: Free Press, 1988), 245.
42. *Aviation,* 18 August 1924, 889.
43. Hiroyuki Agawa, *The Reluctant Admiral: Yamamoto and the Imperial Navy* (Tokyo: Kodansha International Ltd., 1979), 31–32.

## 2. The Preparation

1. Letter, Subject: "Airplane Flight Around the World" from Chief of Air Service to Adjutant General, War Department, 6 November 1923. National Archives, RWF File, Box 7.
2. Document U-672-A.S., undated, unsigned, Wade/Morrow Collection, Series Eleven.
3. Letter, Chief, Engineering Division, McCook Field to Chief of Air Service, 26 October 1923. National Archives, RWF File, Box 7.
4. Letter, Edwin Denby to John W. Weeks, 14 January 1924. National Archives, RWF File, Box 7.
5. Letter, Secretary of the Army to Secretary of the Navy, 25 January 1924. National Archives, RWF File, Box 7.
6. Ogden was notified he was commissioned as a second lieutenant on 5 June 1924 when the flight reached China. He was sworn in at the Astor Hotel in Shanghai.
7. "Report of Round the World Flight by Airplane While Under the Command of Major F. L. Martin, A.S. 1924," Confidential . . . Wade/Morrow Collection, Series 1, Folder 8, 5.
8. Letter, O. Westover, Commander, Langley Field, to Chief of Air Service, 8 February 1924. National Archives, RWF File, Box 7.
9. "Report of Round the World Flight," p. 7.

## 3. The Adventure Begins

1. Letter, Major J. E. Fechet, Chief, Training and War Plans Division to Clayton L. Bissell, Subject: "Instructions for Duty as Advance Officer, Round-the-World Flight," 14 January 1924. National Archives, RWF File, Box 7.
2. Letter, Major J. E. Fechet, etc., Box 7.
3. Letter, W. E. Gillmore, Air Officer to C. L. Bissell, 22 January 1924. National Archives, RWF File, Box 7.
4. Letter, W. E. Gillmore, etc. Box 7.
5. Letter, Major J. E. Fechet to Lt. C. C. Nutt, 19 January 1924. National Archives, RWF File, Box 7.
6. Letter, Major J. E. Fechet, etc., Box 7.
7. Letter, Major J. E. Fechet, etc., Box 7.
8. Letter, Mejor J. E. Fechet, etc., Box 7.
9. Letter, Major J. E. Fechet, etc., Box 7.
10. Letter, Secretary of the Navy Edwin Denby to Secretary of War John W. Weeks, 22 March 1924. National Archives, RWF File, Box 7.
11. Letter, Lieutenant R. J. Brown to Lt. Clifford C. Nutt, c/o Military Attaché, Tokyo, Japan, 12 February 1924. National Archives, RWF File, Box 7.
12. Letter, Lieutenant R. J. Brown, etc., Box 7.
13. *New York Times,* 7 March 1923.
14. Memorandum, R. J. Brown Jr. to C. L. Bissell at Dutch Harbor, Alaska, 20 February 1924. National Archives, RWF File, Box 7.
15. Letter, Maj. Gen. Mason M. Patrick to Commandant, U.S. Coast Guard, 25 March 1924. National Archives, RWF File, Box 7.
16. Confidential message, CINC Asiatic to OPNAV, 2 April 1924. National Archives, RWF File, Box 7.
17. Letter, F. L. Martin, Subject: "Progress Report to Chief of Air Service," 14 March 1924. National Archives, RWF File, Box 7.
18. "American World Flight," *Aviation,* 11 April 1924, 362.
19. F. L. Martin, "Report of Round the World Flight," undated, 13. National Archives, RWF File, Box 7.
20. Letter, F. L. Martin to Chief of Air Service, 31 March 1924. National Archives, RWF File, Box 7.
21. Lowell Thomas, *The First World Flight* (Boston: Houghton Mifflin, 1925), 19.
22. Marty Martinez, "Magellans of the Air." *Air Line Pilot,* April 1974, 20.
23. Arnold diary, 6 April 1924. Wade/Morrow Collection, Series 2.
24. Letter, L. D. Schulze, Subject: "World Flight Equipment" to Chief of Air Service, 12 April 1924. National Archives, RWF File, Box 7.
25. *San Diego Union,* 8 April 1924.

## 4. Daring the Aleutians

1. Martin, "Report of Round the World Flight," 19.
2. Martin, "Report," 20.
3. Arnold diary, 6 April 1924. Wade/Morrow Collection, Series 2, Folder 1.

4. Harding diary, 6 April 1924. Air Force Museum Archives, Wright-Patterson AFB, Ohio.
5. Alaska was purchased from the Russians in 1867 for $7.2 million. Sitka was its capital until 1900.
6. Harding diary, 10 April 1924.
7. Marty Martinez, "Magellans of the Air." *Air Line Pilot,* April 1974, 21.
8. Martinez, "Magellans of the Air," 21.
9. Harding diary, 10 April 1924.
10. Arnold diary, 11 April 1924.
11. Arnold diary.
12. Martin, "Report of Round the World Flight," 23.
13. Thomas, *The First World Flight,* 62.
14. Thomas, *The First World Flight,* 64.
15. Arnold diary, 13 April 1924.
16. Arnold diary, 14 April 1924.
17. Harding diary, 15 April 1924.
18. Letter, F. L. Martin at Kanatak to General Patrick, 22 April 1924. National Archives, RWF File, Box 7.
19. Martin, "Report of Round the World Flight," 28.
20. Martin, "Report," 30.
21. Harding diary, 15 April 1924.
22. Thomas, *The First World Flight,* 78.
23. Thomas, *The First World Flight, 78.*
24. Harding diary, 19 April 1924.
25. Thomas, *The First World Flight,* 82.
26. Thomas, *The First World Flight,* 82–83.
27. Wireless message from Unimak Island to Associated Press, Bremerton, Washington, 30 April 1924. The local residents believed the fliers should have landed at False Pass. National Archives, RWF File, Box 8.
28. Telegram, Loring Pickering, General Manager, North American Newspaper Alliance to Chief of Air Service, 7 May 1924. National Archives, RWF File, Box 8.
29. Telegram, Loring Pickering to Signal Corps, U.S. Army, Washington, D.C., 7 May 1924. National Archives, RWF File, Box 8.
30. Letter, Mason M. Patrick to Loring Pickering, 9 May 1924. National Archives, RWF File, Box 8.

## 5. *Seattle* Is Lost

1. Martin, "Report of Round the World Flight," 32.
2. Martin, "Report of Round the World Flight," 32.
3. Martin, 33.
4. Alva L. Harvey, *Memoirs of an Around-the-World Mechanic* (1924) *and Pilot* (1941), Manhattan, Kansas: Air Force Historical Foundation, 1978, 12.
5. Martin, "Report of Round the World Flight," 34.
6. Martin, "Report," 35–36.
7. Martin, "Report," 38.

8. Radio message from Martin, Port Moller, Alaska, to Chief of Air Service, 10 May 1924. National Archives, RWF file, Box 7.
9. Martin, *Report of Round the World Flight*, 39.
10. Harvey memoirs, 14–15.
11. Radio message, Chief of Air Service to Major Martin, 14 May 1924. National Archives, RWF file, Box 7.
12. Memorandum, J. E. Fechet for Chief of Air Service, Subject: "Shipment of Additional Plane for World Flight," 13 May 1924. National Archives, RWF File, Box 7.
13. Letter, Major Martin to General Patrick, 3 June 1924, as quoted in *New York Times,* 4 June 1924.
14. Memorandum, J. E. Fechet for Chief of Air Service, 26 April 1924. National Archives, RWF file, Box 7. General Patrick did not send this message.
15. Memorandum, J. E. Fechet for Executive, Army Chief of Staff, 30 April 1924. National Archives, RWF file, Box 7.
16. Archibald D. Turnbull and Clifford L. Lord, *History of United States Naval Aviation* (New Haven: Yale University Press, 1940), 222–23.
17. Harding diary, 2 May 1924.
18. Arnold diary, 5 May 1924.
19. Arnold diary, 5 May 1924.
20. Unpublished, undated manuscript by Leigh Wade, Wade/Morrow Collection, Series Two, Folder 8.
21. James C. Winchester, "First Round-the-World Flight." *Air Facts,* 38:8, 1975.
22. Harding diary, 11 May 1924.
23. Radio message, Commander Bering Sea Patrol to Commandant, U.S. Coast Guard, 19 April 1924. National Archives, RWF file, Box 7.
24. Radio message, Commandant U.S. Coast Guard to Commander Bering Sea Patrol, 20 April 1924. National Archives, RWF file, Box 7.
25. Thomas, *The First World Flight,* 115.
26. Arnold diary, 13 May 1924.
27. Arnold diary, 13 May 1924.
28. Thomas, *The First World Flight,* 107.
29. Letter, Major R. S. Bratton, Subject: "Report on Airplane Base at Hitokapu Wan" to Military Attaché, American Embassy, undated. National Archives, RWF file, Box 8.
30. Linton Wells, *Blood on the Moon,* 194–95.
31. As quoted in anonymous report from U.S. Coast Guard cutter *Haida,* 17 May 1924, 26. Furnished by History Office, U.S. Coast Guard.
32. Anonymous report, 27.

## 5. First across the Pacific

1. Arnold diary, 15–16 May 1924.
2. Thomas, *The First World Flight,* 108–9.
3. Radio message, Bering Sea Patrol at Dutch Harbor to *Haida,* 14 May 1924. National Archives, RWF file, Box 8.

4. Letter, General Patrick, Chief of Air Service, to Rear Admiral Fredrick C. Billard, Commandant U.S. Coast Guard, Treasury Department, 28 May 1924. National Archives, RWF file, Box 7.
5. Letter from General Patrick, Box 7.
6. Letter from General Patrick, Box 7.
7. Radio message, Secretary of War to World Flight, 18 May 1924. National Archives, RWF file, Box 7.
8. Arnold diary, 17 May 1924.
9. Arnold diary, 17 May 1924.
10. Thomas, *The First World Flight,* 119.
11. Thomas, 124.
12. Thomas, 129.
13. Thomas, 131.
14. Welcoming speech by Dr. Yoshinao Kozai, president, Tokyo Imperial University, Tokyo, 25 May 1924. As quoted in Thomas, *The First World Flight,* 135–36.
15. James C. Winchester, "First Round-the-World Flight.
16. Thomas, *The First World Flight,* 139.
17. Wells, *Blood on the Moon,* 210.
18. Harding diary, 30 May 1924.
19. Thomas, *The First World Flight,* 143.
20. Thomas, 146.
21. Thomas, 148.

## 7. To China and the "Paris of the Orient"

1. Apparently Nelson did not know what Smith observed and would state later in his confidential postflight report.
2. Thomas, *The First World Flight,* 157–58.
3. Thomas, 160.
4. Leigh Wade, "Aerial Globe Trotting," unpublished manuscript, Wade/Morrow Collection, Series Eight, Box 39, Folder 4.
5. Thomas, *The First World Flight,* 161.
6. Thomas, *The First World Flight.*
7. Thomas, 168.
8. Thomas, 169.
9. Thomas, 171.
10. Thomas, 172–73.

## 8. On to Calcutta

1. Thomas, *The First World Flight,* 176–77.
2. Thomas, 177.
3. Mitchell made a trip to the Pacific between December 1923 and July 1924. The War De-

partment had ordered him not to visit Japan in an official status, believing that such a visit would strain relations between that country and the United States. He did visit Japan as a tourist in June 1924. Upon his return to Washington the following the month, he prepared a 325-page report in which he stated that a war with Japan was inevitable.

4. Thomas, *The First World Flight,* 179.
5. Thomas, *The First World Flight.*
6. Thomas, 184.
7. Thomas, 187.
8. Thomas, 188.
9. Letter from H. A. Halverson, Constantinople, to Chief of Air Service, 9 July 1924. National Archives RWF file, Box 8.
10. Letter from Halverson.
11. Thomas, *The First World Flight,* 194.
12. Marty Martinez, "Magellans of the Air." *Air Line Pilot,* May 1974, 12.
13. Wells, *Blood on the Moon,* 206–7.
14. Thomas, *The First World Flight,* 200.
15. Memorandum by Lowell H. Smith, Calcutta, India, 29 June 1924. Wade/Morrow Collection, Series 1, Folder 8.

## 9. Paris by Bastille Day

1. Wells, *Blood on the Moon,* 207.
2. Thomas, *The First World Flight,* 203.
3. Thomas, The First World Flight.
4. Arnold diary, 3 July 1924.
5. Wells, *Blood on the Moon,* 210.
6. Erik H. Nelson, Engineering Report of Round the World Flight, undated, 17. Wade/Morrow Collection, Series Two, Folder 4.
7. Arnold diary, 7 July 1924.
8. Story of the Round-the-World Flight, unsigned, undated. Wade/Morrow Collection, Series Eleven.
9. Arnold diary, 8 July 1924.
10. Arnold diary, 9 July 1924.
11. Thomas, *The First World Flight,* 219.
12. Arnold diary, 12 July 1924.
13. Thomas, *The First World Flight,* 231.
14. Arnold diary, 13 July 1924.
15. Thomas, *The First World Flight,* 232.
16. Thomas, 233.
17. Thomas, 236.
18. Untitled commentary by André Viollis, *Le Petit Parisien,* 15 July 1924.
19. Editorial, *Le Matin,* 16 July 1924.
20. Thomas, *The First World Flight,* 237–38.
21. Arnold diary, 15 July 1924.
22. Thomas, *The First World Flight,* 238.

## 10. Preparing for the North Atlantic

1. Thomas, *The First World Flight,* 242.
2. Thomas, 243.
3. Arnold diary, 17 July 1924.
4. Thomas, *The First World Flight,* 248.
5. Unsigned memorandum for Capt. Pinney, *USS Milwaukee,* Indian Harbor, Labrador, 31 July 1924. National Archives RWF File, Box 8.
6. Unsigned memorandum for Capt. Pinney.
7. Arnold diary, 31 July 1924.
8. Signal Corps radiogram, Maj. Gen. Patrick to Lt. Clayton Bissell, c/o Commanding Officer, Cruiser *Milwaukee,* 29 July 1924. National Archives RWF file, Box 8.
9. Thomas, *The First World Flight,* 253.
10. As quoted in Ernest A. McKay, *A World to Conquer* (New York: Arco Publishing, 1981), 145.
11. Thomas, *The First World Flight,* 254.
12. Thomas, *The First World Flight.*
13. McKay, A World to Conquer, 145.
14. Thomas, *The First World Flight,* 256–57.

## 11. North America at Last!

1. Thomas, *The First World Flight,* 238.
2. Marty Martinez, "Magellans of the Air," 14.
3. Report, "U.S. Army Air Service Around the World Flight," undated, 52–53. Wade/Morrow Collection, Series One, Folder 8.
4. James H. Winchester, "First Round-the-World Flight." *Air Facts,* August 1975, 20.
5. Arnold diary, 4 August 1924.
6. Memorandum, Chief of Air Service for Deputy Chief of Staff, 7 August 1924. National Archives, RWF file, Box 7.
7. Memorandum, H. C. Pratt, Training and War Plans Division, for the Executive, Air Service, 9 August 1924. National Archives, RWF file, Box 8.
8. Radio message from Smith to Chief of Air Service, 6 August 1924. National Archives, RWF file, Box 8.
9. Martinez, "Magellans of the Air," 16.
10. Radiogram, Smith to Chief of Air Service, 10 August 1924. National Archives, RWF file, Box 7.
11. Thomas, *The First World Flight,* 270.
12. Quoted in fiftieth anniversary pamphlet titled "First Around the World," published by Douglas Aircraft Company, 1974, 12.
13. Thomas, The First World Flight, 272.
14. Thomas, 273.
15. Thomas, 274.
16. Thomas, 275–76.
17. Thomas, 276.
18. Quoted in Chelsea Fraser, *Heroes of the Air,* 291–92.

19. C. R. Roseberry, *The Challenging Sky,* 73.
20. Thomas, *The First World Flight,* 284.
21. Radiogram, Bissell on USS *Milwaukee* to Chief of Air Service, 26 August 1924. National Archives, RWF File, Box 8.

## 12. Mission Accomplished

1. Radiogram, White House (to be held until released) to Lt. Lowell H. Smith, USS *Richmond,* 14 August 1924. National Archives, RWF file, Box 8.
2. Secret message relayed from Chief of Naval Operations to USS *Milwaukee,* 26 August 1924. National Archives, RWF file, Box 8.
3. Confidential radio message, General Patrick through Chief of Naval Operations to USS *Richmond,* 28 August 1924. National Archives, RWF file, Box 8.
4. Radio message, USS *Milwaukee* to Chief of Air Service, 25 August 1924. National Archives, RWF file, Box 8.
5. Arnold diary, 31 August 1924.
6. Memorandum, H. C. Pratt, Training and War Plans Division, to Chief of Air Service , 25 August 1924. National Archives, RWF file, Box 8.
7. The residents of Mere Point were proud that the World Fliers had made their first landing on United States soil there. Governor Percival P. Baxter promptly ordered a parcel of land procured for a state park and a large bronze tablet installed on a granite boulder titled "Maine's Tribute to the American Round-the-World Aviators."
8. Thomas, *The First World Flight,* 296.
9. Telegram, Edward P. Syosset, Long Island, to British Consul, Boston, 5 September 1924. National Archives, RWF file, Box 8.
10. Telegram, George R. I., Balmoral Castle, England, to General Patrick, 8 September 1924. National Archives, RWF file, Box 7.
11. Thomas, *The First World Flight,* 298.
12. Letter, Subject: "Instructions to Commanding Officer, Round-the-World Flight," from W. G. Kilner, Executive, Adjutant General's Office, 20 August 1920. National Archives, RWF file, Box 7.
13. Letter, "Instructions etc."
14. *Aviation,* 22 September 1924.
15. Arnold diary, 8 September 1924.
16. Thomas, *The First World Flight,* 302.
17. Arnold diary, 12 September 1924.
18. The Barling bomber made its first flight on 22 August 1923. It had three wings, four rudders, six engines, and ten landing wheels. It could carry enough fuel to stay aloft thirteen hours, was designed for a crew of eleven, and was used by the Army Air Service to set duration and altitude records for lifting useful loads of about 4,400 to 6,600 pounds. But its top speed of 95.5 mph was considered too slow. It made its last flight in August 1925 and was destroyed in 1928.
19. Letter, Chief of Air Service to Commanding Officer, World Flight, 20 August 1924. National Archives, RWF file, Box 8.
20. Thomas, *The First World Flight,* 306.
21. Thomas, 309.

22. *U.S. Air Services,* November 1924.
23. *U.S. Air Services.*
24. *U.S. Air Services.*
25. *U.S. Air Services.*
26. *Los Angeles Evening Express,* 23 September 1924.
27. Thomas, *The First World Flight,* 312.
28. *Los Angeles Record,* 23 September 1924.
29. *San Francisco Chronicle,* 2 September 1924.
30. Editorial, London *Times,* 30 September 1924.
31. *Seattle Post-Intelligencer,* 29 September 1924.
32. Arnold diary, 28 September 1924.
33. Thomas, *The First World Flight,* 316.

## Epilogue

1. Memorandum, Major H. C. Pratt, Chief, Training and War Plans Division, to the Executive, Air Service, 24 September 1924. National Archives, RWF file, Box 8.
2. Thomas, *The First World Flight,* 317.
3. Memorandum, Mason M. Patrick, no addressee, 25 September 1924. National Archives, RWF file, Box 8.
4. Telegram, W. A. Curley to John W. Weeks, 16 September 1924. National Archives, RWF file, Box 8.
5. Telegram, William E. Dever to Secretary of War Weeks, 16 September 1924. National Archives, RWF file, Box 8.
6. Telegram, Frank Carson to Secretary of War Weeks, 4 November 1924. National Archives, RWF file, Box 8.
7. Thomas, *The First World Flight,* 320.
8. "Address of Welcome to the World Flyers," by Eugene H. Angert, Racquet Club, St. Louis, 18 November 1924. Wade/Morrow Collection, Series 8, Folder 1.
9. Message, Secretary of War to Commanding General, Ninth Corps Area, Presidio, San Francisco, 12 October 1924. National Archives, RWF file, Box 8.
10. Bill sent to the Senate as H.R. 12064, 68th Congress, 2d Session, 17 February 1925. Wade/Morrow Collection, Series One, Box 8.
11. Lt. Lowell H. Smith, "Official Report of the United States Army Air Service Around the World Flight." Wade/Morrow Collection, Series 1, Folder 4.
12. Lt. Erik H. Nelson, "Appendix A, Engineering Report of Round the World Flight," undated. Wade/Morrow Collection, Series 1, Folder 4.
13. Lt. L. P. Arnold, "Appendix C, Finance Report of Round the World Flight," undated. Wade/Morrow Collection, Series 1, Folder 4, 1.
14. Arnold, Finance Report, 2–3.
15. Lt. Lowell H. Smith, Commanding Officer, "Appendix D, Confidential Report, Round the World Flight," undated. Wade/Morrow Collection, Series 1, Folder 2, 2.
16. Smith, Confidential Report, 3.
17. Smith, Confidential Report.
18. Second indorsement, Letter, Subject: "Disposition of Airplanes of the World Flight," from

Major W. G. Kilner, Executive Officer, Air Service, to the Adjutant General, U.S. Army, 28 April 1925. National Archives, RWF file, Box 8.

19. Letter, H. C. Pratt, Chief, Training and War Plans Division to Chief, Information Division, 9 February 1925. National Archives, RWF file, Box 8.
20. Letter, Major W. G. Kilner, Executive Officer, Air Service, to Clarence J. Bertler, Milwaukee, 12 June 1925. National Archives, RWF file, Box 8.
21. Unsigned letter, Engineering Division, McCook Field, to Commander, Langley Field, Va., 16 June 1924. National Archives, RWF file, Box 6.

# Further Reading


Cunningham, Frank. *Skymaster: The Story of Donald Douglas.* Philadelphia: Dorrance, 1943.

Driscoll, Marjorie. *Wings around the World.* Los Angeles: Pacific Geographic Society, 1939.

Fraser, Chelsea. *Heroes of the Air.* New York: Thomas Y. Crowell, 1940.

Glines, Carroll V. *The Compact History of the U.S. Air Force.* New York: Hawthorn Books, 1973.

———. *Round-the-World Flights.* Princeton, N.J.: Van Nostrand Reinhold, 1982.

Harvey, Alva L. *Memoirs of an Around-the-World Mechanic (1924) and Pilot (1941).* Manhattan, Kansas: Air Force Historical Foundation, 1978.

Gwynn-Jones, Terry. *Farther and Faster.* Washington, D.C.: Smithsonian Institution Press, 1991.

Mason, Herbert Malloy Jr. *Bold Men, Far Horizons.* Philadelphia: J. B. Lippincott, 1966.

Maurer, Maurer, *Aviation in the U.S. Army, 1919–1939.* Washington, D.C. Office of Air Force History, 1987.

McKay, Ernest A. *A World to Conquer.* New York: Arco Publishing, 1981.

Morrison, Wilbur H. *Donald W. Douglas: A Heart with Wings.* Ames: Iowa State University Press, 1991.

Patrick, Mason M. *The United States in the Air.* Garden City, New York: Doubleday, Doran, 1928.

Roseberry, C. R. *The Challenging Skies.* Garden City, New York: Doubleday, 1966.

Tessendorf, K. C. *Wings around the World.* New York: Atheneum, 1991.

Thomas, Lowell, *The First World Flight.* Boston: Houghton Mifflin, 1925.

Wells, Linton. *Blood on the Moon: The Autobiography of Linton Wells.* Boston: Hougton Mifflin, 1937.

# Index


Abbot, John S., 81, 82
Aberdeen, Maryland, 148
Adler, Elmer E., 13
Akyab, Burma, 99–100
Alcock, John, 10 n, 68
Aleppo, Syria, 109–10
*Algonquin,* 53, 57, 76
Allahabad, India, 105
Ambala, India, 105–6
Amoy, China, 86
Andrews, Richard, 165
Angert, Eugene, H., 163–64
Angmagssalik, Greenland, 130, 131, 132, 134
Aomori, Japan, 21
Arland, Louis J., 154
Arnold, Leslie P., 26, 30, 40, 41, 159; career, 27–28, 171; departure, 42; Distinguished Service Medal, 164; finance report, 167; French Indochina incident and, 89–90, 92; Icy Tickle flight, 140–42; in Rangoon, 98, 99; shopping, 118; weather and, 56
Attu Island, Alaska, 24, 35, 45, 68, 69, 70, 73

Baghdad, Mesopotamia, 109
Bahl, Joe, 160–61
Bandar Abbas, Persia, 108, 109
Bangkok, Siam, 96–97
Beck, Johannssen, 68, 75, 166
Beires, Sarmiento, 88, 165
Bellinger, Lowell H., 170
Beltrame, Felipe, 66, 165
Bertler, Clarence J., 169
Bertrandias, Victor E., 143
Billard, Frederick C., 69
*Billingsley,* 124–25, 127, 134
Bissell, Clayton L., 24, 34–35, 122; in Alaska, 55, 77; in Greenland, 131, 133, 139
*Black Hawk,* 83
Blair, William R., 25, 28, 37, 55, 67
Blake, W. T., 102
Bolling Field, Washington, DC, 149
*Boston,* 41; capsized, 129; engine exchange, 55; engine problem, 124–25, 126–28; generator problems, 93–94; Sitka landing, 48–49; takeoff from Kirkwall, 122–23
*Boston II,* 138, 143, 156, 157, 162; disposition, 169–70
Boston, Massachusetts, 145–46
Braccine, Giovonni, 132
Bratton, R. S., 71
Brockhurst, John A., 151, 153
Broome, L. E., 35, 65, 81, 165
Brough, England, 24, 117, 118, 121
Brown, Abie E., 158
Brown, Arthur Whitten, 68
Brown, G. H., 10 n
Brown, Robert J., Jr., 9–10, 13, 28, 36–37, 145
Bruel, M., 92

Bucharest, Rumania, 111
Budapest, Hungary, 111
Bushire, Persia, 109

Cabrál, Sacadura, 10 n, 65
Caffrey, Jefferson, 18, 19
Calcutta, India, 24, 100–101, 102, 103
Cason, Frank, 162
Chahbar, Persia, 108
Chevalier, M., 90, 91, 92
*Chicago,* 41, 159, 162; disposition of, 165, 168, 169; engine problems, 79, 87, 89, 90; fuel pump failure, 140–41; Kirkwall takeoff, 122–23; punctured pontoons, 138, 139
Chicago, Illinois, 152, 162
Chignik, Alaska, 51, 54, 59
Chittagong, Burma, 100
Collier, Robert J., 166
Connell, Auwilda (Mrs.), 41
Constantinople, Turkey, 24, 110
Coolidge, Calvin, 18, 21, 30, 37, 41, 142, 148, 149, 157
*Corey,* 51, 52
Cotinho, Gago, 10 n, 65
Cotton, Lyman, 128, 134, 137
Crozio, Tullio, 132
Crumrine, Clarence E., 12, 14, 17, 20, 24, 118, 129, 130
Curley, W. A., 162

Dallas, Texas, 153
Dargue, Herbert A., 8, 9, 12
David, Evan J., 57
Davidson, Howard C., 117, 120
Davis, Dwight F., 8, 142, 168
De Jean, Louis, 158
Denby, Edwin, 25
Dever, William E., 162
d'Oisy, Pelletier, 65, 114, 165, 168; crash, 82
Doolittle, Jimmy, 14
Douglas, Donald W., 15, 16, 31, 168
Douglass, William B., 108
Doumergue, Gaston, 114
Dutch Harbor, Alaska, 54–58

*Eider,* 67, 69, 75, 166
El Paso, Texas, 153
Eugene, Oregon, 39, 157–58

Fechet, J. E., 13–14, 35–36, 64–65
*Ford,* 69, 71, 76
Foulois, Benjamin D., 8
Frank, W. H., 11–12
Fredricksdal, Greenland, 131, 132, 133, 136
Frost, Holloway H., 69, 70, 71, 72, 76
Fulcinelli, Bruno, 132
Fuller, George, 109

*Gertrud Rask,* 130, 131, 133
George V, King of England, 146
Gilmore, W. E., 35
Goddard, George, 147, 151, 153
Goto, Yukichi, 21

*Haida,* 54–55, 56, 57, 67, 69–70
Haiphong, French Indochina, 87–88
Hale, Willis, 129
Halverson, Harry A., 24, 101–2, 109, 110
Hansen, Eilor, 48
Haraguchi, Hatsutaro, 31
Harbord, J. G., 10–11
Harding, John T., 39, 84, 150; career, 29, 171; Distinguished Service Medal, 164; Tavoy flight, 98
Harmon, Millard F. (Mrs.), 41
Harris, Harold, 150
Harvey, Alva L., 29; crash, 59–63; Distinguished Service Medal, 164; on downed *Seattle,* 51–54; postcards, 169; Prince Rupert landing, 47, 48
Hawkes Bay, Newfoundland, 143–44
Hensley, William, 148
Hines, John L., 31
Hitokappu, Yetorofu, Japan, 71, 77–78
Hong Kong, 87
Horna Fjord, Iceland, 123–24, 125, 129
Hue, Annam, 90–91, 92
Hughes, Charles Evans, 19, 21
*Hull,* 51, 52

Icy Tickle, Labrador, 24, 139, 140, 141
*Island Falk,* 136
Isoda, S., 70–71
Ivigtut, Greeland, 138, 139, 140

Jones, Bradley, 25, 28, 179

Kagoshima, Japan, 24, 82–83
Kampongson Bay, French Indochina, 96
Karachi, India, 107
Kashiwabara, Japan, 24, 36, 76
Kasumigaura, Japan, 78–79
Kelly, Oakley G., 12, 14
Kilner, W. G., 147
Kirkwall, Orkney Islands, 121
Koenig, Robert, 169
Koenig, Theodore J., 39
Koenig, Theodore J. (Mrs.), 41
Komandorski Islands, 68–73, 74–75, 76
Kozai, Yoshinao, 80
Kuni, Prince, 80
Kushimoto, Japan, 82

Langley Field, Virginia, 25
Lawton, Malcolm S., 24, 85, 90
Lee, Willis A., Jr., 81
*Leif Ericsson,* 131
Leighton, Bruce G., 132, 133
Lewis, Victor Alonzo, 158
Lindquist, C. E., 34
Locatelli, Antonio, 122, 132, 133–34, 136, 165; rescue, 137–38
London, England, 24, 116–17
Los Angeles, California, 156

MacLaren, A. Stuart, 35, 65–66, 88, 100, 119, 145, 165; crash, 81

MacLaren, A. Stuart (Mrs.), 117
Macready, John A., 12, 14
Madsen, Charles, 52
Magruder, Thomas F., 117–19, 130, 133, 137, 138, 142
Mantz, Paul, 156
Martin, Frederick L., 29, 31, 32, 158; career, 26, 170; crash, 59–63; departure, 39; Distinguished Service Medal, 164; on downed *Seattle,* 51–54, 56–57; postcards, 169; Prince Rupert landing, 46–47, 48; publicity, 38, 40, 41; training, 28
Masanao, Hanihara, 21
McClaren, J. W., 71–72
McClelland, H. F., 118
McCook Field, Dayton, Ohio, 150–51; 152, 164, 165
McDonald, George C., 143, 169
Meister, Louis, 148
Mere Point, Maine, 144
*Milwaukee,* 131, 139
Minato, Japan, 78
Mitchel Field, New York, 147–48
Mitchell, William "Billy," 8, 9, 10, 11, 28, 148, 149, 166; in Bangkok, 97
Moffett, William A., 11, 37
Moseley, C. C., 38, 163, 166
Multan, India, 106–7
Muskogee, Oklahoma, 152
Nazan, Atka Island, 66–67
Neblett, Herbert C., 28
Nelson, Erik H., 12, 13, 14, 15–16, 26, 29, 41, 150–51, 161; Alaska flight, 50; in Ambala, 106; career, 27, 171; China flight, 84–85; degree, 166; Distinguished Service Medal, 164; engineering report, 166; forced landing, 148–49; Horna Fjord flight, 123–24; in Hue, 90–91, 92; and icebergs, 135–36; Karachi flight, 107; preparation, 39, 40; Tavoy flight, 98; test flights, 31, 32, 37–38; training, 28
Nelson, Gunnar, 147, 148–49
*New Orleans,* 41, 84, 162; disposition of, 165, 168–69; engine problems, 107, 129–30; forced landing, 148–49; Kirkwall near disaster, 123; Rangoon near disaster, 98–99; Sitka near disaster, 49
*Noah,* 90
Nungesser, Charles, 148
Nutt, Clifford C., 14, 17, 20, 24, 35, 36, 37, 78

Ogden, Henry H., 39, 41; career, 29, 171; on *Barry,* 134; Distinguished Service Medal, 164; *Boston* ditch, 124, 126–29; Prince Rupert landing, 47; on *Richmond,* 129, 130; Tourane departure, 92–93; and Wells, 104, 105
Omaha, Nebraska, 152
O'Neill, Joseph, 163
Osborne, James, 56

Page, Nelson T., 66, 165
Pais, Brito, 88, 165
Paramushiru, Japan, 45, 68, 76
Paris, France, 113–15
Patrick, Mason M., planning, 8–9, 10, 11, 14, 15, 17–18, 30, 37, 38, 40, 143, 145, 147–48; disposition of planes, 168; flight request, 22, 32; Martin and Harvey decision, 64; personnel selection, 25, 28, 29; "talking paper"; 151–52; U. S. Coast Guard and, 75–76
Pershing, John J., 8, 114, 149
Pictou Harbor, Nova Scotia, 143–44
Pirie, John F., 129
Plenderleith, W. N., 65, 165
*Pope,* 69, 71–72, 78
Port Moller, Alaska, 62–63
Pratt, H. C., 144
*Preble,* 86
Prince Rupert, British Columbia, 47

Ragozzino, Robert, 172
*Raleigh,* 129, 130, 131
Ramsey, Logan C., 28
Rangoon, Burma, 98–99
Read, Albert, 68
Reed, Phil B., 52
Reykjavik, Iceland, 130, 131, 133
*Richmond,* 119–20, 121, 127–28, 134, 142, 143; Locatelli rescue, 137
Richter, John P., 26, 154
Robertson, Ashley R., 154
Roosevelt, Theodore, 10
Runyon, Damon, 122

Saigon, French Indochina, 93, 94, 95–96
San Diego, California, 153–54
San Francisco, California, 156–57
Santa Monica, California, 39, 155
Schroeder, Frederick, 35, 69, 70
Schulze, LeClair D., 24, 26, 28, 30, 40, 42, 44, 44; on *Gertrud Rask,* 130, 131
*Seattle,* 41, 46; crankcase hole, 51–53, 54; crash, 59, 61; disposition of, 169; repairs, 47, 48; search for, 57
Seattle, Washington, 24, 39–42, 158–59
Seward, Alaska, 50
Shanghai, China, 19, 24, 84, 85
Shumushu, Japan, 19
Sitka, Alaska, 48
Smith, Floyd K., 170
Smith, Keith, 9, 10 n
Smith, Lowell H., 29, 32, 41, 159; in Boston, 146–47; *Boston* rescue and, 124–25; in Calcutta, 101; in California, 153, 154, 155; career, 26, 170;

Smith, Lowell H. (*continued*), in Chicago, 162; confidential report, 167–68; degree, 166; departure, 39, 41; designated leader, 66; Distinguished Service Medal, 164; flight decisions, 54, 68– 69, 85–86, 97; French Indochina incident, 89–90, 92; in Haiphong, 88; Icy Tickle flight, 140–42; in Japan, 82, 83; Locatelli and, 132; near fatal accident, 119; Prince Rupert landing, 47; in Rangoon, 98, 99; in Russia, 74–75; training, 28; weather and, 56, 73, 134–36; Wells and 104
Smith, Ross, 9, 10 n
Snow, Lorenzo L., 13
St. Joseph, Missouri, 152
Strasbourg, France, 112
Streett, St. Claire, 12, 13, 14, 16, 17, 28, 37, 145
Sweetwater, Texas, 153

Tavoy, Burma, 98
Tchinkoen Bay, China, 86
Thomas, Lowell, 149–50, 153, 166, 171
Tomkin, E. S., 57
Tomlinson, George A., 108
Tourane, French Indochina, 88–89, 92–93
Tucson, Arizona, 153
Turner, Arthur H., 27, 29, 41

Vancouver Barracks, Washington, 39, 157
Vesin, Bernard, 65, 165
Vienna, Austria, 111–12
Villa, Pancho, 26
Volandt, William F., 13

Wade, Leigh, 29, 32, 41, 99; in Alaska, 50; on *Barry,* 134; broken ribs, 155; career, 26–27, 170–71; degree, 166; departure, 39, 41–42; Distinguished Service Medal, 164; Icelandic ditch of *Boston,* 124, 126–29; Leighton and, 131–32, 133; in London, 117; Prince Rupert landing, 47; on *Richmond,* 129, 130; training, 28; Wells and, 103, 104
Wadsworth, James W., 147, 148
Wainwright, John M., 7
Wales, Prince of, 119, 146, 148
Wash, Carlyle H., 24, 110, 113, 115
Washington, DC, 149–50
Weeks, John W., 10–11, 17, 25, 30, 76–77, 164
Wells, Linton O., 70, 71–72, 73, 81, 100, 101, 170; Arctic report, 72, 76; as stowaway, 103–4, 105, 108
Westover, Oscar, 30
Whitcomb, David, Jr. (Mrs.), 41
Whitten Arthur, 10 n
Woods, Cyrus E., 18–19, 80
Wright, Burdette S. "Birdie," 147, 151, 153, 155, 160
Wright, Orville, 161
Wyatt, Ben H., 37

Yamada, M., 70–71
Yonezawa, Minezo, 21

Zanni, D. Pedro, 65, 66, 165